Celebrating Salvation

Celebrating Salvation

About the birth, death, resurrection, and ascension of Jesus Christ and the outpouring of the Holy Spirit.

Epilogue: the return of Christ

by Clarence Stam

PREMIER PUBLISHING
WINNIPEG

Stam, Clarence, 1948
Celebrating Salvation

ISBN 0-88756-066-0

1. Canadian Reformed Churches – Liturgy. Calendars
2. Salvation – Sermons. I. Title
BX9598.Z6S73 1997 284'.271 C97-920069-5

PREMIER PUBLISHING
ONE BEGHIN AVE., WINNIPEG, MANITOBA, CANADA R2J 3X5

To Rich and Tracey
and Jordan

survivors in the
celebration of salvation.

In loving memory of Ed.

PREFACE

This book is a compilation of material gathered over the course of almost twenty-five years of ministry, spanning two continents and five congregations. This material was used mostly in preparing sermons for festive occasions. Therefore, perhaps, in the course of this book some things may be repeated. But like the Sunday sermons, the truth is worth repeating. The selection of material follows no prescribed plan, except to focus on the direct passages which give us the main events.

There are not many publications available which take a concerted look at the main facts of salvation, the birth, death, resurrection, and ascension of our Lord, as well as the outpouring of the Holy Spirit. Publications of this kind have appeared in Dutch, for example, *De Verborgenheid der Godzaligheid*, J.H. Kok N.V., Kampen, 1957. These books cover material from Advent to Pentecost. Although advent material has not been included here, a section on the return of Christ was added.

The idea for this book has long been in my mind, but began to take concrete shape and form after the reading of *Proclaim Salvation*, by David Ewert, Herald Press, Waterloo, Ontario, 1992. Having enjoyed the main gist of this book, I thought that perhaps a more in-depth treatment of some Bible passages would be helpful.

I wish to express my thanks to the congregations which have during the past years endured my preaching. This material, now published, may be helpful for those who wish to study Scripture and focus on the main facts of salvation as presented in the Word of God. I am grateful to Premier Printing for taking up the publication of this work. Special thanks to Tony and Dini vanderHout without whose encouragement and support this book would not have been published.

A special word of thanks is due to my friend and mentor, Dr. Frieda Oosterhoff of Hamilton, who was willing to spend many hours in proof-reading the manuscript and offering expert advice. Thanks also to Steve Bremer of Hamilton who offered his time and expertise in formatting the manuscript.

May this publication serve to help us experience our Christian faith truly as a celebration of salvation.

Clarence Stam — Stoney Creek, March, 1996

OTHER PUBLICATIONS BY THE SAME AUTHOR:

None Like Thee, the Prophecies of Micah of Moresheth (Premier Printing, Winnipeg, 1977).

Everything in Christ, The Christian Faith outlined according to the Belgic Confession (Premier Printing, Winnipeg, 1979).

Living in the Joy of Faith, The Christian Faith as outlined in The Heidelberg Catechism (Inheritance Publications, Neerlandia, Alberta, 1991).

TABLE OF CONTENTS

INTRODUCTION

Each year most churches work their way through some kind of "preaching schedule." Some of these schedules are set out in a common book and must be rigidly followed, while other schedules are more flexible, allowing local pastors a good measure of freedom.

In the centuries preceding the great Reformation, the ecclesiastical calendar was packed with rules concerning the observation of the many "feast days" or holy days, dedicated to all kinds of persons and events. Church life had deformed into sheer ritualism, and the Word of God was hardly being preached.

John Calvin particularly spoke out against the "superstitious observance" of Lent and other such traditions. It is well known that on feast days, such as Christmas, Calvin simply continued to preach on the text indicated in the "lectio continua", the regular reading.

Today the ecclesiastical calendar is often determined by the secular scheme of things. Days of remembrance, like Christmas and Easter, have become worldly, commercial events. Therefore many churches, in the line of the great Reformation, have correctly opposed a calendar which places too much emphasis on specific holy days. The only real day of worship for the Christian Church is the Sunday, the day of the Lord, and this day returns at the beginning of each week.

Nevertheless, Reformed Churches have not altogether abandoned the notion that the major events of salvation should be remembered every year. In the Church Order of the Canadian Reformed Churches one can find this stipulation, "Each year the Churches shall, in the manner decided upon by the consistory, commemorate the birth, death, resurrection, and ascension of the Lord Jesus Christ, as well as His outpouring of the Holy Spirit" (Article 53).

It should be noted that this article does not demand that certain events of salvation be remembered on a specific day, for the emphasis lies on remembering the facts themselves. We are not concerned with observing certain *days*, but must focus on key *events* in the history of salvation. In practice, however, these facts are usually remembered at set times, according to the calendar generally in use. In itself, this need not be a problem, as long as the preaching of the Word of God remains central also on days of commemoration.

This book contains material used in sermons which were delivered on the commonly accepted days of commemoration. The purpose was and is to let the Word of God speak about the events being remembered. We may, indeed, celebrate the facts of salvation. God has fulfilled all His wondrous promises in Jesus Christ, our Lord. This gives us reason throughout the year for great joy.

Quotations are taken from the *Revised Standard Version* and from the *Book of Praise* that are still used in the Canadian Reformed Churches.

In an "epilogue" we look forward to the one great promise which must yet become reality: the return of our Lord Jesus Christ.

Maranatha, come, Lord Jesus!

Clarence Stam, Stoney Creek, October, 1997.

The Birth of Jesus Christ

Christmas

GOD'S SOVEREIGN POWER MANIFEST IN THE BIRTH OF JESUS CHRIST

"In those days a decree went out from Caesar Augustus that all the world should be enrolled. This was the first enrollment, when Quirinius was governor of Syria. And all went to be enrolled, each to his own city. And Joseph also went up from Galilee, from the city of Nazareth, to Judea, to the city of David, which is called Bethlehem, because he was of the house and lineage of David, to be enrolled with Mary, his betrothed, who was with child. And while they were there, the time came for her to be delivered. And she gave birth to her first-born son and wrapped him in swaddling cloths, and laid him in a manger, because there was no place for them in the inn".

(Luke 2: 1-7)

In December of every year we remember the birth of our Lord Jesus Christ. It is not that Christ's birth really took place on December 25, so many centuries ago. We remember the *fact*, not the *day* as such, and the church celebrated the fact on December 25 already since the fourth century. It is not the intention here to deal with the reasons why this date was chosen, and whether it was done rightly or wrongly.

We may indeed celebrate the birth of Christ. We should be reminded of what the angel said to the shepherds in the night when Christ was born, "Behold, I bring you good news of a great joy" (Luke 2: 10). It *is* a celebration, isn't it? Is the birth of Christ not the central event of history? Does it not mean for the church of all ages a time of great rejoicing?

But is there not also in Christ's birth the element of humiliation and suffering? Yes, there is, and we will not overlook it. But the main emphasis on this day must be on the joy and gratitude which God prepares for us and asks of us because of this great and mighty wonder! It is a birth which has world-wide, eternal significance for peoples everywhere.

You see, this is the *context* in which Luke describes the birth of the Lord Jesus. He gives us a very sober and simple account, but there is throughout the description of the events an underlying sense of a joy of great magnitude. Luke, who wanted to give an accurate description of the facts, sees the wider *historical* context and meaning of this birth, and realizes how it will come to affect all the world. When Jesus is born, then the great Son of David, the long-awaited Messiah, appears in the flesh on the scene of world history. Here is the Redeemer of the world, the King of kings, the Son of God Who became man, and that fact must be proclaimed and is being proclaimed throughout the world. That is why Luke follows up His description of the Gospel with the book of Acts, in which we read how the Gospel of Jesus the Lord reaches Rome.

Rome. The centre of the empire. Luke 2 begins with Rome, and the book of Acts ends with Rome, where Paul is preaching the Gospel openly and unhindered. We may celebrate Christmas, indeed, when we see it in this wider and beautiful context.

I may summarize the contents of Luke 2: 1-7 as follows: God shows His sovereign power in the blessed birth of His Son Jesus Christ. Two main aspects will have our attention. First, we note how an imperial decree serves a heavenly purpose. Secondly, we see how an obscure beginning serves a glorious end.

AUGUSTUS AND QUIRINIUS

Luke begins the story of our Lord's birth by giving us a specific historical setting. Verses 1 and 2 state: "In those days a decree went out from Caesar Augustus that all the world was to be enroled. This was the first enrolment, when Quirinius was governor of Syria."

We find here the names of two important figures: the emperor Augustus, and the governor Quirinius, a keen and honoured Roman general and diplomat. Two men of great power and fame. These were the ones who had the authority and the power to make the laws and enforce them in no uncertain terms. They are two representatives of the supreme and central authority of the vast Roman empire. And immediately the question arises, what influence can the birth of a Jewish infant in distant Bethlehem have with respect to these great power-brokers, Augustus and Quirinius?

We should pay close attention to these two persons, so that we know why Luke mentions them. The first, Augustus, whose real name was Octavianus, was a grand-nephew of the almost legendary Julius Caesar. Octavianus had managed to end the civil wars among the Roman factions and unite the empire under one throne. He came to power approximately 30 years before Christ was born and ruled until A.D.14, covering a span of 44 years as emperor. This was certainly no small feat.

In the year 27 B.C., he took the title "Augustus," which means: the mighty one or the elevated one. Augustus did so for a very specific reason. He wanted to assume total, almost godly power over the entire empire. In order to create an aura of divinity around the emperor and to establish his power as almighty, this title functioned excellently! Augustus presented himself as the god-king, the one destined by the deities of Rome to rule the entire world. Imperial decrees were treated as orders coming almost from the gods themselves. Here lies the beginning of the emperor-worship which would later become a main cause for Christian martyrdom.

To be sure, Caesar Augustus really tried to live up to his name. He united the empire under a solid structure of Roman law, and set up a smooth imperial organization. There was law and order, a common currency, a good system of roads and transportation, and a flourishing world economy. Augustus was an autocratic despot, shrewd and tough, but revered by many.

He also followed a careful foreign policy in the lands under Roman occupation. Mostly he let local rulers govern over their own people, as long as they submitted to him and paid proper tribute. So, for example, the land of Israel was governed by the family of Herod the Great. The Roman garrisons intervened only when the local authorities could not keep things under control, but then they acted swiftly and without mercy.

At this time the general area of Palestine was under the supervision of Quirinius, who had his residence in Antioch. Quirinius had been commander-in-chief of the Roman forces in that area already in the year 9 B.C., and later officially became governor. He was the man immediately and directly responsible for law and order in Palestine.

It is important to know that the Middle East was one of the most difficult areas for the Romans to control and govern. There were many zealots who constantly rebelled against Roman authority, and one cause of these rebellions was the severe Roman taxation. Judea was not a highly desired posting for a Roman diplomat. Many governors could not handle the population and the problems, and their terms in Palestine were generally short.

But Quirinius is known as a man of great efficiency and organizational talents. Shrewd and ruthless, he managed to enforce the policies of Rome. Quirinius was the real power-broker in the area, not king Herod, who often had problems with the emperor.

Why elaborate on these two characters? So that we may see whom and what the Lord Jesus faced when He had come into the flesh. The dynamic duo of Augustus and Quirinius was virtually invincible. It seemed that the political scene had been carved in stone, never to be changed, certainly not by the birth of child who claimed to be of the house and lineage of David. Augustus did not know of or reckon with the counsel of the Lord most high. He did what pleased him and whatever furthered the cause of his empire.

AN IMPERIAL DECREE

For we read that "in those days" (namely, after John the Baptist was born), "a decree went out from Caesar Augustus that all the world should be enroled." Let us call it a "census." Everyone was to be properly registered.

The purpose of this enrolment or census is clear. Augustus needed money to run his massive empire, and money is raised through taxation. In order to determine the amount of taxes from each region, everyone had to be registered, filing his income or net worth, so that a suitable tax amount could be determined. Therefore an imperial decree was issued that everyone was to be registered for taxation purposes. Who could oppose it?

We read in verse 3 that "all went to be enroled, each to his own city." Everyone had to go to his place of birth to be registered there. Now this rule may not have functioned throughout the empire, but it was necessary especially in the land of Israel. There are some simple reasons for this.

First, many Jews were scattered about, not only in Palestine, but also throughout the empire, and it was hard to determine their net worth, unless they went to their own villages and towns. Secondly, many Jews, though living elsewhere, still had an inheritance or land in their area of birth, and this could only be sorted out when everyone was in the right place at the right time. Someone's real net worth in Israel was determined within the framework of the family inheritance. So this measure was put in place, and a decree issued: everyone must go to his own city.

Augustus did not care that this measure caused much hardship for many families. He did not consider the upheaval and displacement a significant factor. He simply gave the command, an imperial decree of the highest order, and woe to anyone who disobeyed. We can imagine that especially the Jews, who considered themselves a free nation under God, were incensed at this imperial decree. They also hated the taxes. Remember how they later asked Jesus whether it was lawful to pay tax to Caesar? Because of its connection with taxation they hated the census even more. Many Jews tried to avoid it, and some zealots even attempted armed resistance. But to no avail. The imperial decree stood and would be fully enforced.

A HEAVENLY PURPOSE

This decree, issued in Rome, also affected Joseph and Mary, living in Nazareth. We read in verse 4, "And Joseph also went up from Galilee, from the city of Nazareth, to Judea, to the city of David, which is called Bethlehem, because he was of the house and lineage of David." Joseph's ancestral area was Bethlehem in Judea, so that is where he, according to the imperial decree had to report for the census.

We do not know whether Joseph and Mary had ever lived in Bethlehem before. Nor do we know how or why Joseph wound up in Galilee, in Nazareth, so far away from his home turf. It does seem a bit odd, doesn't it, that he should leave his ancestral territory. Many explainers suggest that Joseph and others of the "house of David" had left the area of Bethlehem because it was too dangerous for them to live there. The Romans as well as King Herod were much afraid of any competing claims to the throne of Israel. To be a known descendent of David, perhaps even an heir to the throne, could mean being arrested and executed. Therefore, perhaps, the remainder of David's descendants had fled to the far north, to Galilee (see also Matthew 3: 22).

But now Joseph is forced to return to Bethlehem. The imperial decree issued in far-away Rome affects even a poor carpenter in little Nazareth. When the emperor decrees, people move. But notice in what triumphant terms Luke describes the reason for Joseph's journey to Bethlehem, verse 4: "because he was of the house and lineage of David." House and lineage! He not only belonged to the "royal family" generally, he was directly in line to the throne particularly! The line to the throne of David went via Joseph.

We know that the great Son of David, the Heir of the royal house, had to be born in David's city. Thus his rightful claim to the throne of David would be even more clearly established. And that is the real reason behind Joseph's trip to Bethlehem. The imperial decree serves a *heavenly purpose*! The whole empire is set in motion, and the emperor in Rome has his own motives for this, but God's purpose is: to have the Son of David born in the city of David! Augustus and Quirinius have no idea of the fact that they are really subject to the sovereign power of Almighty God and are fulfilling His purpose.

GOD'S EDICT

We therefore see in these verses a clear antithesis and a mighty claim, which had sounded forth many centuries before in Psalm 2, by David: "O peoples, listen to the LORD's *decree*. . . : 'Thou art My Son, I have begotten thee. . .'. Take heed, O rulers of the earth, and hear; Be wise, O kings, and let His *edict* warn you" (from the rhymed version).

God's sovereign decree and His heavenly edict supersede the imperial decree from Rome. Mighty men are unwittingly serving the purpose of Almighty God. That is why we can say: on Christmas, God shows His sovereign power. Not Caesar determines where people go, but God does. He moves rulers and nations so that everyone is in the place which He has determined in His eternal counsel of redemption!

Here also the real *stage* is set: the battle will ultimately be waged over the whole world. God will set His kingdom over against the empire of Rome. Christ will be victorious from Bethlehem on, where He is born as Son of David. Luke specifically places the birth of Christ in this wide historical context, and proclaims in that way: here the Saviour of the *world* is preparing to be born; here, in His own city. Luke 2 is not the endearing story of the birth of a poor child with royal aspirations, but the mighty proclamation of the official arrival of the King of kings. Here the battle lines are drawn with a decree from heaven, "Thou art my Son, I have begotten Thee / This very day. To Thee I'll give the nations" (Psalm 2, rhymed version) The Almighty God shows His sovereign power in the birth of His Son there where He wants Him to be born.

We see this more often in the history of salvation. Time and again worldly rulers and mighty powers are used by God to serve His purpose. The Pharaoh of Egypt, the kings of Babel and Persia, and the emperors of Rome could do only one thing: serve the purpose that God has set. Is it any different today? No, it is even truer today. For Christ has been born, and died, and arose from the dead to ascend into the glory of heaven. Seated at the Father's right hand He, as Head of His church, governs all things.

AN OBSCURE BEGINNING

Luke shows the heavenly purpose in Jesus' birth at Bethlehem. At the same time, he does not hide the *obscure beginning* which is made in the birth of this child.

The word "obscure" means something that is not clear. It is covered, and its real impact is not yet seen. The true meaning of the event is not readily understood. Light is needed to make clear what is really happening here.

The question has been raised why *Mary* went along with Joseph to Bethlehem. Officially, in the case of a census, the wives did not have to come along but could stay at home. Did Joseph know of God's underlying purpose? Surely he did know from Mary the words of the angel Gabriel that the child would receive "the throne of His father, David" (Luke 1:32). Furthermore, Joseph himself had been addressed in his dream as "son of David" (Matthew 1: 20). So surely Joseph must have made some connection between the birth of the child and the city of David.

Maybe this is why he took Mary along. Some explainers suggest, however, that the real reason was her condition. She is called here by Luke, "Mary, his betrothed, who was with child." From Luke's phrasing it is not clear whether

Joseph and Mary were at this point officially married. Matthew's description gives us the sense that this was indeed the case. In any event, we do get the impression that it would not take long anymore for the birth to take place, and it would not do to leave Mary behind to have her child without Joseph being present. She might be open to ridicule and danger. Joseph and Mary will have talked about the matter: to go or not to go.

It could be a dangerous journey. Although the distance from Nazareth to Bethlehem is not much more than 100 kilometers, the road goes through difficult territory. The journey, by foot, would be long and slow, especially for a pregnant woman. One would think that Joseph may well have hesitated before making a decision. But the point is: Mary does go along!

NO ROOM IN THE INN?

As it turned out, the trip apparently did not cause great problems for this young couple. They arrived safely in Bethlehem. We read in verse 6, "And while they were there, the time came for her to be delivered." This may give the impression that they had been in Bethlehem already for a while, before the time of birth came. But, in view also of verse 7, where we are told that there was "no place for them in the inn," I rather conclude that relatively shortly after the arrival in Bethlehem, Mary went into labour. This, of course, complicated the search for a place to stay, for not everyone can accommodate a woman who is about to give birth!

There has been much ado about the words that there was "no room for them in the inn." Some modern explainers suggest that this information about lack of room simply cannot be true. The ancient world, and especially ancient Palestine, was noted for its hospitality. The Jews always opened their houses to travellers and refugees, especially to those in need. Therefore, some say, this text is probably proof of the "anti-semitism" which is said to have been present in the early Christian church. And "anti-semitism" (hatred of Jews) is wrong, of course.

One explainer suggests, however, that there may not have been room in the official *inn,* but that certainly some family took Joseph and Mary in and even gave them the main lodging room, where also some of the animals were kept during the colder months. We should therefore not conclude that this text gives proof for the idea that the people of Bethlehem (Israel) were inhospitable and at this point already rejected the Christ.

I think that there is truth in these remarks. No one knew that the child to be born was the Messiah. To say that the Jews in Bethlehem were inhospitable because they hated Jesus at this point is incorrect. It is true that Jesus was rejected, as John writes, "He came to His own, and His own received Him not." But here the beginning is still so obscure that no one really knew "what child this was"!

We have to look at it this way. The "inn" was not as we might imagine it today, something like a fancy motel. It was a gathering place, an open place, possibly at the outskirts of the town, where the travelling caravans and merchants stayed for the night. It was near the mountain just outside Bethlehem, against the cliff walls, where there were also many caves.

Now Joseph and Mary upon arrival probably went to this "inn," this lodging area, where there was a fire and water. There they found some room and comfort.

But when Mary went into labour, it was not possible anymore for them to stay in that public place. A child cannot be born in a public square where people are milling about, coming and going! In that sense there was no room for them in the "inn." So Joseph hastily had to seek another place. Where did he go? He retreated with Mary into one of the caves adjacent to the public area.

A CAVE AND A MANGER

It should be noted here that the oldest tradition claims that Jesus was born in a *cave*, just on the outskirts of old Bethlehem. That is where today a famous monument stands to mark the place of birth. About those caves we can also note the following: they were used by the shepherds of Ephratah as sheepfolds to keep their flocks in the cold season. These shepherds had built "mangers" in these caves, troughs dug out in the cave walls. It is in one of these troughs that Jesus was laid.

When we look at the verses in this way, many things fall into place. Now it also is clear why the shepherds knew exactly where to go, when they heard from the angel that the child would be found lying in a manger! They simply went to the caves where they sometimes kept their sheep. They knew the place quite well, and the last thing anyone would expect was to find a baby there, lying in one of those mangers! It was a clear sign to the shepherds that the angel spoke the truth (Luke 2: 12).

Christ started His life in a dark cave. The great Shepherd was born in a lowly sheepfold. It was a very *obscure* beginning indeed. Who could ever see in this child, in that dark cavern, the King of kings? The shepherds came and saw because of the *light* which the angel had cast on the event; otherwise they, too, would not have known. Special revelation was needed to understand Who this child was!

Indeed, it was an obscure beginning. Somewhere, just on the outskirts of the city of David, in a cave where normally sheep were kept, the Saviour of the world was born. And no one knew, except Joseph and Mary, and some shepherds later! We ourselves would not have known if Luke had not written about it.

A GLORIOUS END

Christ was born in a cave. He was also buried in a cave. He was laid in a sepulchre owned by Joseph of Arimathea. It ended as it began, in a dark and damp cavern.

But the obscure beginning did serve a glorious end! The child was born alive and in good health. He could grow up to fulfill His earthly task. He came out of that cave to reveal Himself mightily to His people. And He went from that sepulchre to the throne in heaven, after He had comforted His church.

An obscure beginning. Many did not and do not see the real meaning of this birth. They refuse to see it in the light of God's full revelation. Jesus had a tragic life, they say, with a sad ending. And they refuse to see his *death* in its true light. Therefore they cannot properly celebrate Christmas. It is for them not a true celebration.

But we may see from Scripture itself how an obscure beginning did lead to a glorious end! We see in Him and receive in Him our great Lord and King, our Saviour and Redeemer. This obscure beginning was not without reason. It was no fluke. God wanted it this way! The reason is that our faith should not rest on outward pomp and circumstance but on the real meaning of the ministry of Jesus Christ; that we should see His true glory.

It is a matter of faith that this baby, born in a cave, laid in a trough, is the one and only Saviour of the world. He rules the world by His almighty power. It is obscure no more. It is fully clear from the Scriptures. The real meaning of Christmas is unclear only to those who do not know the Bible.

We may rejoice that in the light of the Scriptures we may fully understand the work and the glory of this Saviour.

The True History of the Birth of Jesus Christ

"And she gave birth to her first-born son and wrapped him in swaddling cloths, and laid him in a manger because there was no place for them in the inn".

(Luke 2: 7)

There is only one proper manner in which to remember and celebrate the birth of our Lord. Certainly, we may make a happy day out of it with family and friends. There is nothing wrong with a festive meal with fellowship and sharing. But this may not become a goal in itself, which obscures the true meaning of Christmas. We must let the Word of God and the true worship of God determine everything from beginning to end.

Having focused earlier on the first seven verses of Luke 2, I now want to devote more attention to verse seven by itself.

We know the story of Christ's birth so well, and yet every year it must strike us, on the one hand, how amazingly simple the description of Luke really is. Never before has anyone like Christ been born, and never will anyone like Him be born again; yet Luke describes it to us in such simple terms. But on the other hand, these simple terms are deeply stirring: you cannot escape the solemnity of the biblical account.

As to the biblical simplicity: usually the birth of great people is surrounded by fantastic legends. There are some apocryphal accounts of Christ's birth which are nothing more than elaborate embellishments – "tasteless and unedifying", as one commentator aptly put it – of what the Bible tells us. Fact is mixed with fiction, and human imagination is added to divine revelation so that the truth is obscured.

The birth of Christ is to be proclaimed in truth and without embellishment. It must be done in simple and yet stirring terms, for so the Holy Spirit has revealed it. Perhaps we could summarize the message of Luke 2: 7 as follows: **the true history of the birth of Jesus Christ**, and note that it is both a simple history and a special one.

A SIMPLE HISTORY

It is not easy to tell the story of a birth in a clear and yet a restrained manner, paying attention to necessary detail and still preserving dignity. We can easily say too much or not enough. Although most of us know well the process of birth, there are also little children and perhaps older people who have not experienced or witnessed such an event.

Now Luke could have made quite a story out of it. In a lengthy first chapter he has built up the tension. Now the moment of the birth of Christ has arrived, and that has been the focal point of everything. Should Luke not now go into great detail and in depth describe to us the birth of our great Lord and King?

There is indeed detail and depth, not in the sensationalistic manner of the world, but in the quiet manner of the Word. We read about the decree of Caesar Augustus that everyone was to go to his place of birth for proper enrolment, and that also Joseph and Mary, who was pregnant, undertook a journey to their town of origin, which was Bethlehem.

And there in Bethlehem the Lord Jesus is born. In verse 6 we read, "the time came for her to be delivered," which simply means, she was "full term," her due date had come. Christ's birth was not premature or delayed, but came after a regular, full term pregnancy. When Joseph and Mary arrived in Bethlehem, the time had come for the child to be born.

Verse 7 tells us about the birth itself. It says: "she gave birth to her first-born son. . . ." That's it. That's all. It is indeed such a simple history. It does not say whether it was a very difficult or lengthy labour and delivery. We are not told how much the baby weighed at his birth and whether he was immediately healthy and strong, or not.

A FIRST-BORN SON

We do read that Mary gave birth to her "first-born." It was for Mary a first child, her first labour and delivery. It is generally agreed that the first time is often the most difficult, but the point is here not so much that it was a first delivery (the process) but that the child himself was her first-born (the result). It says nothing about the birth itself.

Now, giving birth is under the best of circumstances a difficult experience. In this case, for this young couple, having been displaced and cut off from their supportive and familiar surroundings in Nazareth of Galilee, being all alone, young and inexperienced, with no one to help, it must have been quite an ordeal!

Still, it is told in simple terms. "She gave birth to her first-born son." "First-born" implies that she later had more children, and even though this first birthing process was unique for Joseph and Mary, unique in many ways – as we will see more clearly later – yet it was simple like those that would follow.

THE SWADDLING CLOTHS

Now it was the custom in those days that right after a child was born it was washed, rubbed with some kind of body salt, and wrapped in cloths. It is clear that a new-born baby needs to be washed. It does not say whether Mary was able to use the body salt – perhaps she had none – but it does say that she wrapped him in "swaddling cloths."

The verb "to swaddle" means simply to bind or to wrap. The idea was to wrap the child snugly in these cloths to keep it warm. In the famous hymn about the shepherds watching their flocks by night (which is Hymn 17 in the Book of Praise of the Canadian Reformed Churches) there was a line about the babe being "all meanly wrapped in swaddling cloths." All meanly wrapped? As a child I thought, "How awful to wrap up this newly born child so tight that it almost suffocates." Was He maltreated from the moment He was born? But in truth it is quite simple: he was properly clothed for protection and warmth. There was nothing strange about it: it happened to all new-born infants in Israel. One family may have had nicer and newer swaddling cloths than another, but Christ, just like all other babies in His time, was properly washed and clothed.

In this light we can appreciate that the newer version of Hymn 17 – as we now have it – reads: ". . . Not as a King arrayed, but *humbly wrapped* in swaddling cloths. . .". Indeed, humbly, for "meanly" means commonly, in humility, without riches.

It says that Mary did all this. She gave birth, she wrapped, and she laid the child in the manger. She is on her own. We do not read that any other women came to help her. Of course, she will have received the loving help of Joseph. But most men are quite at a loss when it comes to labour, delivery, and post-natal care, certainly the first time around. Mary had to do the main portion of the work of post-natal care herself, despite her weakness and fatigue.

Many children have been born under difficult and poor circumstances. So it was with our Lord Jesus Christ. In simple terms, his was the normal birth of a healthy child, but one who was born in extreme poverty and under difficult circumstances. We can take it literally when the apostle Paul says that Christ who was rich (in heaven) became poor (on earth) in order that He might make us rich in him (2 Corinthians 8:9).

Back to our main point, then: it is a simple history. Until now, we have discovered nothing significant, nothing out of the ordinary. Luke tells it all in a restrained manner, with tasteful discretion, and yet in such a way that we know all we need to know about what happened that day.

Christ, our Saviour, came in the natural way of labour and delivery; He was born of woman, like all people, and His birth was very common. It is true, Christ came in a different sense than all others – for He alone is the eternal Son of God – but He came in a natural way, for He truly is son of man!

In no way may this be obscured or embellished. It has been told as it really happened. These are the facts as we must know them for our salvation. Christ did not come into the world in any spectacular way with a grand entry, but in the normal way of pregnancy and birth. In this manner He became truly one of us, flesh of our flesh and bone of our bone! And so He could begin in our flesh to overcome sin.

A SPECIAL HISTORY

It is indeed a simple story. But yet it is a special story. For this child, who was born that day in Bethlehem, is nevertheless the Son of God, the Saviour of the world. And indeed, it must be said of Him that He suffered from the *beginning* of his life to the end. We see this element come to the fore in the second part of verse 7.

For Luke adds something here that is indeed different: "[Mary] laid Him in a manger, because there was no place for them in the inn." This lying in a manger may be considered significant also in view of what the angel says to the shepherds: this will be a sign for you: you will find a babe wrapped in swaddling cloths – thus a new-born infant – and *lying in a manger.*

The manner in which Jesus is born may not be different from that of other births, but the place where He is laid is of great significance; it constitutes a sign!

THE NATIVITY SCENE

You have perhaps seen reproductions of the "nativity scene," and no matter how these scenes differ from each other, they all have this in common: the place looks so cosy and warm. A quaint little stall, a nice wooden crib with clean straw, a baby with healthy, rosy cheeks, proud parents and smiling shepherds, even interested animals looking on with a sheepish grin. Not a bad atmosphere at all, really, in which to be fostered as an infant.

I do not want to poke fun at these scenes, but I do have to point out that they hardly reflect the reality of Christmas. We do not know exactly where Jesus was born in Bethlehem – and the commentators differ greatly on what is the proper explanation of the words in which the event is described – but from our text a few important matters do become quite clear.

It says that there was "no room for them in the inn." What we have to understand by the word "inn" was explained in the previous chapter. The word used for "inn" meant, as we saw: a place to let down, tie down the animals and lie down yourself. It was a rest-area, as we sometimes have them at the roadside. The area was generally divided into two sections: one for the people, around a fire, an open hearth, and one for the animals in a type of cave. And the word used for "manger" means indeed "feeding trough." "Manger" is derived from a verb (think of the French "manger") which means "to eat". This, as we saw, was for the shepherds a clear sign of identification. For you do not normally find babies in a manger. In a manger you find slop, not sucklings. Shepherds knew all about animal feeding areas, how dirty they were. Every barn or stable, let alone those in a public area, is filled with bacteria and filth. The shepherds also knew where these mangers were. They didn't have to go checking all sorts of places, asking whether a baby was born, for there was only one place to look: the public rest area. And that was indeed where they found the infant: it was exactly as the angel had told them.

And to think that this child, lying in that manger, is indeed Christ, the Lord, the awaited Messiah, the Son of David! Here is where the history becomes special and different from any other birthday story. Here the extreme poverty becomes a humiliation, an emptying, which will lead to the final humiliation on the cross of Golgotha.

I think now of Hymn 19 in The *Book of Praise*, "For though God's equal, though eternal King, He did not to His rightful glory cling. . . Himself He *emptied* that He us might save. . . ."

The Son of God comes out of the glory of heaven into the Bethlehem slop; He comes from a heavenly throne to a feeding trough, because now already He begins to bear the wrath of God for our sins. That is the special history of Christmas! And if this is His beginning, what will His end be? He will go from manger to tomb, from rock bed to rock bed, enduring even the agony of hell, for our sake, because of our sins.

LACK OF HOSPITALITY?

Often, in connection with this verse, a verse from John 1 is quoted, "He came to His own home and His own people knew Him not." And frequently you can read as commentary: how awful, the King was born and no one knew!

But the people in Bethlehem could not know initially that in this way and in that place a Saviour was born to them. The Lord God used the shepherds for that purpose later: they made known to Bethlehem and surrounding area the birth of the Messiah. What John refers to when He writes "His own people knew Him not" is that the people *when told*, refused to acknowledge Him as their Saviour! The expression, "They knew Him not" does not mean: we didn't know about Him, but it means: we knew, yet we said, No! We don't want such a Saviour. And that rejection has to do with the fact that they never knew their own misery, never acknowledged the depth of their own sin. No one did identify the poverty of the babe in the manger with the extreme misery of his own sin.

Meanwhile, the process of emptying Himself has begun. And He will have to go all the way, drinking the cup to the last drop.

We see here something of the great, inexplicable love of God that He gave His only-begotten Son, who from the beginning had to bear the eternal wrath of God. We see here something of the immeasurable love of Christ who, though He was Father's everlasting Son, did not despise the virgin's womb. We see here something of the great love of the Holy Spirit, who alone does guide us to understand and to know Him, receive and acknowledge Him, as our Saviour. I think here of the old hymn, "Te Deum" (Hymn 2 in the *Book of Praise*), the Hallelujah of the New Testament church.

SHOPPING MALL YULETIDE

The world, too, knows that the "Christmas story" is simple, yet special. Many would agree if you told them that the history of Christ's birth is one of stirring simplicity and special depth. They would say: yes, it strikes a tender chord with us, too. It strikes a chord, but it does not lead to an eternal song, for the world has made this feast into a celebration of human kindness and good cheer in bad days. People do not want to know the truth about Christ or about themselves. Therefore Christmas makes no real difference in their lives.

The trouble with most shopping mall and yuletide "nativity scenes" is that they focus the attention on one aspect and do not give the living history. The trouble with most people is that they never really get beyond the shopping mall and mistletoe mentality. But is not the trouble with *us,* Reformed people, that we do not let the reality of Christ's earthly ministry encourage and motivate us to a newer and better service?

Slowly but steadily, we are taking over the Christmas style celebration of the world around us. Our manner of celebrating Christmas is already much more integrated with our society than was that of our parents. And it is being said: it's only a matter of style, not content! What's wrong with a festive atmosphere? With some lights, some boughs, a Christmas tree? That's only atmosphere, indeed. But be careful that the main issue is not lost among us, that the true story is known, the real meaning of Christmas not obscured!

The main issue is our dedication and commitment to the Lord, who went from the manger to the throne; it is our seeking first the kingdom of heaven and the righteousness of God in Christ. Here is where the devil wants to wean us away from the truth of God's Word. He tries to do it in his own special, deceptive way, by giving lots of atmosphere, but no room to breathe spiritually; by providing lots of trees, but not the tree of life, and lots of lights, but not the Light of the World.

For the devil likes to make Christmas into a carnival. He is the great pretender, the great deceiver, who takes away the Word and gives "atmosphere" instead. The devil takes this special story and vulgarizes it, makes it romantic and endearing, a story of human kindness and of men of goodwill. He commercializes it, neutralizes it, paganizes it, packages it and then says: here you have it, Merry Christmas!

We may never separate style from content, for the one is reflected in the other. Keep combining simplicity with depth. Especially on Christmas Day. Then it will remain for us and our children indeed a very special history, which leads us to sing of the victory of Christ over death and satan's power infernal. And the true history will motivate us to greater service.

The Glory of the Lord in Ephratah's Fields

". . .and the glory of the Lord shone around them, and they were filled with fear."

(Luke 2: 9B)

On Christmas Day, as our text says, "the glory of the Lord" shone round about the shepherds in the field of Ephratah. I cannot see this "glory" as being anything else than a brilliant light. God is light, says the Bible. He dwells in an impregnable light, and therefore His "glory" is also manifested in terms of "light," an incomparable, majestic brilliance that makes everything in it glow and shine.

The darkness of the night was suddenly removed by the brightness of the glory of God. There was no gradual transition from dark to light, as in the early morning or evening, no dawn or dusk, but it was as if someone had suddenly switched on mighty floodlights. Dark one moment, light the next!

I suggest that the appearing of this light was an altogether unique and special event. It never happened in this way before Christmas, and it never happened in this way afterward.

THE BURNING BUSH AND OTHER MANIFESTATIONS

Certainly, the glory of the LORD was seen before on this earth. We can think, for example, of the time when the Angel of the LORD appeared to Moses in the burning bush (Exodus 3: 2). That was also a manifestation of light, a fire burning by itself, without consuming any fuel. Fire too is light.

Think of other appearances of God, for example the one at Mount Sinai, when Israel had been led out of the house of bondage. In Exodus 19: 18 you can read how the LORD descended on Mount Sinai "in fire." That fire was wrapped in smoke, contained as it were "in a kiln," an oven. The glory of the LORD in the bush and on the mountain was limited and obscured, because people could not bear to see the full light of God.

At that time, after Moses had ascended the mountain to receive the Law, he came down and "the skin of his face shone," because he had been so close to God, and the people were afraid to come near him (Exodus 34). The light was so bright that Moses required a veil over his face whenever he spoke with the people!

And when God's glory descended into the tabernacle, upon the ark, we read in Exodus 40: 35 that even Moses was not able to enter, because "the glory of the LORD filled the tabernacle." Even Moses could not stand *in* the light of this glory!

Are you beginning to get the picture? Never before have any persons, not even Moses, been so taken up in the glory of God as these shepherds were! It says in our text: the glory of the Lord shone *around* them, and that means: God's glory, God's brilliant light completely enveloped and surrounded them. All around them was this light, like a wall of fire, and they were standing right in the middle of it.

Compare again the situation of these shepherds with that of Moses at the burning bush. Here is Moses, and there is the bush. Here is Moses, and a little farther off is the light. Moses is not standing in the light at all, but outside it. Indeed, the Lord even warns Moses not to come closer. Moses may not come near the fire, let alone be taken up in it. And he is reminded that he is a sinful man who cannot stand in the presence of a holy God: "Take off your shoes from your feet." We see in Exodus 3 a remarkable distance between Moses and the light of God's presence. God is still far, even though He is close.

But in the fields of Ephratah it is different. Here are the shepherds, and here is also the light! There is no longer any distance between the presence of men and the manifestation of God's glory. God's glory illuminates the shepherds. God has come so close that *men* are for the first time fully taken up in His glory. They are not even told to take off their shoes or sandals. They are taken up in the glory of God just as they are, where they stand.

As you see, the history of redemption never repeats itself. There is always progression in the work of God. The LORD God has made another mighty leap in the history of salvation. God has come closer to His people; He is closer than was ever seen before.

And let us not say now: but God Himself was not present there in the fields of Ephratah as He was in the burning bush; it was only an angel, not God Himself. For this is not true. The expression, "the glory of the Lord" denotes the majesty with which God Himself appears on this earth. God is indeed seated on the throne of heaven, but He is also present in the fields of Ephratah with His glory, majesty, grace, and power! Where the glory of God appears, there God Himself is manifest.

MEGAPHOBIA

The shepherds are taken up, suddenly, in nothing less than the glory of God. In one instant they stand in the presence of almighty God and share in the heavenly glory that normally is seen only by angels. There is no cloud of smoke to obscure the brilliance of that glory, there is no veil given to block out its penetrating power; they see it as it is, and it surrounds them. Can you understand that it is said of these men, "They were filled with fear"? Literally it says: they feared with a great fear! Two Greek words are used which we also know in English: *mega-phobia!*

All the young people know the word "mega." There's even a rock group called "Megadeath." When someone makes a lot of money, we say that he makes megabucks. Megaphobia: a fear that is so great that it grips you to the core of your existence, so that you cannot so much as move. Phobia, also in our language, is a fear that controls you, so that you are virtually paralysed and cannot function as you should.

We sing "Silent night, holy night, all is calm, all is bright." It's bright all right, but not very calm. Who can be calm when he suffers from megaphobia? Christmas is not some kind of peaceful "interlude" when even perpetually warring factions have a brief ceasefire. The first Noel led to great fear, to hearts that pounded with an all-pervading sense of dread.

Why this megaphobia? How would *you* have felt if you had stood in the shoes or sandals of these shepherds? If you experienced the sudden switch from pitch dark to brilliant light? If you saw the luminous figure of an angel suddenly before you, and the whole area lit up, with everything around you appearing like a surreal landscape? And it happened without any warning. It was not as if a faraway light had caught the shepherds' attention and they watched it come closer. The angel, it says, appeared, that is, he materialized out of nowhere. Suddenly he stands before you, and with him comes the splendour of heavenly light never seen before. How would you react?

Why such megaphobia? There is, of course, the element of surprise, the sudden happening of the unknown. But I think that we must go a step further to understand this fear. The shepherds were perhaps not gifted or learned men, but they knew all about light and dark, sunshine and moonshine. They knew when they saw something that was not "of this world." For them this brilliant light could mean only one thing: it was the manifestation of the living God. And that being so, they feared that they now stood face to face with their doom. Every Israelite knew: no one can see God and survive. Their megaphobia is a matter of knowing that they cannot live, for all flesh must wilt before the fire of God's presence. It is the fear of God that fills them with this unspeakable dread. For God is the Judge, who can sweep them into eternal darkness.

A SIGN OF CELEBRATION

They experience this light as a sign of condemnation, and therefore cannot understand that it is in fact a sign of celebration! They do not yet see that the "glory of God" which envelopes them is evidence that God has come to dwell with mankind in a way never seen before. They do not yet see that God here starts a new chapter in the relationship with His people, and that this chapter begins with the birth of Jesus Christ.

For there is only one explanation for this pouring out of the glory of God. God has come down to us, to dwell with us, rich in mercy and in love. The heavenly light does not consume the shepherds but illumines them. They are not destroyed by it; they are taken up in it. This manifestation of God's glory is a celebration of the work of salvation in the birth of Jesus Christ, our Lord. When the Son of God comes into the flesh, the glory of God does not stay behind, but spills out of the heavens over the fields of Ephratah, and in its rising tide takes up the shepherds. One angel appears, but soon more follow: suddenly (verse 13) there is with the angel a multitude of the heavenly host, praising God! It's almost as if the distance between heaven and earth, between God and creature, between men and angels is wiped out altogether. The earth may share in the glory of heaven, and men may hear the song of angels.

MEGA-JOY

For God has come down to deliver His people through Him Who is greater than Moses, from an enemy mightier than Pharaoh, and now the light of heaven will decisively break through the darkness of this earth. For unto us a Son is born, unto us a child is given, and the government shall be upon His shoulders! God has come down to man, in the flesh; and the glory of God shines around simple men. This has never happened before. God has decisively broken through the darkness with the light of heaven.

Therefore the angel can also say: fear not! Do not let this heavenly light fill you with dread! For I bring you good news of a great joy! Instead of megaphobia, let there be mega-joy! Instead of mega-death, let there be mega-life! This glory, this light, is not the ominous sign of eternal condemnation, but the glorious dawn of the era of salvation. To you is born this day in the city of David, a *Saviour*, Who is Christ, the Lord. Now is the time, not to flee from the light, but to stand in the Light. Savour the moment, bask in the warmth, draw near to the burning bush, for the day of salvation has come. The people who in darkness walked, have seen a glorious Light!

THERE IS DARKNESS. . . .

Yes, but what about sin and death? How can sinful men stand in this light and live? Notice that there *is* darkness on Christmas Day. There's no light at the manger. The Son of God has cast off His glory, which he had when He was at the bosom of the Father, and has entered into our darkness. The weight of our sins is already pressing upon Him, and the curse of God is taking its effect on Him.

The light and glory are not where they should have been, there where the Son of God is. For the Son has become a servant, and has emptied Himself, and will be obedient unto death, even the death of the cross. Darkness will cover Him all His days, and ultimately, on the cross of Golgotha, the darkness will enshroud Him and swallow Him up. He will face mega-fear and mega-death so that we may experience mega-joy!

The glory of God which shone around the shepherds is something that we have not seen. It is only described to us. It did not last, either. When the angel choirs withdraw and retreat to heaven, the fields of Ephratah are dark again. Once more the glory of God is shrouded behind the clouds, contained as in a kiln in the confines of heaven.

GLIMPSES OF GLORY

The glory of God that appeared on Christmas Day was never again seen in the same manner. When the people saw Jesus walking, they saw no glory. I know, on the mount of transfiguration a few disciples, Peter, James, and John, saw a remarkable change in Jesus' outward appearance. It says in Matthew 17: 2, "And He was transfigured before them, and His face shone like the sun, and His garments became white as light." It was again a brief glimpse of things to come. And when Stephen later stood before the Jewish council, we read (Acts 6: 15) that "all who sat in the council saw that his face was like the face of an angel." Another brief glimpse of things to come. And when Stephen had finished speaking, we read that, "gazing into heaven. . . he saw the glory of God, and Jesus standing at the right hand of God" (Acts 7:55). Here we have a glimpse of a tremendous reality: Jesus appears in glory!

These glimpses are reminders to us that the glory is still there. But never did it shine so brightly on earth as in that night, when Christ was born.

God does not tell us of this light so that we may concentrate on what once was, but to encourage us to look forward. The glory of the Lord shone around them. Yes, it did. But something greater is about to happen. The glory of the Lord will shine around you. One day you will see this light. One day you will hear these angels. For we are children of light. We have been called out of the darkness, writes Peter, into His marvellous light. This light is our destination! And its powerful effect must now already be seen in our lives. The light that is from heaven must now be reflected in our hearts, in our deeds.

It is not without significance that the glory of God was again withdrawn. Even after Christ's resurrection, God's glory was not seen by men. The glory is still contained within the kiln of heaven. There is much darkness here below.

On Christmas Day we often are struck more by the existing darkness than by the light that once shone. There is the darkness of war, sickness, loneliness, sorrow, and death. For some, maybe even some of us, Christmas time is filled with unspeakable sadness because of the brokenness of life. During these times, more than at other times perhaps, we miss those taken from us. Where is the light and the glory that once illuminated the shepherds?

I'LL BE HOME FOR CHRISTMAS

But we must understand that this text is not nostalgic, but prophetic. People wax nostalgic, "I'll be home for Christmas, if only in my dreams." But God's Word is prophetic! You *will* be home for Christmas, and it won't be in your dreams!

Where is home? There is a city, a paradise, of which it is written, "and night shall be no more; they need no light of lamp or sun, for the Lord God will be their Light, and they shall reign for ever and ever" (Revelation 22: 5).

The glory of the Lord will shine around you, and you will be filled with mega-joy! *Mega*, a nice word for Christians! As long as you connect it properly. As I mentioned, *Megadeath* is the name of a worldly rock-group. It is a well-chosen name, really. They may not know it, but that's precisely where they are headed, unless they repent. Without Christ, it's mega-death. Eternal death. Mega-phobia. Eternal despair. Praise God that you are not a member of that cult of doom.

For we celebrate mega-joy! That's what makes Christmas so wonderful, every year again. That is why we can hang in, even in dark days, for the Light just won't disappear. It's there, and one day the glory of the Lord will shine around us, we'll be taken up in it, fully, eternally, because Jesus Christ lived and died here for our sake. And the shepherds will tell you: this is even better than Ephratah!

Ephratah, they will say, you should have seen that light, man, we were so scared! It came so unexpectedly. Jesus was then still in a manger. What did we know? Man, we had megaphobia! But this is greater, for Jesus is now on the throne in glory, for ever. This is better than Ephratah. We expect the light of Him Who sits on the throne. We'll be so close to the Lord we can actually see Him, touch Him, walk with Him. In the brilliant light of the new earth.

That is our real joy on Christmas Day.

> He sent His Son with power to save.
> From guilt, and *darkness* – see that word? – and the grave.
> He through this world will guide His own,
> And lead us to His holy throne!
> His mercies ever shall endure
> When this dark world shall be no more!" (Hymn 61, *Book of Praise*).

The Reaction to the First Proclamation of the Birth of Christ

"... and all who heard it wondered at what the shepherds had told them. But Mary kept all these things, pondering them in her heart. And the shepherds returned, glorifying and praising God for all they had heard and seen, as it had been told them".

(Luke 2: 18-20)

Practically everyone in some way or another celebrates Christmas. I cannot think of anyone who is not at least to some extent affected by the seasonal "Christmas spirit." There may be the die-hard cynic who says that "Christmas" means nothing to him, but deep down everyone shares something of the feeling of Christmas. It is hard to escape it with all the commercial hype and seasonal sentimentality.

As I have stated before, do not think that it is wrong to enter the Christmas "feeling." If you are, like me, a romantic at heart, you cannot help being sentimental at such occasions. And for children, especially, it is an exciting time of the year. Youngsters can have strong feelings about Christmas.

The late Dr. K. Schilder, a well-known Reformed scholar who died in the early fifties, once wrote an article on the topic: "Feeling" and Christmas. He agreed that we may at Christmas time experience a sense of particular joy, even if this joy is based in part on enjoying the cosiness of family gatherings.

CHESTNUTS AND JACK FROST

Christmas does have its own cozy atmosphere, with "Chestnuts roasting on open fire, Jack Frost nipping at your nose." Christmas is indeed the time to be with family and friends, a time of sharing, out of which great memories are born.

At the same time, Dr. Schilder warned that Christmas must not be merely a matter of *feeling*, but essentially a matter of *faith*. It is not a feast determined by fantasy but governed by facts. He remarked that many people who like to emphasize the feeling often deny or neglect the facts of Christmas. The romantic idealists of the previous century were among the first to deny the virgin birth.

In this connection Schilder warned that we do not "romanticize" Christmas because of its cozy atmosphere. We cannot just "feel" Christmas, we must believe Christmas. We must see its significance, not as an isolated event, but within the framework of God's work of salvation. On Christmas Day we must note the facts and place them in their proper biblical light. We must reflect on the meaning of the facts for us today. We must *reflect*, not reminisce or merely pause, but deeply ponder, and come away, amazed, with praise and thanksgiving!

This is the direction in which the Bible itself points us in Luke 2. The narrative concerning Christ's birth ends with the praise of the shepherds, people who came away from Bethlehem with the faith that a great and mighty wonder had occurred, and who were *therefore* filled with a special feeling.

We want to take a look at what the Bible tells us about the reaction of the people who were directly involved with the first Christmas to the public proclamation of the birth of Christ in their midst. What did they do with it? How did it affect and change their lives? And from there on we want to see how it must affect us who have greater knowledge and deeper insight.

THE HESITANT AMAZEMENT OF THE PEOPLE

Admittedly, it is not easy to reconstruct exactly how everyone reacted. Besides, people often react wrongly or later change their minds. People are fickle; you can't really do much with their initial reactions. But still it is not without reason that Luke records these reactions. He does so in order that we may learn what is pleasing to God, and what reaction He requires of us. That is what we want to discover: what is the LORD God telling us in this passage of Scripture?

The shepherds' initial reaction to the message of the angels was one of great enthusiasm.The appearance of the angels was too majestic to ignore. And so we read that these simple men went with haste to Bethlehem (verse 16), and after some searching, they found Mary and Joseph, and the babe "lying in a manger," just as it had been told them.

We read in verse 17, "And when they saw it, they made known the saying which had been told them concerning this child." Undoubtedly the shepherds told Mary and Joseph what had happened in the fields of Ephratah, and they, in turn, will have been told by Mary and Joseph the circumstances leading up to the birth of Jesus. There must have been an excited interchange of information.

Apparently the shepherds had no difficulty accepting the truth of what they had seen. They may not have fully understood every aspect, but it was clear to them: this child is the promised seed of David, the Messiah of God! And faith led to a public confession. The shepherds became evangelists. Indeed, when you want an example of spontaneous evangelism, look for it on Christmas morning: they made known the saying which had been told them concerning this child. They went out and spoke of the message of the angels. They had no direct mandate for this, but it was a matter of course: they could not do otherwise but proclaim the Word concerning this child.

Now shepherds were generally not the most respected and trusted types in Israel. As a matter of fact, they were held in very low esteem. Still, it will have come as a great surprise to the people who heard them speak to hear such a message. What? Our great King, born here, in a stable? What is it these men are telling us?

It says in Luke 2: 18, ". . . and all who heard it wondered at what the shepherds told them." It does not say how many people heard the testimony of the shepherds. There are many details which Luke does not mention. But we may safely assume, given the way words tend to travel, that a good number of people in Bethlehem and vicinity heard about what had happened. And, as one explainer notes, since Jerusalem was only six miles from Bethlehem, it is quite possible that even some of the citizens of Jerusalem heard stories about the strange happenings in and around Bethlehem.

Luke does not say that all these people outrightly rejected what was told them by the shepherds. On the contrary, the Jews were quite open for supernatural occurrences. It says that they wondered; literally, that they marvelled. They were amazed by the whole story. This means that it was something completely unexpected. It became the talk of the town. Perhaps some of the villagers went to look for themselves to see whether the stories of the shepherds about a babe in a manger were true. If they went, they could indeed see the child and hear what Mary and Joseph had to say. But it is possible that not that many took the trouble to go and look. The shepherds' tale may have appeared too fantastic and incredible.

Still, people wondered. They did not shrug it off without any further thought. They did not reject it immediately. And they were puzzled by the whole thing: what could it possibly mean?

Imagine this conversation taking place, somewhere in Bethlehem. Did you hear what these shepherds were telling in the village this morning? What do you make of it? I don't know, but it doesn't seem plausible to me! Why would the angels appear to them, the shepherds, and not to us, the citizens of Bethlehem? Yes, come to think of it, the whole thing is rather strange, isn't it?

I suggested that people generally reacted with hesitant amazement. They did not conceal their surprise; they may even have been moved by the story, but it does not appear that their lives were really affected. There was a hesitation which led them away from the importance of the facts. Soon they would go on with the things of everyday life. The testimony of the shepherds caused a ripple on the pond of life in Bethlehem, but that was about it. In the end, people shrugged their shoulders and carried on as before.

CHRISTMAS: FLEETING FASCINATION

All who heard it, wondered. Now I ask myself if this is not the most common reaction to the Christmas happening, also today. People are generally fascinated by the Christmas story. It has all the ingredients of an amazing tale. At Christmas time many people may even think for a moment: isn't it remarkable that this child was born in such a manner? Such a lowly birth and yet such lofty ideals!

People wonder about this birth. They may not immediately shrug it off as nonsense, but they often do not come much beyond "wondering." There is also today a hesitant amazement. There may be agreement in principle about at least some of the facts, but without commitment in practice. Many people around us will "believe" that Jesus was born on Christmas Day. But they hesitate to go any further; it has no impact on their lives. Therefore, they soon forget and move on to more important things. In fact, then, Christmas does not really function in their lives. It is merely a fleeting fascination.

It's not that most people do not know. But they only pay attention to what they themselves like to hear. They have made the real history into a sentimental story, as a setting for a man-centred feast, in which also some homage is paid to God. Never do we hear more carols or hymns on our television and radio stations than at Christmas time. But what effect does this really have on society? People will have to come further than expressing just a hesitant amazement. They will have to stop and think about what has really happened.

MARY'S PONDERING

But we see a certain progression here in this passage. The people wondered. But, Luke writes, indicating sharp contrast, ". . . Mary kept all these things, pondering them in her heart." There's a lot of difference between "wondering" and "pondering," is there not?

Mary does come a step further than most other people. Now, of course, you can write that off as maternal love and care. Every new mother (especially with her first child) is very keenly tuned in to whatever is said about her child. It may be that Mary was at first somewhat disappointed at the circumstances in which her son was born. The angel had said to her (Luke 1: 32 ff.), "He will be great, and be called the Son of the Most High, and the LORD will give to Him the throne of His father David. . . ," but it surely did not look that way at all. It was no birth fit for a king! Therefore, the arrival and the testimony of the shepherds will have given Mary a lift and strengthened her weary soul: it is true, my son is destined for great things after all! What mother would not carefully note all that is said about her first-born child?

A HIGHER SPIRITUAL LEVEL

But perhaps we should place this on a higher spiritual level. Mary's reaction is indeed maternal, typically that of a mother, but it is also more than that. We read first: she kept all these things. This means: she observed and listened very carefully. There was no detail which escaped her that morning, despite her weakened condition. And she accurately committed all these things to her mind and memory. Whatever she will forget in life, not this! She will have other children, but none of them will be born under these circumstances and be surrounded with such testimony.

It was very important that Mary committed these things carefully to memory. For did she not have to testify later about the facts and their sequence? It is quite possible that Luke, who writes this account, himself heard it from Mary. When Luke wrote his Gospel, Mary could very well have been still alive, an elderly woman of about eighty. In any case, Luke himself tells us in chapter 1 that he "followed all things closely," that is, he conducted a careful investigation, using reliable sources. One of the sources used in the gospels was the careful and detailed knowledge of Mary.

But Mary does more than just memorize the facts. Committing something to memory does not necessarily mean that you understand what is happening. To know the facts is one thing; to interpret them is another. Luke says: Mary kept all these things, pondering them in her heart. "Pondering" means that you give a matter some deep thought. The original Greek verb means something like: bringing together, collecting. Mary notes the facts, and tries to piece things together. How does the testimony of the shepherds accord with her own experiences? Is there a clear line? Is there a significant and consistent development?

DIGESTING IN FAITH

Mary is asking herself: what does it mean? What does it tell me about this my child? It says that she ponders all this *in her heart.* The heart is the core of life. I believe that these words mean that she is digesting also these new developments *in faith.* She already believes that her Son is the Messiah, the Son of God. The angel Gabriel told her so. And what now happens is a clear confirmation of that early message. Mary knows that the long and difficult months of pregnancy have been vindicated . The Lord God has remained true to His promise. Even if the outward circumstances of this birth do not bear it out, this child is indeed the Son of David, Christ the Lord!

We are in this passage not presented with the thoughts of a proud mother, but we are taught that the Lord God caused Mary to piece things together, to tie in previous revelations with new revelations, and so to get a good view on the entire matter! For this is the activity of the believer. See how it all fits. See how it all points to one inescapable conclusion: Jesus is the Christ, the Son of the living God. And that is how we must receive this Word of God today.

Maternal pondering, yes. But it is certainly done in a spiritual manner: facts are put together in the perspective of divine revelation. Mary is here more than just a mother; she is already a believer. And we must be more than spectators, for we, too, must put things together in the light of God's entire revelation.

Now I know that Mary still had a long way to go. She had to learn to divest herself of motherly pride. She had to learn not to stand in the way of the Son of God. She had her plans and expectations which did not always accord with God's plans. She had to step back so that He could step forward in His own time. She had to learn that, although He was her son, He was also her Lord! She had to come to confess Him as her Saviour. She would have to stand at the foot of His cross. She would also have to experience the outpouring of the Holy Spirit. Mary was just a beginner on the path of faith. But there was a decisive beginning.

Faith always begins with hearing the Word, with keeping it in mind and pondering it, with piecing the facts together in the light of all God's revelation. We must accept this, no matter how much we have to deny ourselves. Believe me, Mary had to learn self-denial! So do we! It begins on Christmas Day: we must see in this child the Saviour of God and receive Him personally as such. And then we must go and glorify God for what He has given us in his Son.

EXUBERANT PRAISE OF THE SHEPHERDS

For there is yet one reaction which we must consider in this passage, namely that of the shepherds, with whom we started. We saw how they went to Bethlehem in haste, and how they proclaimed to all whom they met what they had heard and seen. Of these shepherds we are finally told, "And the shepherds returned, glorifying and praising God for all they heard and seen, as it had been told them" (verse 24).

The way this is stated indicates joyous *exuberance.* These men are really filled with great excitement and happiness. They cannot cease to talk about it and they constantly relive each moment of that wondrous night and day. I imagine an exuberant, boisterous group of men returning to their flocks filled with a deep wonder which cannot be hidden. Glorifying and praising God is usually a visible and audible affair, don't you think?

I think that we have here the *climax* of the Christmas story. This is what the Lord God envisioned from the very beginning: that His Name would be praised, not just by angels, but by His people! Here we see the real height of the progression in "the first Noel," if I may use that term.

Remember how it started? With a mighty angelic choir singing: Glory to God in the highest! That must have been wonderful music in God's ears! But this is how it ends: joyful men going on their way rejoicing and glorifying God. And it is the praise of His people that God seeks! More important to Him than the beautiful songs of the angels is the simple praise of His children on earth. That's the teaching of the Bible. And when this is combined, angels and men glorifying God together, is there any symphony more exalted?

The shepherds have to go back to their flocks, of course. Life goes on. Their task waits. But they return vastly different from the way they came. It says that they go glorifying and praising God.

Now these two words, glorifying and praising, basically mean the same. The first word glorifying means to magnify, to make great. And it has the connotation: to make great on the basis of the facts. It is not really the shepherds who make God great. God shows His greatness in the facts of salvation!

The second word, praising, has in it the notion of granting joyous approval to something. It means to *concur* with the facts! It implies a deep sense of agreement. So take that together: the shepherds go on their way, recognizing that God is great because of what He has done, and they give their agreement and assent to this work. God is great! The facts demonstrate it. They concur with it, and so they share in it.

Notice also how it says: glorifying God for all they had heard and seen. First *heard*: from the angel and the angelic host. The heavenly Word precedes the human vision. But also *seen*: for the eyes see what God has said. The facts bear out the truth of the Word. It is not the other way around: first seeing and then perhaps hearing an explanation later, but first hearing and then seeing that it is exactly as it had been told them.

I repeat: the revelation of God has priority. If the shepherds had not first heard the message from heaven, they never would have "seen" in this child their King and Saviour. But now they return glorifying and praising God. For He shows that His Word is Truth. He causes His people to see things which they otherwise never would have noticed. So the Word becomes flesh.

On Christmas Day we have the calling to start with what God has said and has been proclaimed also to us. This is what we must believe. And whoever believes will also see! For us this means that we will see Christ, not as a babe in a manger, but as glorified King, seated on the throne of heaven. If we believe this, we, too, will come to the level of praise that is required. We will acknowledge the greatness of God in His work of redemption in Jesus Christ, born in such a simple yet wondrous manner.

ENDURING JOY?

I have often wondered about these shepherds. We do not read about them anymore in the Gospels. Did their faith withstand the test of time? Did their great joy endure? Or were they, like many others, later greatly offended at Christ's ministry? Perhaps several of them never lived to see the day, some thirty years later, that He was crucified, perhaps some did. What happened to these first witnesses, these first evangelists, these first confessors of Christ?

We do not know. And is it really important for us personally? The question for us is: what is *our* reaction? In light of all that we know today, do we earnestly believe with our whole heart, and truly love the Lord Jesus? Will our faith withstand the test of time in our days? Will our joy endure? We have not seen the babe in the manger, but we do have the completed revelation of God. We have access to a Saviour Who is now glorified in heaven after having finished His work on earth. Let these shepherds not one day testify against us because of our unbelief or lack of commitment. But let their praise lead us to stand in greater awe of God's great work of salvation in Jesus Christ. Let us praise God's Name exuberantly, with audible and visible joy! Let us pray for a childlike and enthusiastic faith, which leads to joyous testimony and life-long commitment. Then the feeling of Christmas never ends, but carries over to the marriage feast of the Lamb, where we may mingle our voices with those of the angels in never-ending praise: glory to God and peace on earth!

Jesus Christ Received into the House of David

"When Joseph awoke from sleep, he did as the angel of the Lord commanded him; he took his wife, but knew her not until she had borne a son; and he called his name Jesus".

(Matthew 1: 24, 25)

We turn now to a passage from the Gospel according to Matthew, a Gospel which has aptly been called "the royal Gospel." For Matthew's purpose is to proclaim Jesus as the promised Messiah, the Son of David, the seed of Abraham. Matthew wants to demonstrate very clearly that God has fulfilled the prophecies of old in Jesus the Christ.

In our text Matthew establishes the *legitimacy* of Jesus. That is, he shows that Jesus lawfully, according to the Scriptures, takes the place assigned to Him as the Messiah. Matthew was writing first of all for the Jews in Palestine, and it was very important to convince these Jews that Jesus was truly and lawfully the Christ, Son of David, seed of Abraham.

This is why we have in Matthew 1: 1-17 the famous genealogy or list of names. Here is also the reason why in Matthew's account *Joseph* receives such a prominent place. While Luke devotes more space to Mary and to her experiences, Matthew concentrates on Joseph and his role in the birth of the Lord.

Joseph and Mary each have their own place and task in the history of revelation. Most often attention is concentrated on Mary, and on what she has done. We know that she has become the object even of idolatry. Usually Joseph is left somewhere in the background, as if he had little or nothing to do with the birth of Christ.

It is of course true that neither Joseph nor Mary must stand in the centre of attention. They are only serving their God and ministering unto their Lord. It is Christ who must receive all attention.

But it remains true that Joseph has an important task to fulfill. As husband of Mary and as head of the royal house of David, Joseph must officially receive Mary's child as his own, into his family. Joseph must do so *prophetically*, giving to the child the designation which God Himself has determined.

We may see God's wonderful providence in leading all things in such a way that Jesus Christ takes His lawful place on earth and so becomes our Saviour, our Emmanuel. For that is the true joy of Christmas. And in that context we may and must pay attention to the work of Joseph with respect to the birth of Christ. Through this work, Jesus Christ is officially received into His earthly family, the house of David. This is done in submission to God's Word, in recognition of God's holiness, and in confession of God's grace.

JOSEPH'S PROBLEM

We can fully understand that Joseph has a problem when he hears that Mary, his betrothed, is pregnant and will have a child which is not his child. This is not a fairy tale, but real life, and Joseph has to deal with a very complicated situation.

Most explainers feel that Joseph believes that Mary has been untrue to him, and that he therefore wants to divorce her (verse 19). The procedure of divorce, as regulated in the Law of Moses, required a public ceremony. But, we are told, Joseph was considering to divorce her "quietly," because he was "unwilling to put her to shame." The explainers say that Joseph loved Mary too much to make a public spectacle out of her; he was too kind and compassionate a man.

But it does not say anywhere that Joseph did not believe Mary's account and that he suspected unfaithfulness. Mary will have told him exactly what happened. Joseph will also have heard about what happened to Zechariah and Elizabeth, as described in Luke 1. Joseph himself expected the coming of the Messiah, and there is no reason why he should disbelieve Mary. He knew of the wondrous works and almighty power of God.

STEPPING BACK?

Being a "just man," that is a God-fearing man, Joseph simply does not know what to do. He recognizes that God has claimed Mary for an important and unique task. He obviously feels that he must now step back. He thinks that he cannot play a role here anymore. Their relationship will have to be terminated, but how?

Since Mary is not guilty of adultery, he does not want to cast even a shadow of suspicion on her. So he considers that he'll have to do it quietly, without public ceremony.

Joseph is prepared to let Mary go, now that God has a special purpose for her. This will have been difficult for him, but he does not see anymore how their marriage can function. We read in verse 20 that the angel says to him, ". . . do not fear to take Mary your wife." Do not *fear*, which indicates that Joseph's fear was a fear of the Lord. For whom else should Joseph fear? A verb is used here that is also used for fearing the Lord. Joseph will step aside in wonder, awe, and reverent fear.

So Joseph is pondering the question: how do I end this relationship without bringing any shame to Mary? We can imagine him, at night, tossing and turning in a restless sleep, after having considered all the angles and not having found a solution. In that situation, an angel appears to him in a dream.

And what the angel does is simply tell Joseph what his task is in all this. He is addressed very honourably as "Joseph, son of David" (verse 20). He need not out of fear step back. God does not at all want this relationship terminated. Instead, He wants the marriage to be solemnized.

It is true that Mary's child is "of the Holy Spirit," and that Joseph has no task here as a natural father. But he does have another task: to receive this child into his family, and to recognize it in earthly terms as his own child. Joseph will have to function as the earthly father of the child. He will have to give it a legitimate place and an official name.

A CONVINCING DREAM

We read, "When Joseph awoke from sleep, he did as the angel of the Lord commanded him. . . ." Joseph vividly recalled the essential elements of the dream. What is more, he recognized the contents of the dream as being the Word of God.

We might not let ourselves be so quickly convinced by such a dream. After all, in our view dreams are deceptive. We would wonder and say: did I really dream that? Does God really require this of me? But we must understand that God did not reveal Himself in the same way then as He does now. Joseph was quite aware that a dream could contain divine revelation. And he accepted this dream because it also accorded with the facts that he had witnessed. In doing so, Joseph submitted to the Word of God.

We can speak with admiration about Mary, who so willingly says to the angel, "Behold, I am the handmaid of the Lord; let it be to me according to your word" (Luke 1: 38). But Joseph is no less obedient; he shows himself to be a true son of David, also according to the Spirit, for he too says, "Behold, I am the hand-servant of the Lord; I will do according to your word."

Nor does he waste any time. Now that he knows his task, he makes haste to fulfill it. The very next day, "when he awoke from sleep," it says, he began to take the necessary measures and to prepare for the marriage. There could now be no delay. And this was not so much for the good name and reputation of Mary as for the sake of the name of the Christ. The glory of God is at stake here, more than the honour of men.

The name of this child must be without blemish. He must in His birth be legitimately received into His earthly family. He shall not be a child born out of wedlock, with no name and place of His own. He shall, instead, be known as the son of Joseph of Nazareth, the carpenter, who is lawfully the son of David.

From Luke 1 we get the impression that right after the appearance of the angel Mary goes to visit Elizabeth, and that she marries Joseph after her return from Elizabeth's home. She stayed with Elizabeth for three months. So she may have been about three months pregnant when Joseph married her.

SUBMISSION TO THE WORD

Be that as it may, it is clear that Joseph wastes no time. We read, "He took his wife." The next step to complete the marriage covenant is taken. The official wedding occurs, and Mary is now Joseph's lawful wife. And the point is: when Joseph takes Mary as his wife, he also consciously accepts the child as the Son of God.

It is important for us to appreciate this. Joseph and Mary were not ignorant victims of God's mysterious ways. See how open and frank the Scriptures speak about this matter. The man Joseph was not deceived, fooled, kept in the dark! He knew exactly what he was doing. He may not have understood all the implications and consequences, but he acted, in the knowledge he had, in sincere faith. We see here in the house of David the triumphant power of faith. We see what truly characterizes the house of David: submission to the Word of God.

Joseph and Mary did not do what they did in their own strength. They were prepared by the Word of God to act in simple and childlike faith. There is no other way for the Christ to be received in His earthly family than in the way of submission to the Word, the way of faith.

And in essence it is still the same today. Christ is now in heavenly glory and does not need an earthly family to be born in. But we must receive Him in our families and homes, and in our lives as individuals, in the same faith as Joseph and Mary. Indeed, our faith must even be deeper, since it is based on a far greater knowledge than Joseph and Mary ever had. Joseph dreamed a special dream, but we have the entire revelation of God, so that we may know: this child is truly the Emmanuel, the Saviour of our lives, our joy today and our hope for eternity!

We should be amazed that the Son of God in this way will enter into our earthly situation, and we should understand Joseph's reverence for the *holiness of the Lord.*

GOD'S HOLINESS RESPECTED

Notice how it is emphatically stated that the marriage, although officially solemnized, is not in fact consummated, for it says, ". . . but [Joseph] knew her not until she had borne a son" (verse 25a). He "knew her not" means that he had no sexual relations with her.

This may surprise us. Since Joseph and Mary were now lawfully husband and wife, did Joseph not have the right to have these relations with his wife? We know today that such relations, with love and care, are not at all dangerous to the mother or the expected child until perhaps the last month of pregnancy. We do not read anywhere that the Lord had forbidden Joseph to have this relation with his wife. It could very well have been Joseph's own position in the matter.

We must appreciate that this cannot have been easy for the couple, especially not for Joseph. If Mary was two or three months pregnant when they married, it meant a wait of at least eight or nine months. These people had normal desires and needs, and we must understand, when we read this simple statement in our text, that it did mean a great sacrifice which could only be made by the power of faith.

What is the reason for Joseph's abstinence? It has to do with his being a God-fearing man, a man who indeed stands in awe of God's mighty work. It is inspired by nothing less than a great reverence for the holiness of the Lord.

Joseph knows that the child is conceived by the Holy Spirit. He realizes that the power of the most High has "overshadowed" Mary. She is in the special service of Lord at this time. It must remain absolutely clear that this child is not born in any way by the *power* or the *will of man*, but that it is indeed born of the Spirit.

The Jews in Matthew's time could have scoffed and said, "Jesus was probably just Joseph's natural son, conceived before marriage maybe, but still Joseph's natural son." Therefore, Matthew must explain: in no way can this child have been conceived by man, for there was no sexual union between Joseph and Mary "*until* she had borne a son."

Joseph abstains in recognition of the power of the Holy Spirit, in reverence of God's holiness. Here man must indeed step back. Here the work of God must first be completed. And it is written so that we today will know without any doubt: this child is conceived by the Holy Spirit, and born of the *virgin* Mary!

NO OTHER CHILDREN?

You probably know what the Roman Catholic church has done with this text. Rome contends that Joseph and Mary *never* had any sexual relations and that Mary remained a virgin mother until her death. How could the same womb which had borne the Holy Son of God also bring forth sinful children? And when the Bible speaks about Jesus' "brothers," Rome explains that these must have been children of Joseph from a previous marriage, not sons of Mary.

But our text does not require this explanation. If he knew her not *until* she had borne a son, it is to be understood that he *did* know her *after* this son was born, after the time of purification and healing had taken place. Joseph abstained not because Mary was so holy and even beatified (as Rome says), but because of the child, Jesus. In brief, we need not make this a complicated matter. The simplest and most logical explanation is usually the best. It was out of reverence for the holiness of God and the power of the Holy Spirit that Joseph knew: until the child is born, I must stand back, completely. So Joseph learned to reckon with the special character of this child before it was born. With how much awe will he have received this child into his family after it was born!

Christ was received with great reverence, even though He came by the way of the womb, was born of a woman, into the weakness of human flesh, in humility. How much more, then, shall He be received with reverence today, now that He has a glorified body and dwells in heavenly glory! Shall we not stand in awe of Him Who on Christmas became like unto us in every respect, except sin? Shall we not revere Him Who showed forth the holiness of God on our behalf in a corrupt and wicked world? And Who is coming with the clouds of heaven to judge the living and the dead?

GIVING A NAME

Joseph showed his reverence for the holiness of God, and for the holiness of the child conceived by the Spirit. He also confessed *God's grace* at the birth of this child. For the text continues, "and he called His Name Jesus." It was in Israel the father's official task to give a name to each child, and so to give that child a place in the family and in Israel.

We have to understand that when Joseph gave this name to the child, he was acting in obedience to the command of the angel of the Lord. Joseph may not have understood the deep implications of this name, as we do today. Still, being a just and devout man who expected salvation from God, he did understand that this was a very significant and special name. He knew that when he gave the child this name, he officially designated Him as the Saviour of Israel, as the promised Messiah.

The name "Jesus" – as the angel explained – means Saviour: "for He will save His people from their sins"(verse 21). When Joseph gives this name to the child, he does a prophetic deed. For the name Jesus is prophecy, proclamation from above, concerning the purpose and the task of this child. All Israel will hear the prophetic claim which lies in this name.

The name Jesus, or Joshua in Hebrew, designated those who led Israel out of the house of bondage and into the land of promise. Here it means a spiritual liberation and renewal: deliverance by the blood and Spirit of Christ; salvation from sin and from death, the wages of sin.

When Joseph gives that name, he is not only the first *prophet* of the New Testament, but also the first *professor.* A professor is someone who makes an important declaration of faith. Joseph is the first one to present this child as the Saviour sent of God. He is the first to receive it publicly as a gift of God's grace, and the first to proclaim the appearance of God's grace to Israel in the birth of this child.

Whenever we read these Christmas stories, every year again, it should strike us how privileged these people must have felt, how unassuming they appeared, and how deeply they understood that God's unmerited and unexpected grace was manifesting itself in their lives through this child! God did something so wonderful and amazing in their lives through the child Jesus, that it never ceased to amaze them.

NO FRINGE PLAYER

Sometimes we tend to think that Joseph got a bad deal, that he was no more than a fringe-player at the manger of Bethlehem, upstaged by ecstatic shepherds and adoring wise men. But Joseph is prophet and professor of God's grace in Christ Jesus, and our confession today is based on his prophecy, which he received from God Himself: this child is our Saviour, our Redeemer. And in this manner Joseph, too, was used by God to put Christ in the centre.

In naming Jesus in humble confession of God's sovereign grace, Joseph proclaimed that all who want to be saved must embrace this child, this Son of David, as their Saviour. That is the prophetic claim which must be preached every Christmas morning again: there is salvation only in the Son of God. Let us then with the same wonder, recognizing God's awesome and amazing grace in Christ, say with even more conviction and insight than Joseph: He is truly our Saviour. Let us with this profession receive Him into our lives, into our homes, and say with all our heart, "Thou hast become, LORD, my salvation; all those who seek Thee wilt Thou bless."

The Decisive Breakthrough of Light in the Darkness

"The light shines in the darkness, and the darkness has not overcome it".

(John 1:5)

In the Egreja Reformada, the Reformed Church, in Maragogi, Brazil, you can find the first words of this passage from John 1: 5 on the wall behind the pulpit: "a luz resplandece nas trevas," the light shines in the darkness. When I saw those words there, I was moved. Brazil certainly is a place of ignorance and poverty, indeed of darkness. And yet, also there, it is publicly testified and confessed that "the light shines in the darkness."

Christmas in Brazil is of course quite different from Christmas in Canada. Most people there do not have the money to give presents to one another. There often is no special Christmas dinner. You will not find snow or mistletoe, nor are there many colourful lights and decorated trees to mark the festive season. We did see in the large shopping centres – already in November – the odd ribbon decoration, but for the common people these centres are virtually inaccessible.

Do you think that these people really miss much? In a country that is largely dominated by Roman Catholicism, the birth of Christ will certainly be celebrated in various rituals, although in a more sober manner than in Europe and North America. It may be that, in the absence of rampant commercialism, for some the real truth of Christmas will become clearer. For indeed, the light shines in the darkness.

FROM ETERNITY AND HEAVEN

The text from which I took these words is from the Gospel according to John. As you know, John starts his version of the Gospel in a manner quite different from that of Matthew and Luke. We find no mention of Zechariah and Elizabeth, Joseph and Mary, angels and shepherds, Herod and the wise men. The birth of Christ is not described at all.

John does not start in the fields of Ephratah but in the spacious expanse of heaven: in the beginning was the Word, and the Word was with God. He does not begin with a certain point in time, but with eternity. John provides a deep perspective and a broad outlook, and lets us see that the coming of Christ into the world is of cosmic, world-encompassing significance.

The Gospel of John is from the start majestic. When Jesus was born, John writes, the true light was entering the world. Christmas is a key moment, a decisive occurrence in the history of the world.

The eternal Word, the everlasting Light became flesh.

LEADING TO A DECISION

John shows us that Christ comes from eternity as the great Light that always was present, and that now decisively breaks through in this world. There is a sharp antithesis: if you have Christ, you are in the Light; if not, you are in the darkness. This means that the coming of Christ places all people before a key *decision.* Christ Himself saw His ministry as being final and conclusive.

Listen to the terms in which He spoke of Himself, as recorded by John: I am the Bread of Life. I am the Light of the world. I am the Door. I am the Good

Shepherd. I am the Resurrection and the Life. I am the Way, the Truth, and the Life. I am the true Vine. I AM. I am all this and more. We do not gather on Christmas day to party. We celebrate the victory of Light over darkness, the birth of Him Who said, "No one comes to the Father except through Me." It is with this message in mind that John was instructed to write the Gospel. He proclaims the birth of Jesus Christ as the decisive breakthrough of the Light into the darkness. He writes about the constant presence and the mighty victory of that Light.

LIGHT AND LIFE

The apostle John often uses the word "light" to describe Christ and His ministry, and employs the contrasting term "darkness" to describe this world which lies in the power of sin and death. Light versus darkness, it is a constantly returning motif in John's Gospel (we meet it at least 23 times!).

The word "light" is sometimes used in the same context as the word life. Light and life go together. That is so in nature: if there is no (sun)light, nothing can flourish; everything must die. And what applies to nature applies to the spiritual realm. As darkness is symbolic of God's judgment and of death (think of the darkness in Egypt), so light is symbolic of God's grace and mercy (think of Goshen). Life and light go together.

When John writes, "the light shines in the darkness" (verse 5), he has in the previous verse already used the word *life.* Let's look at that: "In Him [the Word that became flesh, the Son of God incarnate] was life and the life was the light of men."

In Him was life. When John uses the word "life" (also a term frequently met in his Gospel), it is often a reference to everlasting life. When he says that "in Christ is life," he means that Christ has life in Himself, since He is God almighty and eternal, the Creator. It also means that He *imparts* life to others, graciously gives life. And this does not just refer to His gift of temporal life and breath to all creatures, but it means that He alone can and does give to people the gift of everlasting life.

The text continues: the life was the light of men (verse 4). This means that "men" (people) can only see (live, walk, function) through the life which Christ imparts to them. What makes people tick, what keeps them going and enables them to progress is the light of God, who takes them up in his fellowship and covenant.

The truth of the matter is, says John, that people can only really live through Christ (in Him was life) and can only function in fellowship with Him (the life was the light of men). It is through Christ alone that people live and function. It has always been so and it will always be so.

DARKNESS AND DEATH

John writes that the light shines in the darkness. We know from Scripture how darkness came into the world. There was the fall into sin, with the resulting curse on creation. The kingdom of the earth became a kingdom of darkness, governed by the prince of darkness, the devil. People who were meant to live through Christ and in Him with God, now came to live for themselves and by themselves.

Darkness descended. Now do not think that after the fall all was dark. For, says John: the light shines in the darkness, and he means that this light shone also from the beginning. He writes: the light *shines* (present tense). That means: it is constantly and always shining. John does not want us to get the impression that there was no light until Christmas Day, as if Christ was not active before then. On the contrary, looking at things from the perspective of the beginning, he says, the light shines in the darkness of the ages.

LIGHT VERSUS DARKNESS

The light shines in the darkness. We must realize that "light and darkness" are two contrasting and mutually exclusive powers. They cannot co-exist. The one always seeks to overpower and destroy the other. Light opposes darkness and expels it. Wherever the light shines, the darkness must draw back. Similarly, wherever the light recedes, the darkness takes its place. You cannot really be in the twilight, you are either in the light or in the dark.

When there is light, you can see, discern, look ahead, and therefore also move ahead. Light is a condition for progress and motion. Light means that you have fellowship with your surroundings. But if it is dark, you cannot see, you do not make progress, you stumble and fall. You are out of touch with your environment.

What John is saying, then, is this: in the beginning was the Word, the Son of God. He not only gave life, but He is also the Light which shone from the beginning. He is the one Who enables the people of God to progress in their life with God and with each other. Christ has always been the Light of the world.

ALWAYS LIGHT

After the fall into sin, when everything seemed utterly dark, God came with the Gospel of salvation by promising the seed of the woman.The light shines in the darkness! When the "first world" perished in the flood, and again all seemed dark, God saved Noah and his family. When people rebelled against God at Babel, God dispersed them and called Abraham, promising to make him into a great nation. When Israel was enslaved in Egypt, God led them out from there with a mighty hand. He surrounded them with His light. And when the people of Israel fell away from Him in the time of the Judges, He raised up David, the theocratic king. When the dark era of the exile had come, He brought back a remnant, which He protected, so that Jesus Christ would be born. The light shines in the darkness! When we look at the history of the church as described in Scripture, we see that the light shone brightest when everything seemed to be plunged into utter darkness.

PREPARING FOR THE INCARNATION

And all this happened because of what John describes in verse 9: the true light that enlightens every man was coming into the world. In all this previous history, Christ was preparing for His incarnation, for His birth on Christmas Day. The true light was coming into the world, John says, the light that is real light and not some temporary, artificial product. It is the light that enlightens every man, that is: the light upon which everyone depends for true direction and progress.

The understanding of Christmas does not begin at the manger of Bethlehem, but in the Garden of Eden. The real struggle of the darkness against the light dates from that time. And the victory of the Light was already assured at that time.

For John adds, "and the darkness has not overcome it." The light shines victoriously. And you may believe that the darkness did what it could to dim it. Darkness cannot stand light and must battle it. And so the devil and all powers that are against God did everything in their power to prevent the continuation and spread of the light! The devil wants darkness. When it is dark, evil creatures, predators can move about freely to seek their prey.

PEOPLE PREFER DARKNESS

John expands on this thought in chapter 3: 19-21. He has said that the light has come into the world but adds that "men loved darkness rather than light." People prefer darkness! Can you imagine that? What kind of people prefer darkness? Only those who want to do evil. That's what John says: people loved darkness rather than light, because their deeds were evil. Mankind needs darkness as a cover-up for sin. John writes, "For everyone who does evil hates the light, and does not come to the light, lest his deeds should be exposed."

The light exposes evil. When we are examined in the brilliant light of Christ and His Word, every spot and blemish is visible and we are seen in all our ugliness and filth. And since people cannot stand this, they do their utmost to have the light snuffed out. Turn off the light! Then no one can see how filthy and evil we are!

You will understand, then, why there has been from the beginning great opposition to this light. In our text John says that the darkness tries to overcome the light. The word that he uses here can be taken in various ways. The King James Version has: and the darkness comprehended it not. Then it would mean: the light did shine, but the darkness could not understand it. In other words, the darkness is not able to receive the light because it is cannot grasp its meaning. One might refer to what Paul wrote to the Corinthians: the unspiritual man does not understand the spiritual things of God.

The NIV follows the same kind of translation as the King James Version: the darkness has not understood it, but in a footnote it allows also for the translation: the darkness has not overcome it. The word that is used means "to take hold of" something. The darkness could not take hold of the light. And there is in this verb the notion of holding something down in order to control it. Some have suggested the translation: the light shines. . . and the darkness has not mastered it. That is perhaps, seeing also the context, the proper translation. The darkness did not fail to *understand* the light, but (understanding quite well the implications of the working of the light) it actively *opposed* the light, trying to control, master, subdue it, and so prevent it from working.

THE LIGHT PREVAILED

The darkness did everything possible to keep the light from shining. Satan transplanted the truth with the lie. He led Israel from true worship of God to idolatry and apostasy. Time and again he caused God's people to stray from the way of truth. In all this, he sought to prevent one thing: the coming of the Son of God into the world. Satan said: the Word shall not become flesh. It will never be Christmas Day.

Satan has attempted to prevent the birth of Christ ever since the fall into sin. Often it seemed that he would succeed. And indeed, except for the covenant promises and the sovereign grace of God, Satan would have succeeded. But he failed. Our text speaks of the great victory of the light. The darkness has not overcome it. Christ entered into our flesh so that He might fulfill all the righteousness of the divine law and redeem us from our sins.

THE DECISIVE BREAKTHROUGH

The birth of Christ is the decisive breakthrough of the light in the darkness. That is how the prophets spoke of it: the people who in darkness walked, have seen a glorious light (Hymn 15, *Book of Praise*). It is also the manner in which Simeon spoke when he saw the baby Jesus: mine eyes have seen thy salvation, a light for revelation to the Gentiles and glory for thy people Israel (Luke 2: 32, Hymn 18: 2).

Christmas means that the light of God, which was always present, has broken through into the world. This has consequences for the world and for us. In John 3: 21 we read, ". . . he who does what is true comes to the light, that it may be clearly seen that his deeds have been wrought in God." Whereas darkness attracts criminals and predators, the light attracts those who love and seek truth and purity. Now that the light has broken through on Christmas Day, we are all faced with a tremendous responsibility: can my life stand the scrutiny by the Son of God? Can I stand in that light? Will it be seen that my deeds have been wrought in God? For the light which has broken through on Christmas illuminates everything and shines into the deepest recesses of our life and heart.

YOU ARE THE LIGHT OF THE WORLD

You see, to celebrate Christmas can mean various things: nice, festive season, family get-togethers, Christmas dinner, and what not. But we must realize in the midst of all this that Christ is the true Light that enlightens every man, and when the question is asked, "Can you stand in that light?" you must be able to answer, "Yes! I have nothing to hide. I am attracted to that light. Let it shine, also in my life." When you do what is true *you come* to the light, and do what can be seen in the light. You do not try to overcome the light, but indeed comprehend it, take it up within yourself, so that it illuminates you, and you become one of the children of light.

I want to conclude this section on the Light with another passage of Scripture that is closely related to our text. The light shines in the darkness, and the darkness has not overcome it. Jesus is the Light of the world. That is number one. That always comes first. But Jesus said to His disciples: you are the light of the world. *You* are (Matthew 5: 14). That is number two. That always follows. To celebrate Christmas means to take up the light of Christ into ourselves by faith through His Spirit and to be light-bearers ourselves. We must reflect the light of Christ. Christmas does not have meaning for just one day, but for all of life.

The light shines in the darkness, and it shines on you, so that you may reflect it in your surroundings. Do you know what we are called in the Bible? Children of Light. We must shine as lights in the world. Never mind the lights on the Christmas tree. Our whole street is lit up with colourful lights, but that's all artificial. If only everyone who lives on our street would reflect the light of Christ. Paul writes: you are light in the Lord, walk as children of light. And the fruit of light is found in all that is good, according to God's law.

Satan and the world still oppose the light. Satan, we are warned, does so, even though he often disguises himself as an angel of light. Now that we live in the age of the true Light, we must all the more show ourselves to be children of light, and discern the spirits in the light of God's Word. Watch out for the prince of darkness who pretends to be an angel of light and seeks to turn you away from the Word of God. That is the calling which comes to us when we celebrate Christmas.

Soon the Christmas lights in our street will go out. The Christmas trees will be dumped in the driveway for pick-up by the trash company. The festive atmosphere disappears. Don't let the light go out in your house. Keep the festive atmosphere. Otherwise you've had only a worldly Christmas. Believe in the light and walk in it. And do not fear the powers of darkness: God is my light, my refuge, my salvation, whom shall I fear? (Psalm 27).

Sometimes it can seem so dark, also in the life of Christians. Sometimes it may seem that you cannot progress, that there is no way out of the difficulties. You may say: I cannot see a way, O Lord! But Jesus says: there was always light. And especially now, since Christmas, the light has broken through. Do not be afraid of the darkness. Do not hide in it, either. Keep coming to the light. For the darkness could not and cannot win. The light shines, forever, also in your life. Receive it, believe it, work with it, and so reflect it!

God is my light. One day we will see a light that is unimagined. The book of Revelation speaks about the new Jerusalem and says: the city had no need of sun or moon to shine upon it, for the glory of God is its light, and its lamp is the Lamb. By its light shall the nations walk.

One day no more darkness or powers of darkness, but light everywhere. Also for me. There is the mighty victory of the light, of which Christmas is the assurance. In that victory we may stand every day in all our trials and defeats. God is my Light. Whom should I fear?

The Lamentation at Bethlehem

"Then was fulfilled what was spoken by the prophet Jeremiah: A voice was heard in Ramah, wailing and loud lamentation, Rachel weeping for her children; she refused to be consoled, because they were no more".

Matthew 2: 17, 18

Whenever we celebrate Christmas, we remember the birth of the Lord Jesus Christ and we read and sing about "peace on earth" among the people of God's good pleasure. We partake of the great joy that was shared by the shepherds and others in the little town of Bethlehem.

In this passage, however, we read about the massacre of the infants, about blood on earth, and we are confronted with the great sorrow of those who lived in and around Bethlehem. From peace and quiet to bloodshed and clamour, indeed a very severe contrast! Does it really belong in one and the same Gospel?

When we place the death of these many children over against the birth of that one Child, we ask ourselves, "Why did these children have to die?" Is all this bloodshed not deeply infuriating and totally senseless? Why did the Lord God allow this to happen? Perhaps an even more important question now is: what meaning can it possibly have for us today?

A MEANINGLESS INCIDENT OR MIGHTY PROPHECY?

The matter gains great significance when we read that not only an act of violence is committed, but that prophecy is being fulfilled. It is not just an unfortunate, isolated incident which might have been prevented and which is really quite meaningless, but here the *Word of God* finds fulfillment. King Herod retains his specific responsibility in the affair, but the Lord wishes to use this event to instruct His people unto salvation.

Christmas leads to a crisis, and in that crisis we need consolation. Here the Church of Christ is directed by the lamentation at Bethlehem to its only consolation in the latter days. We will focus on the cause of the lamentation and the content of the consolation.

JEREMIAH AND MATTHEW

You wonder how the prophecy of Jeremiah 31 can be fulfilled in Matthew 2, when there are two totally different situations involved. The cause of the lamentation in Jeremiah is the exile of Judah to Babel. Certainly, in the war which preceded the actual exile, there will have been casualties (and even infants may have been killed), but how can that compare with the massacre of infants which is perpetrated by the soldiers of King Herod? How can the one lamentation be linked to the other?

I may mention that also in Matthew 2 mention is made of an exile, namely the exile of Christ to Egypt. In Jeremiah 31 the battle is directed against the people of God, who are forced into exile because of their sins. In Matthew 2, however, the battle is against the Messiah of God, who is forced into exile although He is without sin. But we may leave that matter for the time being, although it's good to remember the connection.

In order to understand our text well, we have to pose a few important questions concerning the link-up of Jeremiah 31 and Matthew 2. What do Ramah and Rachel have to do with Bethlehem Ephratah? Why does the Holy Spirit lead Matthew to refer to Jeremiah 31?

A MATTER OF GEOGRAPHY?

It cannot be a matter of geography. It is true that Rachel is buried near Bethlehem, but that hardly seems to the point. Ramah was not close to Bethlehem; as far as we know, it was a town on the border between Northern Israel and Judah. The whole point of the prophecy in Jeremiah is that Rachel stands at Ramah on the border of Northern Israel (Ephraim) and Judah, and bemoans the exile of *both* kingdoms, of the *entire* covenant people. She looks to the North, and sees the children of Israel gone; she looks to the South, and again sees the children of Israel being led away into captivity, and her lamentation is great: O my children, my children! Where have all my children gone? The cause of Rachel's poignant and bitter lamentation is the utter destruction of the covenant people.

The cause of the lamentation in Bethlehem Ephratah is different. King Herod thought that he had made a satisfactory arrangement with the "wise men," but they did not return to Jerusalem to tell him more about the "king of the Jews." So Herod sent in his henchmen with specific orders to kill all the possible candidates for the title – all the male children in Bethlehem and the surrounding region who were two years old and under. Scholars have estimated the population of that area at around two to three thousand, and they think that at most one hundred infants were killed. But that is still a formidable number. It is a mass-murder, a terrible infanticide.

HEROD'S CRUELTY

Herod was known for his furious rage and extreme cruelty. He even killed his own son when he thought that this son was a potential danger to him. The emperor Augustus is reported to have said of Herod, "It is better to be Herod's swine than Herod's son." Indeed, his own family was afraid of him. This murder of infants in Bethlehem shows his deeply cruel character. A whole area is suddenly steeped in grief; hundreds of people are beyond themselves with sorrow; they cannot be comforted.

You must try to picture this. The soldiers are going from house to house, dragging out the infants, and slaughtering them before their parents' eyes. The parents are exclaiming that their son is not "the king of the Jews," but the soldiers are oblivious to their protests and brutal in their actions: orders from headquarters, next house! Picture the sheer devastation, the utter hopelessness of the people left behind with the bodies of the dead children, and perhaps with the bodies of those parents who tried to defend their children's lives. There is wailing and loud lamentation, and Matthew directs us to a similar lamentation in the days of Jeremiah.

Similarities can indeed be noted. There is the suddenness of the happening and the swiftness of execution. There is the merciless and brutal campaign. There is the impossibility of defence and of escape. There is the utter devastation when the troops have left.

WHY RACHEL?

The question is: why is *Rachel* mentioned here? You will recall that Rachel's two sons were Joseph and Benjamin, but Bethlehem was situated in Judah. The reason for mentioning Rachel is that she as one of the *mothers of Israel* so particularly suffered anxiety and grief for her children. She cried out during her life because the LORD first did not give her children, and she died when her second child was born. Rachel, intense, brooding, proud, and yet brought so low because of her children.

Both in Jeremiah 31 and in Matthew 2, Rachel is the symbol of the mother of Israel who suffers anxiety and grief because of her children. It is a grief for the losses suffered in the struggle of the ages, in the history of redemption. When you hear the name Rachel, you think of the struggle to bring forth *covenant children* (Genesis), of the sorrow when the covenant children are carried away into captivity, and now, of the clamour in Bethlehem Ephratah for the covenant children massacred. Rachel embodies the struggle for the seed of the covenant and the sorrow over the seed of the covenant.

When you hear the name Rachel, you think of Jacob, who loved her, the father of Israel according to the flesh. When you hear the name Jacob, you remember his opponent Esau, the disobedient covenant child whose seed became an enemy of the covenant people. When you hear the name Esau, you remember that Herod was an Edomite. Now we have come full circle.

THE WIDER CONTEXT

Rachel mourns the loss of her children. But Matthew must put the event in the wider context of the history of salvation. There is a tremendous struggle going on through the ages. It was there already in the days of Esau and Jacob, Rachel and Leah. It became even clearer in the days of Jeremiah, when the exile occurred. In that struggle children were lost. Many tears were shed by mothers over their children.

But now that prophecy of Jeremiah is *fulfilled* (verse 17), which means that now this word reaches its fullness, for here the *real* struggle becomes apparent. It always was, and certainly is now, the battle against *the* seed of Abraham, Jesus Christ! The devil seeks to destroy the Son of David, and in doing so he will not spare any of "Rachel's children." Herod seeks out his arch-enemy, and he will not show any mercy. The woes and pains of the Old Testament church were many, but it will not be any easier in the New Testament dispensation, for now we have entered the last phase of the great struggle between the seed of the woman and the seed of the serpent! There lies the deepest cause of the lamentation. The church has entered into the last era, and with it also the last woe, "the great tribulation"

(Revelation 7:14), has begun. The serpent who could not destroy the Child goes to make war on the woman and her children (see also Revelation 12), and the cry will rise up to heaven, "How long, Lord, until thou wilt avenge the blood of thy children?" (See Revelation 9).

THE FIRST CASUALTIES

It is remarkable that this story, which comes immediately after the Christmas account, puts us right on the battlefield of the latter days, in the midst of great lamentation. Where only a while before angels sang of "peace on earth," mothers now wail because of the war that rages and the casualties of battle, "O my children, my children." Here we learn that the battle against the Christ involves us and our children, our families.

The bloodshed began in Bethlehem. The first "casualties" fell there. I do not call these babes "the first martyrs," for they did not even know why they were being killed. They are, however, the first casualties in the New Testament era, in the intensified conflict which has come with the birth of Christ. For now – more than ever – the rage of the devil is fierce against the people of the covenant. Rachel, Rachel, if you mourned already under the Old Covenant, now is the real time for your tears, for now begins the great tribulation!

Do we understand the character of this dispensation? The way the world celebrates Christmas can really put you on the wrong track. The way they celebrate it out there, it seems as if the birth of Christ means the end of all woes, whereas it really means the beginning of the woes! Peace on earth will come only in the way of extreme sacrifice, through blood, sweat, and tears, and while it is indeed fully the blood and the sacrifice of Christ alone which will bring redemption, *we are involved*. There will be casualties among us, even "innocent babes," so to speak, will be victimized. For the devil knows of no mercy and his anger is great, and he goes about seeking to devour Rachel's children.

Many tears will be shed between the first and the second coming of Christ. There will be much suffering, also for the church and its youth. It will touch us and our families, our homes and our lives, in many different ways. And it is ultimately not designed against us, but against the Christ, Who is here exiled to Egypt and today is denounced by millions! Our Lord warned us about this situation before His cross, when He said, "If they do this to the Master, what will they do to the disciples?"

This history shows us that we may not become complacent after Christmas, as if there were no battle going on. We are called to be aware of our involvement in the great battle which has intensified since the birth of Christ. We are warned to preserve our Christian lifestyle and to set our Christian priorities in a world that does not understand, and we must do so no matter what the personal cost. For only if we are involved, will be consoled in this struggle.

CONSOLATION REFUSED

What is striking in this passage (and in the one of Jeremiah 31) is the statement that Rachel "refused to be consoled." She refused consolation because "they [the children] were no more."

Refusal to be consoled. Some explainers see this as a *sinful* reaction of Rachel to her woes. When consolation is offered, they say, it should be accepted, but it is typically the reaction of a sinful, proud woman to refuse consolation. However, we should be careful here.

It does not say anywhere that Rachel's refusal to accept consolation is condemnable. As a matter of fact, it is quite understandable. "They were no more. . ." means simply: whatever you say, it does not bring the children back. The loss is definite and devastating, and words cannot change the reality or take away the pain. The only thing that would bring consolation is the return of the children. That's all Rachel thinks of, and that's all she wants!

You can understand this better if you yourself have had to give up a loved one. People come to you from all sides with well-meant words of comfort, but at certain moments it all means so little, for whatever is said, it doesn't change the situation. All you really want is your loved one back. And it is understandable that some withdraw into themselves in their grief and "refuse to be consoled." They do not want to see anybody, not talk to anyone, not hear any words of comfort, for they are governed by their grief.

NO CHEAP WORDS

I think here of the situation of Psalm 77, "By a weight of troubles bowed, to my God my grief I told, *I refuse to be consoled*." The spirit grows restless and is deeply moved and you begin to wonder: "Where is God, who once us blessed?" Why, LORD, did you let them take my children? I cannot live without my children. This is called "being overwhelmed by grief."

Sometimes words, indeed, fail. There are many situations when you discover as pastor: it is so easy to say something, but it is so hard really to comfort someone. This is especially so under truly devastating conditions as in Bethlehem. Is not often small comfort given and are not often cheap words spoken?

This leads us to the question: where will the church in the latter days find its consolation? When the woes increase and the great tribulation begins, where will we go for comfort? What word of comfort will you speak to those wives who have lost their husbands, and those mothers who have lost their children for Christ's sake and for the sake of the Gospel? What will you say to those whose whole earthly lives have been devastated by the enemy just because they are Christians?

There is in this respect, even though we know little of it in our time and country, untold suffering! Believers are being ridiculed, boycotted, persecuted and even killed for the sake of Christ – the earth is red with the blood of the saints. So many have been led like sheep to the slaughter and it continues today, O God!

THE RETURN OF THE CHILDREN

Human words fail. That is why Luke here refers us to the Word of God, the prophecy already given of old, the Word which never fails! Perhaps you noticed that Matthew only gives a part of the prophecy, the part that deals with the exile of the children. But if we read on in Jeremiah 31, we also read of the *return* of the children: "Thus says the LORD, Keep your voice from weeping and your eyes from tears. . . there is hope for your future, says the LORD, and your children shall come back to their own country. . ." (Jeremiah 31: 16, 17).

Jeremiah consoles Israel! And the content of this consolation is that Israel will be restored out of exile to its own land to await the kingdom of God and the coming of the Messiah. That prophecy was fulfilled. The Messiah has come. Now it must be clear also for the church of the latter days where consolation is to be sought. It is to be sought in the sure fulfillment of the Word of God, and in the return of the Son of God, especially now that He has undergone the shame of the cross and been exalted above all kings and broken the power of the devil.

We have the prophetic word made all the more sure today. The content of the consolation today is that Christ has overcome the power of the devil and is now ruling in heaven, putting all his enemies as a footstool beneath His feet. Our comfort is that we, in life and death, in body and soul, belong to this Lord and Saviour, and that nothing can separate us from His love. Our sure hope is that He, when He comes, will *bring back* with Him all the children, and that not one child will be lost. Our great consolation is that all God's children – also those who have gone before us and especially those who have given their life for the sake of Christ – will see the great day of His glory with all the saints.

Christ will gather His entire church. The turmoil of the latter days will be great. The wounds will go deep, for when God cuts, He cuts deep. We will be sorely tested and refined, by trial, through temptation, and it will always be a matter of "sowing seed in tears" (Psalm 129). The church of Christ will go through the great tribulation. But there will also always be peace in the turmoil, balm for the wounds, strength in trials, hope in temptation, and the harvest will be realized. "The sower, bearing grain in sadness, shall certainly come home with gladness."

There is a great lamentation in Bethlehem. For Christ's sake. It is only the beginning of the woes. But there is for the church of the latter days a great consolation in the fulfillment of the Word of God. We are directed to that consolation, which will be our strength all the more now that Christ has been exalted.

GONE IS THE GRIEF

We who must go through the great tribulation may await the certain perfection of the church. This comforts us when difficulties come because we serve Christ. It will not be said of us anymore that we refuse to be consoled, for we are consoled in all trial and strife of life. We are consoled both when the Lord grants times of relief and when there are times of great stress.

Where have all the children gone? All the children will come back. "A seed shall serve Him, and each generation in time to come will hear of His salvation; the unborn too, will hear the proclamation of what He wrought" (Psalm 22:11, *Book of Praise*).

It will not always be easy for the church in the latter days. The devil's attacks and the world's temptations will be with us. Our own weak flesh will be against us, not to mention the moments of deep sorrow and grief, when God really cuts deep. But we have been directed where to seek our consolation, and we may sing already now, though sometimes with tears, "Gone is the grief that silenced me."

Gone is the grief. For the loss of the children. For all the pain. For Christ's sake, whose pain was incomparable, who bore the penalty and paid the price. In Christ, by faith, the grief is gone. And one day it will be gone forever. "I may, delivered from despair, now laud thy Name in song and prayer. Forever, LORD, my God and Saviour, will I give thanks for Thy great favour" (Psalm 30:7, *Book of Praise*).

Gone is the grief. You and I, Rachel, and the children, we shall rejoice forever.

The Messianic Program of Jesus Christ

"In the fifteenth year of the reign of Tiberius Caesar, Pontius Pilate being governor of Judea, and Herod being tetrarch of Galilee, and his brother Philip tetrarch of the region of Ituraea and Trachonitis, and Lysanias tetrarch of Abilene, in the high-priesthood of Annas and Caiaphas, the word of God came to John, the son of Zechariah in the wilderness".

(Luke 3: 1, 2)

The Gospel proclaims the birth of Christ as being of "cosmic" significance, that is of world-wide, global, importance. Does it not say that God so loved the *world* that He gave His only-begotten Son (John 3: 16)?

It seems, however, that after the birth of Christ nothing really changes. The Jews do not know that their Messiah has been born. The world just keeps on rotating despite the birth of the King of kings. Jesus and his family live in Nazareth, leading a life as simple and unknown people.

Time goes on. Kings die, and their thrones are taken by others. Power struggles take place, as always, and there are political changes. New rulers rise to power; new names become famous. The name of Christ, the Messiah, the son of David does not play any role. After the grandeur of Christmas, life goes on in the world without Christ.

Is the passage at hand not an impressive list of worldly names? Tiberius Caesar, Pontius Pilate, Herod, Philip, Lysanias, Annas and Caiaphas. Quite a gathering of nobles, worth a lot of money. Emperors, kings, aristocrats, with a mighty monopoly on world power. What effect will God's initiative in Christ have on this worldly conglomerate of wealth and influence?

There is one more name in this text. We read, ". . .the Word of God came to John the son of Zechariah, in the wilderness. . ." John, son of Zechariah. Luke introduces him with a bit of pride and pathos: and then along came John! Is this God's answer to the apparent monopoly of Satan and the world? But this John is nothing more than a desert hermit: what will he be able to do that has any influence on world events?

Well, John the Baptist is called out of desert seclusion to herald the appearing of the Messiah, and to proclaim the evangelical plan-of-action of Christ in the courts of kings and throughout the land. The world, with all its aristocracy and nobles, will never be the same again. We see here how God unveils the messianic program of Jesus Christ in the calling of John the Baptist. This messianic program deals with the united nations of Rome, the divided kingdom of David, and the deformed priesthood of Aaron.

PROPHETIC HISTORY

As you no doubt know, Luke is writing his Gospel to a Roman nobleman, called Theophilus, to convince him of the world-wide significance of the Christ. It is no wonder, scholars explain, that Luke painstakingly gives a set of dates and a list of names which would be of special interest to Theophilus. Therefore, they say, Luke writes, "In the fifteenth year of Tiberius. . .," etc. He wanted to be historically exact. But, some conclude, you really cannot "preach" on this text, because it is non-essential. It would be a historical survey of little significance to the congregation of Christ.

However, we should realize that Luke's way of writing history is, at the least, remarkable. He writes in a different manner than any other historian, for he is writing prophetically. This means that he gives these names and dates in their relation to God and to Christ's program of action.

At the end of verse 2 we read, "And the Word of God came to John, the son of Zechariah, in the wilderness. . . ." You may call that the climax, the whole point of these verses. Everything is related to it. God calls His spiritual child, John, out of the seclusion of the desert to a public office, to prepare the way for Jesus Christ, the King of kings, not only locally, in Judea, but as John himself says, "*All* flesh shall see the salvation of God" (verse 6). When John is called, he has a divine message first for the Jews, but this same message will affect kings and princes everywhere. Indeed, all flesh will be confronted with the kingdom of God.

John is the herald of Christ, who announces His plan of action for this world. If you know this, you look at the list of names in a different light.

ROME'S GOLDEN ERA

Is it not an ironic beginning? "In the fifteenth year of the reign of Tiberius Caesar. . .," Luke writes. Jesus Christ was born under the emperor Augustus, who has already made way for Tiberius. But meanwhile Christ has passed into oblivion, hidden away in the hills of Galilee. The real power in Palestine belongs to the Roman emperor, who lives in a pompous palace and is surrounded by special brigades.

Tiberius has been emperor now for fifteen years already. This is a significant point. It means that his throne is well-established and his power firmly fixed. When a new ruler is in the process of coming to power, there are always conflicts and opportunities for change. There is an unstable situation then, from which others – perhaps Christ? – could profit. But God does not wish to profit from the world's instability. His Word comes to John in the fifteenth year of Tiberius, when the emperor rules unopposed and when Rome has come to its "golden era." Hardly ever was an empire so wide-spread, so well-governed, and so well-equipped for world dominion as Rome under Tiberius. Here is the peak of Roman power and might.

If you take a brief look at the history of the Roman empire, you note the following. Under Julius Caesar the empire was founded; he was the victorious general who made the mighty conquests. Yet politically, Julius Caesar could not bring stability; he was assassinated. Under Octavianus Augustus the empire was strengthened; he was the keen politician who settled the internal feuds. And now under Tiberius Caesar the empire has been *consolidated*; he is the undisputed head of state and ruler of the kings of the earth.

Under Tiberius Caesar the imperial-Roman economy started to bloom. The famous system of roads, necessary for trade and commerce, was perfected throughout the empire. Foreign policy was carefully planned, and all resistance to Rome in outlying areas crushed. Tiberius consolidated the famous "pax Romana," the peace of Rome: the unity of all nations under one king. And in his fifteenth year, it had all been achieved: there was one mighty, united empire under the only sovereign ruler, Tiberius.

EMPEROR WORSHIP

It need not surprise us one bit that this Tiberius demanded divine reverence and worship as the head of humanity and as the mediator between the "gods" and the people. Everywhere, throughout the empire, children were taught to worship the emperor. Their parents offered weekly sacrifices of incense to their lord and master in Rome. This man had created a religious cult around his person. His imperial decree was divine truth. His will was divine law. His touch meant blessing and health. His anger meant instant death. That is how it was in those days.

Do we see, then, what Luke is telling us? The Lord calls John, but he is not called to operate in some chaotic situation and to use the unstable political climate as an opportunity for revolution. John is not called to organize revolution, but to proclaim reformation, that is, a return to the true religion, to the real relationship to the Living God, to the real peace. John is to proclaim, not the lasting glory of the "pax Romana," but the breakthrough of the "pax Christi," the peace of Christ.

Theophilus must learn to appreciate the plan of action of Jesus Christ, who does not overrun the world in its weakest moments but calls it to reformation in its times of greatest strength. When the civilized world is at its peak and when the nations are united under Rome, when Rome is strong, it is asked to measure its empire against the Kingdom of God, and see if the peace of Rome can withstand the peace of Christ.

THE REAL DECLINE AND FALL

In the fifteenth year of Tiberius, John receives his call in the desert. And that means that there and then the real decline and fall of the Roman empire begins. World government is now being claimed and realized by the true King of kings, Jesus Christ. The real prince of peace is proclaimed, and His plan-de-campagne to unite the nations under His power and to rule from sea to sea is revealed. He begins the process of establishing a world-wide realm of peace and prosperity for His people.

That process continues today, and its progress is proclaimed to us every Sunday. The Kingdom of God continues to make its way into this world, but where is the empire of Tiberius Caesar? Christ is seated on the throne, at the right hand of God, but Tiberius is long gone. God is still worshipped throughout the world, but where is the divine reverence for the Roman emperors? The united nations of Rome could not stand when confronted with the Kingdom of Heaven. In the end, the Roman empire could only serve the proclamation of the Name of Christ. For God will use the mighty empires of this world to serve His purpose: the gathering of the Church of Christ.

A PERMANENT CRISIS ZONE

Despite his claim to divinity, Tiberius cannot be everywhere at the same time. He cannot oversee everything, especially not in the distant colonies, but must delegate authority to others. And Roman politicians developed a very effective policy. We should know the procedure, for it helps us to understand the Gospel.

The policy was as follows. Relatively quiet areas received or retained a king or ruler out of their own people. The idea was: keep the people content by assigning them their own rulers, collect taxes via their own government, and people won't have the idea that they are under occupation. As long as these countries paid their taxes to Rome and cooperated in the affairs of the empire, they were relatively independent. This was a policy which the Romans had copied from the Persian King Cyrus.

The restless areas, the so-called "permanent crisis zones," were placed under direct Roman rule by means of occupying troops commanded by a military governor or proconsul, who sent monthly reports to Rome and was authorized to use force to maintain the peace and collect the taxes.

This helps us understand the situation in Palestine, which was one of those "permanent crisis zones." For a long time, the entire area was ruled by one man, Herod the Great. He displayed the brutal forcefulness required to keep the area relatively quiet. But when Herod the Great died, his descendants fought among each other for power. Therefore the Romans divided Palestine into four smaller sections (and that explains the word "tetrarch" in our text: ruler over one-fourth) and set a tetrarch over each section.

Archelaus, son of Herod the Great, ruled in the South (Judea), Philip in the North (Ituraea and Trachonitis), Herod Antipas in the central area (Samaria and Galilee), and the rest (the present Syria) was given to a certain Lysanias, the son of a Roman general.

DAVID DIVIDED

It is important to note that the southern area (Judea, governed by Archelaus) remained an area of conflict and uprising, and that Archelaus despite much bloodshed could not keep the area under control. It was this violent and unstable situation which prompted Joseph and Mary to resettle in Nazareth after coming out of Egypt (Matthew 2:22). The Romans finally tired of the situation, deposed Archelaus, placed Judea under direct rule, and sent governors from Rome. Pontius Pilate was already the fifth governor to try his hand at keeping Judea under Roman power.

Meanwhile, the important point is that Palestine was completely divided under Roman authority. It is remarkable that Luke describes the entire area of Old Israel, the previous kingdom of David and Solomon. This is Israel as it was in its golden age. By including the entire area of the old kingdom, Luke shows the pathetic situation of the heritage of David. It is politically divided into four parts, either under direct Roman supervision or under Edomite rule. Religiously, there is much internal division, and there are all kinds of parties. And economically the country is being exploited for the Romans and the rich.

Notice that while the world is relatively quiet – "the pax Romana" rules – the former kingdom of David suffers chaos, division, disunity. Is this not a very strong contrast?

A WORLD UNITED – A CHURCH DIVIDED

May we not say here that the world is strong and united because the church is weak and divided? The world knows of peace and rest because it is able to divide and rule over the people of God. The world can only profit from a divided church.

Remember the situation when this whole area was united under the throne of David. It was the complete opposite then: the world around Israel was weak and had to pay taxes to Israel. And the whole area of Israel was "holy land," the inheritance of God's people, which received prosperity and peace from the LORD. In the days of Solomon, people came from far to see the glory of Israel and to hear the Word of Israel's God.

But now Israel is a mockery among the nations. Its cities are mostly ruins. Its people are exploited and oppressed. The sheep are without a shepherd. A country is without a king who loves his people from the heart. Luke shows us this sad scene: the church is broken, and the united nations of Rome have no respect for the messianic kingdom of David.

THIS LAND IS HIS LAND

Why does Luke show us this? Because the Word of God, unveiling the program of Christ, deals with the divided kingdom of David. Is Jesus Christ not the Son of David, heir to the throne of His father, and will He not reunite His scattered nation and restore the one service of the LORD? This is an essential part of the prophecy of John the Baptist: Israel, get ready to receive your King, to greet your Messiah, for the Kingdom of God is at hand.

I want you to notice how our Lord Jesus Christ started in the high north, in Galilee, and wandered the hills of Syria. He travelled down to Samaria, through the area of Herod Antipas, walked the countryside of Judea, and searched the barren deserts of the southern Negev, where Satan tempted Him. He travelled this whole land from north to south and from east to west, and He searched out all the people. He entered into the pain of His people to deliver them from their need and unite them before God His Father.

He does this because He is King of kings and, unlike Tiberius, Son of God. First and foremost He does it because He is the Son of David, Head of the Church, who came to His people like a shepherd to His flock. He came to His own, and how did it hurt Him to discover that His own would not accept Him. But even then, He continued and would not be stopped in His campaign. Nor will He be stopped today. He will gather the true Israel and call the nations to take their place with the children of Abraham. He will gather His church despite all attempts to have it destroyed. He will unify His church in the one true faith despite all attempts to keep it divided. He Himself will as the only High Priest deliver His people from their sins and make them a people holy unto the Lord.

IMPOSTER PRIESTS

Luke mentions two more names, of which Theophilus had perhaps never heard, but which are nevertheless important: the call to John came in the days of the "high-priesthood of Annas and Caiaphas." Luke does not just speak of the political but also of the ecclesiastical situation.

You immediately notice that something is dreadfully wrong here. It says: the high-priesthood of Annas and Caiaphas, two of them; although the Law of Moses permitted only one high priest, who fulfilled his office until he died and was succeeded by his son.

That is no longer the case here. The right of inheritance has been rejected. Annas was not Caiaphas' father but his father-in-law. And Caiaphas was not high priest alone, but they fulfilled this function together. In name it was Caiaphas, but in reality it was Caiaphas and his family who ruled the church.

When imposter-kings sit on the throne of David, that is bad! But when imposter-priests serve in the house of God, that is worse! The church is at the mercy of false shepherds, dominated by a family hierarchy which has deformed itself into a political and religious ruling class. The high-priestly family acts as royalty and lives in a palace!

Imagine a true priest living in a palace. It is noteworthy that Annas was a rich man, a capitalist who profited from both the temple tax and the imperial tax; a shrewd businessman whose company was called "church and state – business and politics." No wonder that Annas and Caiaphas later *have* to get rid of Jesus; He threatens their influence and affluence.This high-priestly clique reasons like the policy-makers in Rome: keep the people busy with a legalistic religion of self-salvation, and also, keep them religiously divided, so that your power is not endangered.

UNCARING HIERARCHY

That is the worst thing here. It is not ideal to live under a foreign emperor, but Tiberius is at least far away in Rome. The country is sorely divided, but at least everyone knows what to expect from the local rulers. But when the church is in the grip of hierarchy and when there is spiritual oppression, that is terrible. When the church is torn apart and exploited from the inside, is that not the worst of all evils?

For then the truth is held under, the faith is destroyed, and the church ceases to show forth the marks of the true church of God. When the offices are deformed, the whole church is weakened, and heresies creep in. If the church is governed by a self-serving family clique, an aristocratic hierarchy, then spiritual slavery replaces the treasures of the covenant.

Here in the high-priesthood of Annas and Caiaphas, the low point of Aaron's priesthood has been reached. Israel now, if ever, needs a *new High Priest.* Do you notice how God is preparing to shove this deformed priesthood aside to give Israel its new High Priest after the order of Melchizedek? That is John's calling: as son of Levi, as priest after the order of Aaron, to proclaim the great High Priest, Jesus Christ.

HE FACED THEM ALL

If you sum all this up, you see Jesus Christ emerging here as King of kings, seated on the throne of David, and as the only High Priest, after the order of Melchizedek. In these two verses is unveiled the whole messianic program of Christ: to oppose the united world of man, to restore the divided people of God, to depose a deformed clergy, and to become Himself the true shepherd of His flock!

The great names Luke listed, our Lord knew them all. He faced the power of Rome when He stood before Pontius Pilate. He endured the mockery of Herod Antipas. He withstood the accusations of Annas and Caiaphas. He knew them all, He faced them all, and He overcame them all.

Today this Christ is in glory, as King of kings, and as head of His church, guiding our lives and the world's history to the goal of perfection. For the messianic program unveiled in this passage of Scripture will be completed. Then Christmas will have reached its conclusion.

The Death of Jesus Christ

Good Friday

Simon of Cyrene Compelled to Bear Christ's Cross

"And they compelled a passer-by, Simon of Cyrene, who was coming in from the country, the father of Alexander and Rufus, to carry His cross".

(Mark 15: 21)

We begin our series on the death of Jesus Christ with the history recorded in Mark 15, about Simon of Cyrene being forced to bear the cross of our Lord. Christ Himself once said that whoever wishes to follow Him must deny himself and take up his (own) cross, that is, accept the consequences and possible suffering of being a Christian.

In this passage we meet a literal cross-bearer, Simon of Cyrene. Only, it was not his own cross that he had to bear, but the Lord's. And he did not do it voluntarily but, as we read, he was compelled to do so.

Do you feel a little sorry for Simon of Cyrene because he was forced to perform what must have been to him an unsavoury task? Or does your heart go out more to Jesus, who is so weak that He cannot even bear His cross to the place of execution? Do you perhaps feel sorry for both; for these two poor, unfortunate souls, who happened to be in the wrong place at the wrong time, as the world would say?

Well, I think we can say that Christ does not want us to feel sorry for Himself or for Simon of Cyrene. We have to watch out here for false emotions and superficial sentimentality. In the days of Lent, we need not seek to relive or replay Christ's suffering, travelling His road to Calvary, as the church of Rome does when the Pope bears a wooden cross along the ten points of the *Via Dolorosa*, the road of sorrows. That's not real cross-bearing, that's dramatization.

Christ does not want our tearful sympathy, He wants our sincere repentance. Therefore we must learn also from this Scripture passage what God reveals to us about our sins and our salvation.

These are the real questions. For this text is not an interesting fact, a little trivia, but it is pure Gospel, proclamation of salvation, and as such it contains a message for us, which we shall seek to understand together. Our theme, then, is: Simon of Cyrene is compelled to bear Christ's cross, and we need to discover what this event meant *for the Lord* in His suffering, and what it teaches *us* about our calling.

BEARING ONE'S OWN CROSS

When they led Jesus out to crucify Him, He bore His cross. You can read this in John 19: 17, "So they took Jesus, and He went out, bearing His own cross, to the place called. . . Golgotha." We should note this carefully: He began by bearing His own cross.

This was apparently the Roman custom. Condemned criminals were made to bear their own cross to the place of execution. It was an extra humiliation, just as in modern times – I think of events in the second world war – condemned people were sometimes forced to dig their own graves.

It is not clear exactly what is meant by this cross-bearing. Some explainers say that the criminal had to carry the entire cross, by bearing the upright beam on his shoulders, while he dragged the cross-beam behind him with a rope. Others say that only the cross-beam had to be carried and that the supporting beam was already erected at the place of execution. In any case, this bearing of the cross was a heavy task, but for a healthy and strong person not necessarily an impossible burden. The other two convicted men most likely carried their crosses all the way to Golgotha, which was not far outside the city of Jerusalem.

Why do I mention this? Because the Lord indeed started out by carrying His own cross, but obviously He did not last long. He could not fulfill this task! The extreme anguish suffered at Gethsemane, the trials before the high priests, Herod, and Pilate during that long night, the flogging and other abuse, had all taken their toll on the Lord and so weakened Him that, on the way to Golgotha, He stumbled under the weight of his cross. There was, perhaps, the danger that He would pass out and even succumb before reaching Golgotha!

The soldiers were not merciful to the Lord, but they did not want to jeopardize the execution itself. Christ had to stay alive so that He would die *on the cross*, not before the crucifixion. Therefore, they had to take preventive measures.

Some explainers suggest that the *Jews* opposed Christ's bearing of His own cross, because He was a native Jew after all, and therefore someone else had to be found, a stranger such as Simon of Cyrene. But we do not read about such an outpouring of Jewish nationalism in our text, and the best explanation is the simplest one: Christ was unable to bear His cross. Being utterly exhausted, He stumbled under its sheer weight, and sank to the ground.

APPROPRIATE MEASURES?

The soldiers, of course, had to take proper measures. They did not want to carry the cross themselves. Neither would they be able to convince any of the accompanying party of the Jews to do it. So they did what occupying forces most often do: simply grab an innocent bystander and force him to do the dirty work!

It says, "And they compelled a passerby, Simon of Cyrene, who was coming in from the country. . . to carry His cross." Simon apparently was coming from the opposite direction, going into the city from the country, and the soldiers simply requisitioned him. We may assume that Simon tried to pass by this raucous band, not wanting to be involved, but they just grabbed him and forced him.

Explainers who suggest that Simon was picked because he showed some sympathy for Jesus or perhaps stepped in to help Jesus up are obviously wrong: the text very clearly states that Simon was compelled. He did not want to do it at all. He was just coming in from the country, minding his own business, and suddenly he found himself face to face with this execution squad, and the next thing he knew was that they put this cross on his back. He was no volunteer, but was forced by the Roman soldiers, probably at spear-point. Pick it up, or else!

We should therefore be careful not to place this man, Simon of Cyrene, on a pedestal, as some have done. He is then portrayed as the last person to show Christ some sympathy and to afford Him some relief, a real saint, as it were. Simon of Cyrene, according to this view, showed Christ love on the road to Calvary. And the application is that we today must show the Lord Jesus even more love and support. But that is not the message of this text.

EXTRA HUMILIATION FOR CHRIST

Since Simon was *forced* to lend this "service," it did not really offer Christ any comfort. On the contrary, we can say that this is an extra humiliation for our Lord. When He must see how Simon is compelled to assist Him, He is made to feel even more helpless. No one comes forward to help Him voluntarily, and He is not able any more to demand that someone of his own choosing helps Him. Our Lord is in no position to get Simon "off the hook," but must watch how Simon is forced to perform a very unappealing task on His behalf.

Don't you think that this must have been very difficult for the Lord Jesus to accept? Here his last shred of self-respect and pride was torn away from Him. It was not His style to let others do the dirty work for Him. And I am not talking about foolish, human pride, but the proper respect for His holy office as Messiah. He did not come to have anyone suffer in His place, but He came to bear the burdens of others.

Our Lord was always so very much in charge of His own affairs. He always reached out to help others, and He did so with messianic dignity, authority and power. He commanded the wind and the sea to be calm, to save His disciples. He fed the multitudes by multiplying loaves and fishes. He raised up all who were weak and poor. He dared even to make His own requisitions. He simply took the donkey upon which He rode into Jerusalem, and calmly ordered that a guest room be prepared for Him and His disciples for the last Passover. He called unto Himself whomever He willed, and they came to Him, in submission to His sovereign will. All this was part of His glory and power as Messiah, as Son of David.

THE HELPLESS HELPER

But now the great Helper has become utterly helpless. He who cared for others cannot even care for Himself. Don't you think that Christ must have been sorely tempted here to summon the resources of His godly nature, to raise Himself, and to take up that cross and bear it proudly to the hill of Golgotha? Oh, to be able to say: leave this man alone, for I alone bear My cross.

But the Lord Jesus must let it happen. For it is part of His suffering, the total emptying of Himself, becoming devoid of all human strength and power, stumbling forward in utter weakness, not even able to bear His own cross! That is what this text shows us, so that we might know how far He went, how deeply He humbled Himself, how totally He emptied Himself, for the sake of our sins! Indeed, as the apostle Paul wrote in Philippians 2: 7: Christ *emptied* Himself. Note that word: emptied. He poured everything out, even the last vestiges of his own pride, for us.

Of course, in one way it was a relief that He did not have to bear that cross anymore. But it was at the same time a shame for Him that another must take up

His burden. Hear the taunts of the soldiers and the Jews: can't even carry your own cross, eh? Here, let this man take over for you!

A PASSERBY

This man, Simon of Cyrene, is a mere passerby. Let us not say, an "innocent victim," for no one is innocent. But he was certainly a man who was not at all directly involved in the issue but just happened to pass by. The centurion orders, "Hey, you there, come help this weakling."

Many people would like to know who exactly this Simon of Cyrene was. We really do not know much about him. His name "Simon" indicates that perhaps he was a Jew or a proselyte to Judaism. He came from Cyrene, in Libya, where there was a large colony of displaced Jews. Many of these Jews from Cyrene visited Jerusalem regularly. They also made many proselytes who came to Jerusalem. The Cyrenians even had their own synagogue there. Some of them also owned land in and around Jerusalem. This possibly was the case with Simon, who may have been coming back from inspecting his land and returning to the city to prepare for the passover.

Various explainers suggest that the Cyrenians, being from North Africa, were black people. In Acts 6: 9 we read about people who belonged to the synagogue of the Freedmen (as it was called), and of the Cyrenians, Alexandrians, and those from Cilicia and Asia who disputed with Stephen, the first martyr. The synagogue of the Freedmen, to which also the Cyrenians belonged, was perhaps composed of former (black) slaves who had been set free. These black proselytes were segregated in their own synagogue with many others from foreign places, and as is common with converts, were fanatic in their Judaism. Hence their fierce opposition to Stephen.

So Simon may have been a black man, a former slave, and this perhaps explains all the more why the Roman soldiers picked on him to carry Christ's cross. Surely such a man was in no position to protest!

A DISCIPLE OF CHRIST?

There are commentators who think that Simon may have become a disciple of Christ. For it says in this verse that he was "the father of Alexander and Rufus." This may mean that Simon himself was not known to the churches (Mark is said to have written his Gospel especially for the church at Rome), but that his sons were well-known Christians.

Alexander and Rufus. We do not know exactly which Alexander is meant (the name was not uncommon), but in the letter to the Romans the apostle Paul does extend greetings to a certain Rufus: "Greet Rufus, eminent in the Lord, also his mother and mine" (Romans 16: 13). It may very well be that Simon of Cyrene was the father of this Rufus, who later was a member of the church at Rome. Since only Rufus' mother is mentioned by Paul, Simon may then already have been dead, or he never became a Christian.

But these are all assumptions. We have few hard facts about Simon of Cyrene and don't know whether he became a Christian or not. He comes in out of the field, appears momentarily on the scene, and disappears again. All we can know for sure is that he had to be forced to carry the cross. It is quite probable, in fact, that he was greatly embarrassed, perhaps even offended that he was forced into duty, treated like a slave. It will not be easy for a man like Simon ever to confess this man Jesus as His Lord and Saviour. For, "who saw revealed in Him God's power and God's favour?" (Isaiah 53). Not Simon of Cyrene. All he saw was a bloodied criminal, staggering under the weight of his own cross.

Meanwhile, it is Jesus who is the most humiliated. He who had said: take up your cross, must hand over His cross to another. He who had warned His disciples for the cost and pain of following Him, must see Himself crushed under the weight of the cost and the burden of pain. At this point He cannot do anything, not even for Simon of Cyrene. For the weight of our sins and of the wrath of God, which pressed out of Him the bloody sweat already in the garden of Gethsemane, is here beginning to crush Him totally. We will never understand what it meant for Christ to hand over that burden of cross-bearing to another, even to Simon of Cyrene.

BEARING OUR OWN CROSS

What further message comes out of this text to us in our time? We see Christ here in His suffering. We see Simon of Cyrene toiling under the Lord's cross. What does this mean for us?

We are not asked to do what Simon of Cyrene was compelled to do. No one today needs to bear Christ's cross to Golgotha, the place of the skull. Christ was crucified, dead, and buried, and on the third day He rose again from the dead. He does not need any help or assistance from us in the fulfilling of His ministry today.

We do not have to bear *His* cross. But now Christ's word about our bearing our *own* cross receives all the more depth and significance. Simon of Cyrene was an exception. The rule is that we must take up *our* cross cheerfully, and deny ourselves, and so follow Christ.

And the emphasis for us must lie on the word *cheerfully*, that is, we must carry our cross willingly and with joy. Simon of Cyrene was compelled by the Roman soldiers. His act was not voluntary. Therefore he did not do it cheerfully. He was glad when it was over and he could go home, about his own business. But that may not be the way we bear our cross!

THE GREAT CONTRAST

Perhaps that is where the great contrast lies. No one compels us to take up our cross; that is, no outside, human power. But we know that Christ demands it of us and that the Holy Spirit works the willingness in us. To us comes the calling: take up your cross, and do so joyfully, cheerfully, willingly. If we are compelled, it is by the sovereign grace and power of God! But in all this, the Lord seeks our joyous commitment, our sincere participation.

When we see Christ staggering under the weight of His cross, unable to bear it further, we are reminded of our own cross. And we know: cross-bearing is for us not a form of atonement for sins, for Christ has fully paid for all our sins. The Gospel attests to this clearly. Cross-bearing is for us not a segment of the road to Golgotha, for we do not have to travel that road. Cross-bearing is for us: accepting joyfully the consequences of being a Christian, even if this means publicly suffering for Christ's sake, public ridicule, shame, and persecution.

We will have to tell our children that being a Christian is not easy in this world filled with satanic evil and opposition. From all sides we are attacked, opposed, deceived, and ridiculed. We must make sacrifices which other people never make, set priorities which others never set, and live a lifestyle that is not understood by people around us.

And there may come a time when we, too, stumble under the weight of that cross and when we can no longer bear the load. Then we do not have to look around to find some passerby to help us. We cannot compel others to bear our cross for us. There is no Simon of Cyrene today who can be forced to bear our cross. Instead, we may look to our Lord Jesus Christ, Who today is seated in glory at the right hand of the Father and who by the power of His Spirit strengthens us in our cross-bearing.

Have you ever said to the Lord Jesus: it is so hard for me to bear my cross? Lord, I just cannot carry it any further? Have the demands and difficulties of being a Christian sometimes worn you down? We need not be afraid of admitting this. For would the Lord Jesus, who stumbled under the weight of His cross, not fully understand our predicament?

Oh yes, He gives us many helpers on the way. He grants us a place in His congregation, the communion of saints. We may bear the burdens together. He gives us God-fearing parents, Christian teachers, responsible office-bearers, and a supportive fellowship. We may bask in the warmth and the care of many fellow-Christians and be strengthened together at the table of communion. It is something that Christ did not experience in His trials. He was left all alone, except for the one unwilling man who bore His cross for Him. The help we receive in carrying our cross is something we do not deserve. He earned this for us by His suffering.

OUR ONLY HELPER

But at bottom, only the Lord Jesus can help us to bear our own cross. This is truly the message which comes to us in this passage: I, your Lord and Saviour, who know by experience how difficult it is to be a cross-bearer, I will sustain you, support you, and help you to bear your cross. Christ is not compelled by anyone or anything to do so. He does it in His great love and sovereign grace, because He wants to.

That is our joy today. The very same man, whom we see in our text succumbing under the sheer weight of the cross, today has received all power in heaven and on earth, and He uses this power for our benefit. He says today: I am with you, every step of the way, and I will help you lift and bear that cross, so that you can persevere in your life as a Christian.

This promise comes to us already at our baptism. Children are not cross-bearers in themselves, but cross-bearers through Christ. They share in the riches of the covenant of grace. Christ says at every baptism – what a comfort also to parents, who must nurture and educate these children – I will strengthen you to bear your cross cheerfully. On that basis we live and work. We may always direct our children to the great Helper, the great cross-bearer, and say: our help is in the Name of the Lord!

And every time we celebrate the Lord's Supper, we may all see and hear it again: I, the Lord, am the One Who enables you to bear your cross. To Him we go for all help and strength. Yes, precisely when we use the sacraments, we may pray: grant us your grace that we may take up our cross cheerfully, deny ourselves and confess our Saviour. In the signs and seals of baptism and Lord's Supper, we receive the added assurance that He will never forsake us. He is right there, whenever we should stumble, to lift us up.

He knows what it is to crumble under the burdens.

He knows also how to lift us up. Voluntarily and gladly He does it, compelled only by His grace and love. Time and again, our whole life through. Therefore the church confesses:

> "LORD, though I walk 'mid troubles sore,
> Thou wilt restore my faltering spirit,
> Though angry foes my soul alarm,
> Thy mighty arm will save and cheer it." (Psalm 138: 4, *Book of Praise*).

And one day we shall see that multitude of cross-bearers, who in Christ's strength alone crossed the finish line to stand around the throne, the saints, in countless myriads, of every tongue, redeemed to God,

> "Through tribulation great they came
> *They bore the cross*, despised the shame."

And their song is a simple song, yet a profound one:

> "Worthy the Lamb for sinners slain. . .
> Thou has redeemed us by Thy blood,
> And made us kings and priests to God." (Hymn 52: 1, 3, *Book of Praise*).

CHRIST ON GOLGOTHA

"And they brought Him to the place called Golgotha (which means the place of a skull)"

(Mark 15: 22)

In the time of Lent, the church pays special attention to the scriptural account of Christ's *via dolorosa,* His road of sorrows, to the cross. We saw how Christ had to be helped by Simon of Cyrene to bear his cross to Golgotha.

In Mark 15: 22, we read how Christ arrives at Golgotha, the end-point of the road of sorrows. Here He will be crucified and die.

Now it is remarkable how little we really know about this place called Golgotha. No one can tell us exactly where it was located. The early Christian church apparently was not much involved with the place. It was not until more than 300 years later, under the emperor Constantine, that a basilica (a small church) was erected on the site where supposedly the crucifixion had taken place. It could very well be the proper location or close to it, although it is not certain. Since then, pilgrims from all over the world have been flocking to that basilica to meditate and pray. But the fact remains, we know very little of the exact place.

MANY LEGENDS

It is understandable that many legends have come into existence concerning Golgotha. To give you an idea, let me mention two of them. Some say that Golgotha is the same place where once Abraham was making preparations to offer Isaac. That is a nice touch, perhaps, but it is unlikely. Others say that the skull of Adam was buried there. But the connection between the first and the second Adam should not be made so superficial. Legends do not really help us much.

It is also rather remarkable that the name "Golgotha" does not appear anywhere in the Bible except in the accounts of the crucifixion. It is not mentioned in any of the letters of the apostles, nor do you find the name in the book of Revelation. Ought we, perhaps, to conclude from this that the Lord wanted to prevent any superstition or idolatry to be associated with the place? The event of Christ's death is mentioned throughout the New Testament, but, apart from the Gospels, not the place where this death occurred.

GOLGOTHA AND CALVARY

Perhaps this is the reason why we also do not have any direct references to Golgotha in our hymn section of the *Book of Praise*. Have you ever noticed that? There is one hymn where we find the name Calvary. In Hymn 33 is the line, "Our Surety and our Lord is He Who shed His blood on Calvary."

Where does the name "Calvary" come from? It is the Latin translation of the Hebrew "Golgotha." We find in our text that Golgotha means "the place of a skull," and the Latin word for skull is "calvaria," hence the name Calvary. Via Latin and English, the name "Calvary" has become popular in many later hymns. But that name does not appear in the Bible.

However this may be, when we follow our Lord Jesus Christ on His *via dolorosa*, His road of sorrows – we see that it ends at a place named Golgotha. And we are interested in the location of that Golgotha and in its meaning.

A WELL-KNOWN PLACE?

If in what follows we want to say something more about the location of Golgotha, then it is not because we want to go there to erect another monument. We want to pay attention to the location in order to understand better the meaning of Golgotha. For it is not without reason that this place was chosen.

In New Testament times the place seems to have been a well-known one. Notice how in our text it says: "And they brought Him to the place called Golgotha. . . ." Not "a place," but "the place." If in those days Golgotha was mentioned, everyone familiar with the area knew where it was. That is important, as we will see further.

Notice also how it says that they *brought* Christ to Golgotha. Some explainers feel that this word suggests that Christ had to be supported on the last leg of the journey. He had earlier been unable to carry the cross. Now as they come near to Golgotha, Christ is so weak that He can hardly walk and is in need of support. However this may be, the use of the verb "to bring" also suggests that this place was chosen ahead of time.

This leads us to the question: how far Golgotha was from the city of Jerusalem. Could it have been so far that Christ may have had to be supported during the latter part of the walk? In fact, it cannot have been very far. The apostle John tells us (John 19:20) that the place where Jesus was crucified was near the city. Indeed, we may conclude that it was just outside one of the city gates, where people were going in and out.

THE PLACE OF THE SKULL

This also helps us to understand the name "Golgotha," the Hebrew word for skull. Many speculations have been made concerning the implications of that word. Some have suggested that the place was named "place of the skull" because it was where the skulls of executed criminals were buried. But it is more likely that it was called "skull" because Golgotha was a place that from a distance looked like a skull. It was probably a small, bare, rounded hill, located just outside the city of Jerusalem, along which ran various roads leading to and from the city.

And that is an excellent place for a public execution. For the crucifixion – any crucifixion, but especially this one – was not a quick death somewhere out of the public view, but a public affair. The Romans had the custom of executing criminals along busy road sides and at busy intersections, so that everyone would see it and take notice. The crucifixion was to be a public display and example, meant to be seen by as many people as possible. For only in this way would a crucifixion function as a deterrent for other would-be criminals. And that was precisely the purpose: a punishment which functioned as a deterrent.

PUBLIC EXECUTION

Therefore, what can we say about the location of Golgotha? First, that it was nothing really special. No high mountain. No sacred, historic spot. Just a small, bare hill outside Jerusalem. The first convenient place, really, where a public execution could be conveniently held. The slight elevation would mean that no one could miss it. The busy intersection would ensure lots of traffic, a multitude of witnesses.

You can almost picture the scene. As the multitude comes out of the city, through the gate, the Roman captain, the centurion in charge, looks around, sees a little rise, and says, "Here, this is the place." Little hill, bare, nothing to be cleared away, no trees blocking the view, lots of traffic, what better place could be found? It was chosen because it was suited for a public execution, and for no other reason.

As a matter of fact, it is quite possible that Golgotha could be seen from the city itself. We can read about the women who followed Jesus from Galilee, and were watching from afar (see verse 40). These women may have been standing, with others, on the walls of Jerusalem, from where they had a unencumbered view of what was happening at Golgotha. For this crucifixion was to be seen by many people, from near and from afar.

That is why this location was chosen, and then not just by the Roman centurion, but by God Himself! For that is the conclusion we draw here. Ultimately, the Roman centurion was not in charge, for everything was done, as Peter says at Pentecost, by the "definite plan and foreknowledge of God." It was God Who wished to make the crucifixion of the Lord Jesus into a public display. Christ was to be crucified in such a way that all could see how the curse over sin took its full effect.

NOT IN A CORNER

Later, the apostle Paul, when speaking with King Agrippa about the suffering and death of Christ, says to the king (Acts 26:26): "For the king knows about these things. . . . I am persuaded that none of these things have escaped his notice, *for this was not done in a corner.*" These are keys words: it was not done in a corner!

Christ was not led away in the dark of the night to be executed or terminated in an unknown place, without witnesses. He was not assassinated in some dark alley, where no one saw what happened. His death did not take place in some obscure little village, far away from the centre of things, but right outside the gate of the great city, Jerusalem, on a hill with an unobstructed view. That is the message of Golgotha!

That is also why the sign was nailed above Him in three languages, Hebrew, Greek and Latin, as we read elsewhere, so that *all the world* could see and read: Behold, the Lamb of God who takes away the sins of the world.

Golgotha. The place itself is nothing special. After the corpses were buried and the crosses taken down, no one who passed by would be able to see that a crucifixion had taken place there. No memorials were erected, no markers planted. It was just a bald hill, as there were so many in Judea. As a matter of fact, if it wasn't for the Word of God, no one would understand the meaning of the place.

FURTHER MEANING?

The fact that Christ was crucified on Golgotha, just outside the gate, has a further meaning, which we must also explore. To do that, let us turn to Hebrews 13, the part of Scripture which should be read in connection with this passage from Mark 15.

The letter to the Hebrews was written to explain the greater riches which the New Testament church has over the people of the old dispensation. Christ is greater than Moses. We are richer than Israel. In chapter 13, the writer makes this clear also with respect to the *place* where Christ suffered and died.

He writes in verse 10, "We have an altar from which those who serve the tent (or tabernacle) have no right to eat." Normally the priests were allowed to eat of the sacrifices which were brought to the tabernacle. But they were not allowed to do so on the great day of atonement! For then the remnants of the bull and the ram that had been slaughtered, as it says in Leviticus 16: 27, "shall be carried forth outside the camp; their skin and their flesh and their dung shall be burned with fire."

OUTSIDE THE CAMP

Outside the camp, remember those words. Also on the day of atonement, a goat was chosen, named Azazel, and the high priest was to lay his hands on the head of this goat. He was to confess over him all the iniquities of the people of Israel, all their transgressions and sins, and then the goat was to be sent away into the wilderness. It says: the goat shall bear all their iniquities upon him to a solitary land. The goat, indeed the *scapegoat,* laden with the sins of God's people, was banished and sent *outside the camp,* to die in the wilderness!

The writer to the Hebrews refers to this day of atonement and says in verse 11, "For the bodies of those animals whose blood is brought into the sanctuary by the high priest as a sacrifice for sin, are burned outside the camp." And now notice the connection with Golgotha, verse 12, "So also Jesus suffered outside the gate in order to sanctify His people through His own blood."

Do you notice this? Anything that was brought outside the camp of Israel to be burned there, was unclean. To be sent out of the camp meant to be *excommunicated!* Outside the camp was the place where the garbage and the dung was left, because it did not belong in the camp. It was the place of ultimate destruction and final excommunication.

DAY OF ATONEMENT

Golgotha. Day of atonement. The Lamb of God, bearing our sins, all our sins, is led outside the gate of the city of Jerusalem. This happens because Jerusalem is the city of the tabernacle, the temple, the dwelling place of God most holy. Jerusalem is where the LORD God dwells in the midst of His people. Jerusalem is the holy city, and He who bears our impurities and defilement has no place with God in His city! As Christ goes out through the gate to nearby Golgotha, He is excommunicated, and then publicly cursed as the One who bears all the sins of His people.

Golgotha. Christ is crucified not far from the city; in fact, as we saw, probably even in view of the city, but certainly outside the city, so that He and all the people may know: this one is expelled from the presence of God, excommunicated from the people of God, and so cut off from the land of the living.

Day of atonement. Here the greatest sacrifice of the ages is made. He was made sin, for us, utterly cursed, so that we might inherit the blessing of God, live in fellowship with Him, and enter His holy presence with joy and thanksgiving. At Golgotha the law of atonement is completely fulfilled, so that we may be reconciled to God in Him!

Golgotha, the place of the skull, has become the place of atonement; the place of the greatest sacrifice ever made, by the One who did not die for His own sins, but only for ours! That is the real meaning of this place. "So Jesus suffered outside the gate in order to sanctify the people through His own blood."

WHERE TODAY?

We do not have to go to Golgotha today, even if we could find the exact spot. Do you know what we have to do? We are told it in Hebrews 13:13: "Therefore, let us go forth to Him outside the camp and bear the abuse He endured." Let us bear the consequences of being Christians.

Let us go forth to Him. We today may benefit from His sacrifice. We may eat from the altar called Golgotha. We can have access to the Father through Christ. We *do* have access to the Father through Him. Indeed, as it says in Hymn 33: our Surety and our Lord is He. Every time we celebrate the Lord's Supper, we do not repeat Golgotha, but we partake of the blessing of Golgotha. We go forth to Jesus to share in His sacrifice.

But, it says, go forth to Him outside the camp. We know that He was despised for our sake, and bore the hate of men and the wrath of God for our sake. "Outside the camp" means for us that we may have to become outcasts for His sake. As the writer to the Hebrews states it: that we bear the abuse He endured.

You know, the Hebrews to whom this letter was first written, were being ridiculed and abused by Jews and Gentiles alike. What kind of religion do you have, people scoffed, for you do not bring sacrifices and you have no altar. Well, the author replied, we have a sacrifice: Jesus Christ and Him crucified. And we have an altar, and that is Golgotha. We seek our entire salvation outside of ourselves in Jesus Christ alone, who brought the perfect sacrifice.

DESPISED RELIGION

And this is the religion which the world and the false church despises. Who can believe in a man crucified as a criminal, a failed "king," excommunicated from the people of God, an outcast, left to hang outside the gate? Of course, I know that today many people love to speak of Calvary. But do they accept that there was brought the one and only sacrifice, the complete and perfect sacrifice for sin? "Golgotha" is not enough for many today; it must be supplemented by our own good works and free-will gestures.

The Christian faith is, in essence, totally different from that of all other religions, for it seeks its entire salvation in one place: Golgotha, and in one Person, Jesus Christ. There the one sacrifice for sin was made, once for all.

Therefore, the writer to the Hebrews goes on: when we go forth to Jesus, outside the camp, outside the lines of conventional human religion, we leave everything behind that this world has to offer us. We do not seek our salvation here. Not even in the earthly Jerusalem. See verse 14: "For we have here no lasting city, but we seek the city which is to come." We have no horizontal faith – directed to this world – but we lift up our hearts to heaven, where Christ is, seated at the right hand of God, from where we also await Him. We are not bound to earthly places or institutions: we may serve Him wherever we are. And we do not feel threatened at all when we are for His sake cast out from the places where the religious people of this world congregate. Let the world persecute and the false church ridicule, we will go forth to Jesus outside the gate, and bear the abuse, for His Name's sake. "Our Surety and our Lord is He, Who shed His blood on Calvary."

OUR SACRIFICE OF PRAISE

And if we are to bring any sacrifice, says the letter to the Hebrews, it is not a sacrifice for sin. That would undo the meaning of Golgotha. What sacrifices are we to bring? Verse 17, "Through Him, then, let us continually offer up a *sacrifice of praise* to God, that is, the fruit of lips that acknowledge His Name." We shall worship and praise Him alone, constantly, for His great love shown at Golgotha.

He brought the one sacrifice for sin. We bring the constant sacrifice of praise. And that is not just a matter of words, but also of deeds. Verse 16: "Do not neglect to do good and to share what you have, for such sacrifices are pleasing to God." We must bring the sacrifice of service to the neighbour, to show love and kindness, to share with those in need.

If we truly want to honour the reality of Golgotha and bring an acceptable sacrifice to God, one which really honours Christ, let it be one of praise (worship) and service (love).

What greater joy can there be for a Christian than to worship together with God's people and to devote oneself to the upbuilding of the church and the well-being of the neighbour? Then we are in line with Golgotha. That is what God asks of us. That is the calling which comes to us from Golgotha. Psalm 50: bring God your sacrifices in His house! Which sacrifices? "Blest is the man whom sin cannot entice, who brings *thanksgiving* as his sacrifice." God does not want any more sin offerings, but only thank offerings.

"Redeemed by grace, I'll render as a token
Of gratitude my constant praise to Thee" (Psalm 116).

Then, because Christ was led outside the city of Jerusalem to be crucified outside the gate, we may enter the gates of the holy city, the eternal and lasting city which is to come. We may live in God's presence and fellowship, and say:

"Jerusalem, *within your courts* I'll praise
The Lord's great Name, and with a spirit lowly,
Pay all my vows. O Zion, fair and holy,
Come join with me, and bless Him all your days."

That is the meaning of Golgotha. Christ was cast out of God's city. We may now enter the eternal city through Him.

Christ Stripped Naked on the Cross

"And they crucified Him, and divided His garments among them, casting lots for them, deciding what each should take".

(Mark 15: 24)

We continue to follow the suffering of our Lord on His *via dolorosa*, the road of suffering. Last time we saw Him arrive on Golgotha, where He was crucified.

We do not know the exact procedure which was followed at this crucifixion. In all the texts in the Gospels it says simply that they crucified Him. To understand the extent of Christ's suffering, however, we must know something of what was involved in this manner of execution.

The convicted criminal was most likely first tied down with ropes to the cross. This would immobilize him and facilitate the driving in of nails or spikes. We do not know whether at this point the cross was still lying on the ground or had already been erected. In the latter case, a kind of ladder would have to be used to nail down the condemned.

Most explainers agree that spikes were driven through the hands of the convicted. Whether they were always driven through the feet as well is not clear. Some suggest that the feet were placed flat against the vertical beam, thus forcing the body into a very awkward position, with the knees pushed forward. Others suggest that the spikes were driven through the lower leg, just above the feet. When we read what Christ Himself says later (Luke 24:39), "See my hands *and my feet*, that it is I myself," we may conclude that spikes were driven through the Lord's feet.

A SLOW AND AGONIZING DEATH

The Holy Spirit has not revealed to us all the particulars of Christ's execution, perhaps in order to prevent all kinds of superstitious speculation. What is clear is that death by crucifixion was a very painful death, truly a method of extreme torture. To be stretched out for hours in such an unnatural position must be unbearable. The spikes were driven through the parts of the hand and feet which were the most sensitive, so that every movement caused excruciating pain. Infection invariably swiftly set in, causing fever and delirium.

Because of the victim's position, the blood could not flow properly, and this would cause extreme headache. The lungs would fill with fluid, making breathing an arduous task. There was no way that a crucified person could move to lessen the agony. Even turning the head, the only free moving part of the body, caused severe pain.

Moreover, it says in the verse immediately following our text, that they crucified Him at the third hour, that is at 9.00 a.m. The sun had risen, the temperature was climbing swiftly, as it does in the Middle East, and there was no shadow. Insects began to converge on the victim, stinging, and feeding on the wounds. It does not take long under such circumstances for thirst and exhaustion to set in; yet death on the cross remained a slow and painful process of dying.

I say this not to speculate or dramatize, but these are the hard facts which are known about death by crucifixion. The cross should not become for us some vague symbol of suffering, for it is a gruesome *reality.* What I have described with a few words is a feeble attempt to explain what Christ had to endure for our sake. There is no way anyone can minimize it, or embellish it, or romanticize it as a martyr's death. It was a horrible death to die.

The text gives us another detail about Christ's crucifixion. It tells that He was stripped of His clothes, which were subsequently divided among the soldiers. In other words, He was crucified *naked.* We must pay attention also to this fact. For when Christ was stripped of His clothes and displayed naked on the cross, He lost both earthly honour and heavenly grace.

TOTALLY NAKED?

When you see paintings or sculptures of Christ on the cross, you notice that the artists usually do not portray Christ as totally naked. Perhaps they felt that this would be too shameful. They tried to rescue some of His dignity by covering up His loins. Undoubtedly the intent of the artists is laudable, but the biblical facts give a different picture. And we are not interested in an artist's concept, but in the biblical account.

Admittedly, the opinions differ on whether Christ was stripped of all His clothes. Our text says only this: "And they crucified Him, and divided His garments among them, casting lots for them, to see what each would take." It says only "His garments." Some will argue that it does not say in so many words: all His garments. Yet it is very likely that this is what indeed happened. To strip the victim of all his garments deepened the shame and humiliation of the crucifixion. The Romans therefore customarily let their victims hang utterly naked, and why would they have made an exception in this case? On the contrary, the Roman soldiers had every reason not to make that exception in Jesus' case. I'll come back to that in a moment.

GARMENTS AND TUNIC

The question is first what we should understand by the word "garments." When we look at a more elaborate parallel text in John 19: 23 and 24, we discover that what they took from Jesus was the following: His garments (which they divided into four parts) *and* his tunic. What does that tell us?

The "garments" are generally taken to be the outer garments. We would say our "clothes," again meaning the outer wear. This consisted indeed of four parts: the cloak or mantel (which was also used as a covering at night), the belt or girdle (which was tied around the cloak to keep it closed), the sandals, and the head-covering or scarf. These four necessary items essentially were the "clothes" or "garments" of every Jew. They ensured that the head, the body, and the feet were covered and protected.

Some explainers feel that Christ, perhaps, lost his head-covering or scarf, when the crown of thorns was placed on His head, so that it should not be counted at Golgotha. But there is no reason to assume that this head-covering was not taken along. As to the tunic, that was what we would call the under-garment. It was a frock, made from wool or linen, worn on the body under the mantel. Sometimes a linen shirt was also worn under the tunic, but this under-garment was the basic covering of the body.

For the sake of interest, I mention that we read about this tunic in John 19: 23 that it was "without seam, woven from top to bottom." According to some this indicates that it was a rather expensive item. Some explainers remind us here of the garment of the priest, which was also woven as a single garment. This would be, as some say, an indication of Christ's claim to priesthood. But that is hardly likely, for the priest's single garment was not an under-garment, as is the case here. The priest wore an ornate outer garment woven without seam, and Christ did not.

His outer garments, then, were divided into four parts. This is because every execution squad had four soldiers, and each was entitled to an equal share of the victim's possessions. To determine who got what, the soldiers cast lots. They gambled for it, as soldiers often do. But they did not want to tear up the tunic into four parts, for that would have made it worthless. So they decided to keep it in one piece and cast lots over it as well. Let the dice decide.

LAST DIGNITY REMOVED

John's description, then, confirms what was the Roman practice: the victim was stripped naked. That was part of the humiliation that went with the punishment. For it was the greatest shame for anyone, but especially for a Jew, to be shown naked, and so to be robbed of even the last shred of dignity and self-respect. The only thing a man has left when facing his tormentors is his dignity, and that is in part embodied in his clothes. Strip a person bare, leave him nothing to cover himself, and he becomes totally vulnerable, a laughing-stock over whom even women and children giggle.

Prisoners and ex-prisoners will tell you that among the worst things of prison life are the constant body searches and strip-downs, and the fact that your own clothes are taken from you. It is true, you are given some kind of prison garb, but you lose your personal identity as well as your personal privacy. How much worse it is, however, to be stripped of clothes altogether.

Scripture itself tells us what it means to be rendered naked in public: it is the final humiliation. It was prophesied to Israel as a particular punishment of God. Read what Moses said to Israel in Deuteronomy 28: 47 and 48, "Because you did not serve the LORD your God. . . you shall serve your enemies. . . in hunger and thirst, in nakedness, and in want of all things. . . ."

So it was also among the nations. When the LORD God through Isaiah prophesied judgment over Egypt and Ethiopia (Isaiah 20: 4), he said, "the king of Assyria shall lead away the Egyptians captives and the Ethiopians exiles, both the young and the old, naked and barefoot, with buttocks uncovered, to the shame of Egypt." It was a public shame, and all who trusted in Egypt and Ethiopia for deliverance from Assyria would be dismayed.

If such was the case with "common" people, how awful must it be for royalty, for kings and princes, to be paraded naked as vanquished foes. For that reason especially the Roman soldiers will have delighted in stripping Jesus of His clothes, for did He not claim to be the long-expected King of the hated Jews? This man really needed to be taught a lesson: strip Him down.

THE ULTIMATE INSULT

Do you see what is happening? It is indeed mind-shattering. Here is the Christ, the Son of David, the hope of Israel, and they hang a sign above His head stating, "Jesus of Nazareth, the King of the Jews," and what do people see? A pitiful, wretched shadow of a man, stripped bare of the last shred of human dignity, someone who cannot even cover Himself.

The ultimate insult is, perhaps, that the soldiers make a game out of dividing His clothes. His clothes have no real value: there is a faded mantel, worn-out sandals, a bloodied scarf, and a sweaty tunic. Robes fit for a king? Swearing and cursing, with rude jokes and obscene laughter, they play their game, and mock Him: if you are the King of the Jews, come down from the cross and claim these measly garments! Earlier the soldiers had put a royal robe on Him, borrowed for the occasion, and mocked Him, "Hail, King of the Jews," and now they mock Him again, as He hangs naked.

The king's pride is his royal robe. Think of Psalm 45, the prophetic psalm about the great King, "God, your God, with oil of happiness, has you above all other kings anointed, myrrh and sweet spices for your robes appointed." Yes, you can compose psalms for the King: "In beauty you surpass all men around you, with glory, O our king, the LORD has crowned you," but here hangs a man whose last shred of dignity has been torn away, whose ragged clothes are divided with the roll of the dice.

The Son of God, of whom another Psalm sings, "The LORD is King, enrobed with majesty, He girds Himself with strength and equity," hangs here bereft of majesty, with His girdle crumpled in the dust of Golgotha. This is how the world spits out the Son of God. Naked He came, and naked He shall go; He will depart with nothing but shame.

Pious artists may try to cover the nakedness of Jesus, but in truth the King is here bereft of dignity. It is not simply that He must die. It is that He must die in this way, robbed of all earthly honour; He, the Son of God, through whom all things were made.

ADAM CLOTHED; CHRIST STRIPPED

And now we go one step further. We must! For in biblical light we know that this nakedness of Christ is not just a cruel joke of Roman soldiers, but it is *the work of God.* Christ does not just lose here all earthly honour, but also all heavenly grace!

When you place this event – Christ stripped naked – beside what happened in the Garden of Eden, after the fall into sin, you notice a remarkable contrast. There the first Adam was clothed. Here the second Adam is stripped. And we understand: Adam could only be clothed because one day Christ would be stripped!

Before the fall, Adam and Eve were naked. That was then nothing to be ashamed of. It says in Genesis 2: 25, "And the man and his wife were naked, and they were not ashamed." Not ashamed for *each other*, as the original verb may be translated. Not ashamed *for God* either. Why not? Because there was no sin! There was, so to speak, nothing to hide, nothing to cover up. Nakedness was part of the harmony of a perfect creation. There was nothing encumbered or depraved about the difference between man and woman, that is, about their sexuality. Nor was there anything between man and woman and their God. In Paradise humanity enjoyed total openness and natural harmony.

This changed, however, when Adam and Eve sinned. Then they knew that they were naked. They saw themselves as they now really were. Their outward nakedness had become an expression of their inward corruption. They could no longer go about with one another as before. The harmony had been disrupted. The depravity had become so deep that hitherto unknown forces of evil – also sexually – were unleashed. Their nakedness reminded them not only of their sinfulness, but also of their accursedness. They were utterly vulnerable, open to the righteous wrath of Almighty God.

What did they do? They realized the need for covering. They sewed fig leaves together and made themselves aprons. They needed to be protected against their own depravity and against their accursedness before God. But fig leaves are not very adequate for this purpose.

Then we read that God in His mercy gave to mankind clothes. Is it not a heart-warming scene in Genesis 3: 21, "And the LORD God made for Adam and his wife garments of skins, and clothed them." Garments of skins, that is, durable clothing, solid protection! The LORD God Himself gave a covering for the nakedness of His children.

CLOTHING: GOD'S GIFT AND MANDATE

We must understand that clothes are not a product of cultural evolution. We should not fall into the simple scheme of thinking that primitive people have fewer clothes and civilized people have more clothes because of the difference in cultural progress. In some ways our so-called civilized society promotes more nudity than many so-called primitive societies.

Clothes are a gift and therefore also a mandate of God. God gives clothes to curb and restrain the power and effects of sin, and to cover shame. And wherever you see people shedding their clothes and promoting partial or total nudity, you see the forces of deformation at work. Lack of shame, lack of decency emerge.

When God gave clothes, He was holding back His curse over a sinful humanity. He gave a covering, which would function temporarily. The full harmony of Paradise, however, would be restored only through Jesus Christ. The relationship between God and man, and between man and woman, would find its renewal in the redeeming work of Christ.

Do you see what that means for Jesus on Golgotha? He must pay the price for this covering, by being Himself rendered naked. For at this moment of truth, when the wrath of God against the sin of the whole human race is unleashed in full fury, there is no covering of the depravity of man, there is no escape from the curse of God. The grace shown to the first Adam is withheld from the second Adam!

Yes, the soldiers rip off His garments and tunic. But it is God Who now begins to unleash His fury, stored up through the ages. Here the sinfulness of man will not be covered up, and the full curse of God will not be delayed. Here begins the descent into hell, where there is no grace but only judgment.

On the cross Christ does not lose only all earthly honour, He also loses all heavenly grace! This is what the Roman soldiers with their proud legionnaire's uniforms and the Jewish priests with their ornate gowns do not understand. But Christ knows it. And He undergoes it. For in this way alone can He earn for us the righteousness with which we must be clothed to stand honourably on the new earth and receive grace in the new heaven.

Adam clothed. Christ naked. The second Adam must pay the price for the covering of the first Adam. He must do this so that in Him we may obtain grace, grace forever more. And we will not be ashamed of Him who hung naked on a cross; instead, we may exult in His redeeming work. For He arose from the dead with a glorified body. And today He is seated in glory on the eternal throne of heaven. Indeed, Psalm 45: With glory, O our King, the LORD has crowned you!

ARE WE CLOTHED?

The question now for us is this: are *we clothed* with the righteousness of Christ? The apostle Paul once put that question to the Corinthians, when he wrote to them about the breakdown of this earthly body. He said, "Here indeed we groan, and long to put on our heavenly dwelling, so that by putting it on, we may not be found *naked.*" Dying now, for us, is not a matter of being unclothed, like Christ on the cross, but of being further clothed, receiving the glory of heaven, "arrayed in garments washed in blood" – as kings and priests in holy array, wearing the crown of life.

Indeed, Paul writes, "when our earthly tent" – this body that had to be clothed with perishable garments – "falls to the ground, all worn and rent, our God as gift to us extends a heavenly house, not made with hands!" We will be clothed with eternal glory, through Him Who was stripped naked for us on the cross.

The Repentant Criminal Received into the House of the Father

"One of the criminals who were hanged railed at Him, saying: are you not the Christ? Save yourself and us! But the other rebuked him, saying: Do you not fear God, since you are under the same sentence of condemnation? And we indeed justly, for we are receiving the due reward for our sins; but this man has done nothing wrong. And he said: Jesus, remember me when you come into your kingdom, And He said to him: truly, I say to you, today you will be with Me in Paradise".

(Luke 23: 39-43)

Whenever we remember the death of our Lord Jesus Christ, we must understand that He does not want our sympathy or our tears for His extreme suffering. He said Himself to those who bewailed Him on His day of execution, "Weep not for Me, but weep for yourselves and your children" (23: 28).

He does not want our tears. Don't cry for Me, congregation. What He wants is our confession of sin. What He seeks is our profession of faith. We are not going to re-enact His suffering and walk the *via dolorosa;* but we must hear the testimony of Scripture concerning His work as our Messiah and Mediator.

This is also the case when we look at this passage of Scripture. We'll focus the spotlight of our attention on the fact that Christ was not the only one crucified on Good Friday. We read in verse 33, ". . . they crucified Him, and the criminals, one on the left and one on the right". There were three crosses that day, a fact mentioned by all the evangelists.

THREE CROSSES

Three crosses. Recently when we were travelling through the states of West Virginia and Pennsylvania, I noticed on many hills three crosses, a large one in the middle (signifying Christ's cross) and two smaller ones on each side (signifying those of the two criminals crucified with Him). I thought, on the one hand, that this is a wrong presentation of reality: there is no reason to believe that Christ's cross was any larger or higher than those other two. On the other hand, I thought, it is true, for those two crosses are meant to highlight that one cross.

Being crucified in the middle, between others, certainly means that Christ was considered the most serious criminal. It is clear from the Gospels that all the attention was focused on Christ and His cross. He was the target of all the mockery and derision. Yes, even those crucified with Him mocked Him. The anger and frustration of those two men also was poured out over Him who was hanged between them.

But it is precisely here that we notice a remarkable development. Luke is the only evangelist who specifically notes that one of these two criminals underwent a noticeable change of heart. You might call it "a last minute conversion."

LAST MINUTE CONVERSION?

What are we to make of this "conversion"? There are those who warn us to be very careful with death-bed conversions. It is a proven fact that more than one person who called upon God in a time of need turned away from Him when the need passed. So we should not use this text to conclude: well, I can always repent just before I die. Do not forget that the other criminal, in the same position, also facing death, did not repent. Why did the one turn to Jesus and not the other?

It should also be asked to what extent this one criminal really and knowingly repented. Can we deduce from his words that with his whole heart at the last hour he turned to God?

One thing is clear. These two criminals, crucified alongside Christ, serve to shed more light on the ministry of Christ as our Mediator. We are not really interested in those two fellows as such; we are interested in Christ, for He is our Lord and Saviour. But inasmuch as God uses these two crosses to show us the greater significance of that one cross, we are interested in them as well. And we note that the Lord Jesus reveals Himself on the cross as our true Mediator by receiving the repentant criminal into the house of the Father. We will give attention to the clear confession of this criminal, to his humble petition, and to the certain promise that he receives.

JOATHAS AND MAGGATRAS?

We do not know a great deal about these two men who were crucified that day with Christ. That is not really much of a loss, since these two men are not the focus of attention. Perhaps that is why the Bible does not give us many details about them. I may mention that some manuscripts give the names of these two as Joathas and Maggatras, but the sources are unreliable.

Joathas and Maggatras. If these were their names, what was their crime? What had they done to deserve such a penalty? There are explainers who follow a glamorous exegesis and see in these two men Judaist Zealots. As you know, the Zealot party wanted to liberate the land of Israel from Roman occupation, and they formed cells of resistance fighters who did not hesitate to use force. These Zealots, then, were devout Jews who ardently expected their great Messiah and who had meanwhile begun cleansing the promised land. Call them guerilla freedom fighters.

If that was indeed the case with these two men, it was a timely execution from Pilate's point of view. Crucify some real rebels along with their presumed leader, Jesus; that would really annoy the Jews. Jesus, the king of the Jews hanging between two of his soldiers. That might also explain the fact that these two men themselves join in the mockery of Jesus. Does not one of them say, "Are you not the Christ? Save yourself and us!" (verse 39). These men would be offended and angered at having to hang on the same hill as an impostor like Jesus. They had at least tried to save Israel and were giving their lives, but Jesus had done nothing.

ZEALOTS OR THIEVES?

I wrote that this is the more "glamorous" explanation, especially today, from a "liberation theology" point of view. But in fact the Scripture itself does not at all lead us in such a direction. Matthew and Mark use the expression "two robbers." A word is used there that indicates violent robbers, those who would not hesitate to take a life in order to enrich themselves. It could be taken to mean common thieves or murderers, even pirates or gangsters. Luke uses the word "criminals" (verse 32), and it says literally "evil-doers." This suggests at the very least that these men are hardened offenders, who have made it their profession to rob and steal. Rather than freedom fighters, they may have been terrorists, who killed and plundered. For such criminals Roman law prescribed crucifixion.

It appears that we must think here, then, of hardened criminals, in whose company Jesus did not fit at all. We see here a fulfillment of the prophecy of Isaiah 53 that Christ was numbered among the transgressors, the criminals, who deserved their just reward. These men were gangsters who preyed on the weak and the innocent. It is remarkable that such men escape the wrath of the multitude while Jesus must undergo the taunts of everyone.

CALLOUS SOULS

Now at first both these men reviled Jesus along with the others. This means that they, too, took some evil pleasure in His lot. They, too, rejected Christ's claim that He was the Christ, the Son of God. They mocked with the others: if it is true, then come down from the cross, save yourself and us in the process. This shows you something of the character of these men. To mock someone who is being executed alongside you, while you both face death, is terrible. Only bitter and callous souls act in such a way.

These men must have heard of Jesus and His works. After all, Christ was well-known, and they undoubtedly knew His name and the allegations against Him. But they did not put any faith in Him. They considered Him to be a joke. One of them, it says in this text, railed at Him. Literally it says: he blasphemed Him. This means that he made mocking suggestions about our Lord's claim of being the Son of God. You? Son of God? You, our Messiah? If you are the Christ, save yourself and us.

It seems that these two men kept up the mockery for some time and that one even came to blaspheme the Name of God in the process. But it also is clear that the other in the course of time came to a different conclusion. We read in verse 40, "But the other rebuked him, saying, Do you not fear God since you are under the same sentence of condemnation? And we justly; for we are receiving the due reward for our deeds; but this man has done nothing wrong."

A CHANGE OF HEART

What to think of this change of heart? It is in any case a very clear confession. The blaspheming of his companion has brought the man to a sharp rebuke. He says: man, do you not fear God? You are under the same sentence of condemnation. Soon you, too, will be dead. And then you will have to face the righteous Judge of heaven and earth. Instead of reviling this man here, why not humble yourself before God? Prepare to meet your Maker! Fear God, that is, submit to Him, call upon Him for His mercy and grace. Instead of reviling this man here, prepare to meet God!

And he adds something very important when he says: and we indeed suffer justly, for we are receiving the due reward for our deeds. These words prove that these men were indeed criminals and not Zealots, for a Zealot, who did not acknowledge Roman authority, never would admit to being condemned justly for his rebellion. But this man admits it: we deserve this condemnation. We are guilty as charged, and soon we must face God Himself with our sins.

His final testimony is even more significant. He says, "But this man has done nothing wrong." These words will have cut through the air, and all who heard it will have been stunned. This man vindicates Jesus as being completely innocent, as undeserving of the charges against Him. To revile an innocent man and to refuse to acknowledge your own guilt is the greatest crime. Do you not see the truth? he asks. This Jesus here is innocent!

I consider this to be a clear confession. Some explainers take this man's words with a grain of salt. At this point, they argue, the man was no longer thinking straight; he may have been slightly delirious already. And it is true, in themselves his words do not really constitute a confession of guilt before God. But Christ's answer makes clear that the man indeed fully meant what he said. Christ accepted this confession as truthful, so why should we question it?

You see here what constitutes true repentance, what is the evidence of conversion. Someone who has truly repented will always rebuke a fellow sinner who hasn't repented. You cannot confess your sin and then tolerate it in others. Someone who has truly repented, will confess His guilt before God and men. What is more, he will acknowledge the sentence as being wholly just. It is an unrepentant sinner who does not accept the penalty as being completely justified and who will insist: I do not deserve this.

Is it not a remarkable contrast with the man's earlier attitude and the attitude of all around him? Everyone mocks and blasphemes the Lord Jesus, but this man has come to a different point of view. And in the light of Christ's innocence, he sees all the more the gravity of his own sin.

SILENT STRENGTH

What brought about this change of mind? Wouldn't you like to know? Many explainers say that it was especially Christ's composure on the cross that made this man stop and think. He heard Christ pray for his executioners, "Father, forgive them for they know not what they do." Who has ever heard such a mediating prayer before? Most criminals when being executed curse their executioners to hell. But here is one who prays for them. And the man has also observed how Christ did not revile in return, but remained silent and calm. He sensed Christ's *peace with God.* Even at that crucial point, with his life draining away, silent strength exuded from the Lord Jesus Christ and enveloped this criminal beside Him, so that the man became observant and full of wonder.

All these things may have contributed to the man's conversion. Ultimately it is the power of God, the work of the Holy Spirit, Who uses this man and his conversion, and He does it to vindicate the Son of God. This conversion is a mysterious and mighty work of God which highlights the perfect mediatorial work of Christ. At that moment, as the darkness of Golgotha sets in, there is a light beginning to illuminate one heart. Christ even on His cross, in His dying, snatches one from the jaws of eternal death.

Now the sad part is that it had to come to this point for the man to repent. For the other fellow it was apparently too late. He, too, saw and heard what the first man saw and heard, but it did not lead him to repentance. We should not make this last minute conversion into the rule, for it is an exception. And what is more, we who know of the truth of the saving work of Christ and the reason for His death, may never postpone repentance or cling to sin. Instead we should learn to walk humbly with our God every day.

A REMARKABLE PETITION

Having said what he did, the man turns to the Lord Jesus, and asks, "Jesus, remember me when you come into your kingdom." What do these words mean? Is it really a sincere petition for help? Or is it a last-ditch attempt to escape God's wrath?

It is clear that this man knew something of Christ's teaching concerning the coming of the kingdom of heaven. He had also read the sign, "This is Jesus, the King of the Jews." He knew that the death of Jesus, which was as imminent as his own, did not mean the end for the Lord. It could not mean the end, for will God not vindicate the innocent and the righteous?

What did the man mean when he spoke about Christ coming in or into His kingdom? The expression means that he did expect Jesus to appear again in glory. "Coming into the kingdom" must mean something like coming to power and into the glory which accompanies that power.

Where had the man heard about the coming of this kingdom? Well, it had been a major part of Christ's teaching. He had spoken everywhere publicly of the kingdom of heaven. This preaching, in fact, had started already with John the Baptist, and it been continued by Christ to the end. Christ's last teaching in the temple had been about the very fact that the kingdom of heaven was near (Luke 22).

Christ had consistently taught that the kingdom of heaven had come in *Him* and would be perfected by Him over all the earth. Do you think that this criminal had not heard of these things? He may not have understood everything about it, but he evidently – as his words show – knew that Jesus would come "into His kingdom," that is, would achieve glory and honour from God in heaven and from out of heaven.

NO RIGHTS

Now the man does not presume to have any rights to entering into that kingdom. It is not a kingdom for criminals who have been justly executed for their horrid crimes. But the man does turn to the Lord with a petition, "Jesus, remember me when you come into your kingdom." He doesn't know when Christ will receive this honour and glory. But he doesn't doubt either that it will happen.

He doesn't claim to have any rights to sharing in it. But he nevertheless seeks access to it in true humility.

He says "Jesus, remember me." These words are a plea for mercy. The words "remember me" are *covenantal* language. They are words which Israelites directed to God. I think here of what we find in Psalm 106: "Remember me, O LORD, when Thou Thy own with favour didst endow", or of what we read in Psalm 74, "Remember Thou Thy people in Thy love."

"Remember" does not mean to think of someone occasionally, but it means to consider in grace, to turn to someone in mercy, to restore and to forgive. "Remember me" is a humble petition: please, look down upon me in mercy and forgiveness when you come into your kingdom. For you are righteous and without blame. *I* am guilty and condemned.

This man has no hope left in this life. He is at the end, and realizes the dismal failure. But he has now one hope, one plea: remember me, Jesus. This is the prayer which one would direct to the God of the covenant who always remembers His mercy.

NEVER TOO LATE

The people who stood around the cross heard this. It was a word that was passed on to others. It was passed on to Luke many years later and he recorded it in the Gospel for our instruction and comfort. It is never too late with God. He can form a humble petition in a person's heart in the hour of death.

Here it is clear that this petition is directed to Jesus. No one comes to the Father except through Him. This is made evident also as He hangs on the cross. Jesus is the only mediator between God and men. Oh, I know, it is true, as some explainers point out, the man does not confess Jesus as Christ or Lord. He does not say, "Lord, remember me" or "Christ, remember me." He simply reads the sign and says, "Jesus, remember me." But the name "Jesus" means Saviour, does it not? Is it too meagre a petition? Would you have wanted more from the man?

Well, be prepared to give more yourselves. We who know more are indeed required to give more. We must ask in even greater humility for God's mercy and grace in Christ. We must do this *throughout* our life; we must *thrive* on the grace of God in Jesus Christ. We must also know in even greater measure that we can come to the Father only through the Son, because of His one, perfect sacrifice on the cross. And we must set up our lives accordingly. So that we can pray in full trust and utter peace on the day of our death: Jesus, remember me! and then depart in faith in the certain promise of Christ.

AN UNEXPECTED ANSWER

The climax of this history comes in the last verse. The spotlight – if I may use that word – falls completely on Christ. Listen to what He answers. "And He said to him, truly I say to you, today you will be with Me in Paradise."

Christ's answer will have been totally unexpected to this man, and shocking to all the crowds who stood around. For it is an authoritative declaration of the Lord Jesus. It is a promise so certain that it is introduced with an oath, with the word amen: "Truly, I say to you." Christ puts His full authority as Mediator and Saviour behind what He is now going to say. It is true and certain, anchored in the promises of God.

He says: *today* you will be with Me in Paradise! The man said: whenever. . . But Jesus says: not whenever, *today.* The man says; when you come into your kingdom, but Jesus says: in *Paradise!* Jesus answer is richer than the man could ever have imagined, greater than he would ever have expected. That is usually the kind of response God gives to sincere and humble petitions: beyond imagination.

Paradise. Why does the Lord Jesus here use the word "paradise"? Is that not a vague and obsolete concept? It is not found often in the New Testament. The apostle Paul uses it when he speaks about the fact that he was in the spirit taken up into heaven: "this man was caught up to paradise." And John uses it in Revelation 22 when he writes about the tree of life which is in the paradise of God.

The man on the cross spoke about the day when Christ would come into His glory. But Jesus says: there is already a place where the glory of God is manifest in full measure. Call that place: paradise! Call it heaven. It is the place where there is no sin or grief but only perfection and joy. One day that paradise will cover the entire new earth. But already today you will be with Me in paradise. Today you may enter heaven.

With Me. The man cannot enter on his own. Only in Christ. Only with Christ. Through Christ alone he has access to the house of the Father in heaven. The promise given to His disciples at the last passover – I will take you to Me that where I am you may be also – is extended to this man as well. Access to the Father's house. *Immediate access.* Today, the day you die. Have we not worded this beautifully and properly in Lord's Day 22 of the Heidelberg Catechism, where we confess that my soul, after this life, will *immediately* be taken up to Christ, its Head?

If Christ promises this man access to paradise, entrance into the Father's house, it can only be because his sins are forgiven. He is a criminal no more. He is redeemed from guilt; his dying is an dying unto sin and an entering into eternal life.

PARADISE AND HELL

When Christ said these words and made this promise, He knew that He himself would have to pay for it. He would have to undergo the agony of hell. This man can only go to paradise if Christ first goes to hell. That is the consequence. But our Lord knows – as the darkness falls over Golgotha – that His suffering of hellish agony will bear rich fruit. Here already one is snatched from the jaws of eternal death and promised eternal life.

We must give attention here not first of all to the piety of this repentant criminal, but to the faithfulness of our Lord Jesus Christ, to His solemn promise:

truly, I say to you, today you will be with Me in paradise. We see His willingness to go into hell so that this man may enter into heaven.

This whole event on the cross brings out to everyone, then and now, the truth: Jesus Christ reveals Himself on the cross as the true Mediator. Whoever comes to Him He will not cast out. He does not say to the man: sorry, too little, too late. It is even so: the first will be last and the last will be first. The miracle of the kingdom is that every repentant sinner is joyfully received. He says: enter into the glory of My Father. It is Good Friday after all!

He said this while He was on the cross. How much more can we rest in His promise today, now that He is glorified in heaven and seated at God's right hand. This is the true comfort of every Christian. The forgiveness of sins leads to the life everlasting. Life in paradise. When we die, Christ will take us to Himself. Immediately, the very same day.

But we are like wood pulled from the fire. And there is one major difference between that repentant criminal and us. We are not (yet) in the hour of our death. We are still in the midst of this life. We have the time and the duty – as long as we are here – to show that we have been saved by Jesus Christ. That is the consequence for us. Otherwise the criminal on the cross will testify against us that we did not do what we knew we should do.

Yet the final word of every Christian life is to plead on God's grace in Christ. Remember me, O LORD, a repentant sinner. Remember Thou Thy people in Thy love. Our final act is to trust in God's sure promise, made by His Son on Good Friday: I will remember you. Throughout our life and at its end. He will lead us to paradise, to the tree of life.

CHRIST'S LAMENTATION ON THE CROSS OF GOLGOTHA

"And about the ninth hour Jesus cried with a loud voice: Eli, Eli, lama sabach-thani? that is, My God, My God, why hast thou forsaken Me?"

(Matthew 27: 46)

When we follow the suffering of our Lord Jesus Christ, we notice how He more and more became isolated from his friends on earth. But throughout this time He retained the favour of God, the presence of His Father, the grace of the Holy Spirit. He could always count on God's faithfulness.

Throughout His life and also in His final day Christ put His trust fully in God. He did this, even though He knew that in the end He would lose God's favour. The very thought of losing God's communion already pressed out of Him drops of bloody sweat in Gethsemane. He knew it was coming, and begged: let this cup pass from Me. But the cup could not pass, and now, on the cross, the time came to drink it to the last bitter drop.

And we must realize that the anticipation of this suffering was nothing compared to the suffering itself. To know something is one thing; to undergo it is quite another.

We confess that we cannot understand Christ's suffering. For we do not know what *hell* is. We cannot begin to comprehend what is like to be cast into utter darkness although being righteous and holy.

This text gives us the climax of Christ's suffering, or maybe I should say, the deepest point. Here He testifies that He has undergone the second death – the anguish of hell – before He enters into the first death, the realm of the dead. When He has survived hell, He gives Himself to physical death. Do you know that with all others who are judged by God it is the other way around: first death, then hell? But here it is: first hell, then death.

We would not have known this if Christ had not made it known in the words contained in this passage. For this text gives us insight into the great struggle which He had on the cross. The text is, in fact, a complaint, but not one made in sinful anger. It is an appeal, but not one issued in rebellious rage. It is a lamentation, originating not in bitterness but in deep anguish of soul. It is a lamentation which asks the great question, Why? and provides the only answer to that question: Why? Because! Because of our transgression! This is how we may look at the Gospel concerning Christ's lamentation on the cross of Golgotha. It reveals the depth of His personal suffering and the truth of His messianic ministry.

NOT ORIGINAL

The main words of this passage are, "My God, My God, why hast Thou forsaken Me?" Now we know that these words of Christ are not original; He was not the first to use them. It is a quotation from Psalm 22, spoken first by David. For this reason some Judaist scholars have suggested that this passage cannot be true, for what crucified and dying person would go around quoting Bible verses?

But that is a false suggestion. For is it not true that many believers in the last phase of their earthly life and even on their deathbed refer to specific passages of Scripture and quote texts of comfort? And would not our Lord Jesus, whose entire life was built on Scripture, in His last hours have comforted and strengthened Himself with the Word of God, indeed with the Word that spoke so eminently of Himself and His great suffering? Where else could Christ turn except to the Bible? That's how He started in the desert, saying to Satan: it is written! And that's how He ends on Golgotha, saying: it is written!

The words of Psalm 22 were first spoken by David under very different circumstances, and from a very different background. But here in Christ's mouth they gain an unprecedented depth and meaning. Now we begin to see what these words mean prophetically.

THE SPECIFIC TIMING

Please note carefully how Matthew tells us that Jesus did not speak these words at the beginning of His suffering on the cross but towards the end. It says, "And about the ninth hour, Jesus cried with a loud voice. . . ." And that ninth hour is significant for a number of reasons. First, it is the time when the period of darkness comes to an end. Second it is the time when the evening sacrifice is brought into the temple. Matthew is not going to argue about a few minutes more or less, for he writes "about the ninth hour. . .," around that time. But it is clear that a strong connection is made. After three hours of suffering in the dark, Christ – who has not spoken throughout that time – now suddenly with a loud voice says these words, "My God, My God, why hast Thou forsaken Me?"

This tells us what this suffering in darkness was all about. These words are the result of an intense struggle, an expression of deep anguish, a bitter and loud crying of the soul. Here speaks a man broken to the very core of His existence. After three long and endless hours, finally He speaks, and He speaks these words.

THE DARKNESS

Let us first note something about this darkness. We do not now have to deal with the question whether this day-time darkness was caused by a solar eclipse or the descending of a dark smog (called a "black sirocco"). Let's just call it an exceptional and significant phenomenon. At noon, at midday, the sun turns black and everything is steeped in total darkness.

What is clear is that this kind of darkness is symbolic of God's ultimate punishment, and that it always culminates in death. The Lord Jesus once Himself referred to hell as being a place of "utter" or "outer darkness." It is a darkness so impregnable that there is no light whatsoever. And no light means: no way out, no hope! Psalm 97 speaks of the "joy and light that will dawn for the upright," but this does not apply for Christ: light and joy are removed from Him, and He is totally isolated from contact with those around Him.

Many people – young and old, but especially the very young – are afraid of the dark. Children say: mommy, leave the hall light on. Don't close the bedroom door, daddy! There has to be a way out, a light that offers comfort. Sometimes people who are sick, at home or in the hospital, tell me: the nights are the worst, so dark and quiet, then I feel so alone. Indeed, how the soul is lifted when the sun comes up in the morning over the shimmering hill.

UTTERLY FORSAKEN

Now the text does not say it, but many explainers conclude that when this pitch-black darkness descended over the land and covered the hill of Golgotha, everyone became very quiet. Even the scoffers stopped mocking. People perhaps reached out to each other and held on for comfort. Soldiers stood side by side, grim-faced, weapons poised. Women huddled together, whispering fearfully. And Christ? Well, Christ had only one direction left to go: to God! He Who had lain at the bosom of the Father now reached out to heaven, and found that instead He was plunged into hell. The last door, the only door of real significance, was closed to Him!

And this is His great struggle on the cross. Finally, after three hours of anxiety and anguish, He confesses, yes, laments loudly, that God forsook Him. My God, He says, He in whom I've trusted, whom I have always served, has forsaken Me. And the text indicates: He has been utterly and completely forsaken.

Christ confesses this reality with a loud voice. The Jews had mocked Him saying, "He trusts in God, let God deliver Him now, for He said I am the Son of God." But when our Lord turned to God, there was no help, no support, no fellowship. God did not deliver Him or surround Him with love and kindness. He was left utterly alone.

THE AGONY OF HELL

This means that during these hours Christ was plunged into the agony of hell. For hell is the place where God's love and mercy are not apparent, where only the fullness of His wrath is evident. God is in hell only with His sovereign and righteous condemnation.

When the Lord Jesus takes up that question of David, "My God, My God, why hast Thou forsaken Me?" He reveals to us something of the great struggle which He had on the cross during that time. Forsaken. It's a fact. It's true. The Jews were never more right: cast out as a criminal. But why? Why Me, Oh God? David asked that question too, remember? But David was never utterly forsaken! And David was a sinful person. David had brought about his own fate. Still David asked: why hast Thou forsaken me? Will the great Son of David not ask it all the more? For He did not bring it upon Himself by His sins; it came over Him from God's side. And therefore the question was wrenched out of Him, after three long hours of intensive, fruitless searching: Why Me?

We must understand that it was not a rhetorical question, but a very existential one, a question with deep personal involvement. It revealed a real *struggle*, a going on a route with many temptations. Do not forget that Christ was completely human! So He struggled with the "why" and the "wherefore." He did not just ask the question for the sake of interest as if the answer was a simple: well, you see, I had to forsake you in order to save the church, don't make a problem out of it, we've discussed this before, you know why. Don't ask silly questions.

No, this lamentation reveals the depth of His personal suffering. He really asks about the why. He may know it, but when He experiences it, the question does rise. Our Lord, though perfect, was subject to questions, probing questions, and He had to grow in the struggle to find an answer. Do you think the answer comes easy, even if you know the answer? This is a very real question for the Lord, otherwise Golgotha would have been a sham. Why Me? Of all people, why did you decide to forsake Me? For I am innocent! This is the unspoken claim in the question. I am your faithful Servant. Christ's sense of justice functioned on the cross: He knew that He was innocent.

A BROKEN HEART

And so the Lord Jesus, from out of hell, searched the heavens, but found no response. He hit a wall of silence and was crushed under waves of despair and anguish. It devastated Him, not just physically, but emotionally and spiritually. It broke His heart. And finally it had to come out. After those three hours of intense torment, He shouted it out – not in rebellion but it deep agony – "My God, My God" – twice because He was so shattered – "Why hast Thou forsaken Me"? Why have you left me so utterly alone? For this is hell; I cannot live without you, I do not want to live without you, I love you. Without My God I am indeed totally lost! He asked, but did not receive, He sought, but did not find, He knocked and it was not opened unto Him.

Christ really struggled as a true human being with this great question. He had to find answers, to give them to Himself and so to His church. He was not a machine, but fully human, and so He searched on Golgotha in the darkness, not doubting the Word of God, but growing and maturing in His suffering to this point of lamentation. It was not an accusation, nor a rebellion, and neither was it a being severed from His God! Someone once wrote beautifully: Christ was rejected by God, forsaken by Him, but Christ was never *separated* from God, He never separated Himself from God, for it still was: My God, My God!

WHY ME?

Why me? We, too, sometimes ask this question, although we can never ask it as Christ did. We sometimes know the answer too, but it is never easy to go through the questions and answers personally, to experience the lamentation, to come to rest in the answers which God provides.

As the Form for the Celebration of the Lord's Supper says it so well, Christ on the cross here "humbled Himself to the very deepest shame and anguish of hell. Then He called out with a loud voice: My God, My God, why hast Thou forsaken Me?"

We will never understand the depth of Christ's suffering, for to do that we would have to be perfect and in hell at the same time, and this cannot happen to us. But we must see *something* of what He experienced, we must have an inkling of the depth of His personal suffering, so that we may realize the truth of His messianic ministry.

NOT LETTING GO

"Why hast Thou forsaken Me?" Those who stood around the cross, as the light began to break through again, saw here another cause to scoff. He said "Eli, Eli," clearly Aramaic for "My God, My God," but they joked around and said: ah, now He is calling for Elijah. Yes, God has forsaken Him, obviously, and let's see if Elijah will help. Elijah, you may know, was seen as the forerunner of the Messiah. What mockery: does the Messiah need the help of His forerunner?

No, the misunderstanding is deliberate and the joke is cruel. Christ does not need anyone's help. He admits and confesses that He has been totally forsaken of God, even though He had once claimed "I and the Father are one." But He also maintains: I am innocent of all crime before God and men.

Why Me? Not because I am guilty, for I am not guilty. Well, then it must have another reason. It is because I bear the sins of my people, the wrath of God against the sin of the whole human race, that is why!

What is so beautiful here is that Christ did not let go of His Father, His God in heaven. Even when He was plunged into the agony of hell, He did not abandon His claim: I am not guilty of the things ascribed to Me. I am the true Son of God. I am a true and righteous man. God may cut the bond between Him and His Son, but Christ from His side will not let go. His lamentation is indeed a tremendous appeal to God in heaven.

He did not, in anger and reviling, break the bond with God. That's what some criminals do: they revile and curse at their just judgment. As they are being led away to the execution they scream: damn you all! They raise their defiant chin in anger and set their mouth against God.

And Christ could have become extremely bitter, for He was innocent of all the crimes ascribed to Him, falsely accused and unjustly condemned. He could have cursed God in heaven, and so died in self-vindication. But He did not.

A DECLARATION OF LOVE

We see here the truth of His messianic ministry emerging. The words, "My God, My God, why hast Thou forsake Me?" are a declaration of *love,* a sincere reaching out in truth. He did not break the bond with God, even though God broke the bond with Him. From the darkness of hell Christ looked up into heaven, and He kept knocking at the door: my God, my God! He maintained His innocence and confessed His love even in the hellish agony of the cross. Someone has written that with these words, "My God, My God," a hand reached up out of hell to take hold of the throne of heaven, and for the first time this hand was not soiled but pure!

And so the question already has an answer. Why Me? Because I am the Lamb of God, called to remove the sins of the world. Why Me? Because I bear in my flesh the burden of sin. Because I carry on my head the curse of God, His just curse, His righteous wrath! Why Me? Because this is the truth, the deep truth of my messianic ministry: to give my life, to undergo eternal and temporal death for my people. In these words, Christ, maintaining His innocence, reveals that He is indeed the true Messiah of His people. His forsakenness is *messianic,* His agony is that of a sacrificial lamb slain for others.

MESSIANIC DIMENSION

This does not diminish His personal suffering. But it does give to that suffering a messianic dimension, which we today must fully comprehend. The Lord's Supper Form puts it beautifully when it says: He [Christ] was forsaken by God that we might nevermore be forsaken by Him!

Why hast Thou forsaken Me? God's answer is: so that I can always be a Father to my children. So that the curse which rests on them may be taken away by you, and you may fill them with your blessing!

Christ's struggle was not one in which He doubted His messianic work. That is the false premise, the satanic premise of the movie "The Last Temptation of Christ." Yes, He suffered deeply, intensely, personally, more than we will ever understand, and in that suffering many temptations came His way, but He did know throughout the entire ordeal: I suffer as a lamb, I suffer for my people, so that they will never have to undergo what I am now undergoing for them!

NEVERMORE FORSAKEN

The first thing which He said after those awful hours of darkness was: I have been utterly forsaken – an agony beyond description – for your sake, so that you will nevermore be forsaken of God! For this is the truth of my messianic ministry: that I have earned for you on the cross *eternal fellowship with God!*

And so the day of Christ's death is indeed for us *Good Friday.* It is Gospel, the glad tidings of His lamentation. His lamentation becomes our jubilation. Nevermore forsaken. My God, My God, why hast Thou *not* forsaken me? For I have deserved it. I have so often let go of you, rejected you, forsaken you. I have so often been so angry when I was tried and tested. I have set my mouth against God, instead of appealing to His covenant love and mercy.

Why hast Thou not forsaken me? Because I once, says the Lord, I once forsook Him on the cross of Golgotha. Once is enough. That was totally devastating, and it is enough.

So now I can go on again, knowing that the Father in heaven will never forsake me. Not in any of the trials and temptations of life. Also not in the dreadful hour of my own death, when my life comes before me with all its sins and shortcomings. And not on the day of judgment, when I must stand before the judgement seat of God. He will not forsake me for Christ's sake!

We have to believe this with our whole heart. If we don't, or act as if we don't, we deny the very core of Golgotha, we scoff also at these words of Christ.

But when we do believe this, we will experience it throughout our life. When we look back, we discover it, and when we look ahead we know it: God has not forsaken and will never forsake us, even though we often forsook Him and accused Him in our mind.

Sometimes we can feel so lost and forsaken, even of God. There is a well-known poem about footprints in the sand, two sets of foot prints, those of a father walking with his child on the beach. At a certain point there is only one set of footprints. And later as the child looks back, he says: father, why did you leave me for a while, for I see only one set of prints. The father says: those are my footprints, and I didn't leave you. I was carrying you, for you couldn't walk anymore. Sometimes we think He's gone, but instead He is carrying us through the difficulties, oftener even than we imagine!

There is a sad song that the world sings: you've got to walk that lonesome valley, you've got to walk it by yourself. It's a lie. Only Christ had to walk by Himself through the agony of hell and through the valley of the shadow of death. Only Christ was all alone. Utterly forsaken. So that we never have to walk alone.

Now we may always reach up from earth into heaven and take hold of the foot of the throne with hands washed in His blood, and the Father up above is looking down with love. Now we do not have to ask the question: why must I suffer so? For we have the answer to the question: why did *He* suffer so? Now life becomes livable and enjoyable, meaningful and purposeful, now we can still our restless heart, our disquieted soul, and say to ourselves and to each other: Hope in God, your faith retrieving, He will still your refuge be! (Psalm 42: 7, *Book of Praise*). Now we can pray, with the certainty of being heard: forsake me not, for I on Thee rely. Now we can confess, the LORD is faithful, why then be afraid?

Never afraid anymore. Not of the dark. Not of the agony of hell. Not even of the presence of death. Not of the day of judgment. Never afraid, for My God, my God has never forsaken and will never forsake me! They may say with proud defiance: where is God, your firm reliance? And I say: My God? Don't worry about Him, for He is My God and Saviour. The lamentation of Christ has become the jubilation of the church.

The Work of Atonement Completed

"When Jesus had received the vinegar, He said: it is finished; and He bowed His head and gave up His spirit".

(John 19: 30)

Every time we gather on Good Friday to remember the death of our Saviour, the Lord Jesus Christ, I ask myself this question: what is the purpose of this service? Ought we to express our sadness at this death? Should we become emotional? Should we see and confess our sins more clearly than on any other day, and say: Lord, it was my sin that caused you so much grief?

That is how it is done in many churches. People are invited to go through the whole gamut of emotions which Christ must have experienced. The pope, as we have seen, travels the *via dolorosa*, the road of sorrows, to re-enact the suffering of Christ. In dramatic fashion the whole scene is imitated and repeated. And we may as well admit it, it is impressive to dramatize and emotionalize the suffering of the Lord. Is our remembrance not a bit meagre in comparison?

Well, we have always stressed that also in special worship services the Scriptures must be in the centre. So let us see from the Word of God how Christ died and what He accomplished with His death. We cannot fathom this death, nor will we dramatize and imitate it. Christ does not build His church through dramatic sensationalism but by the simple preaching of His Word.

POWERFUL PREACHING

We must understand, however, that such simple preaching is powerful and demanding. You can go and see a show, a re-enactment, and come away impressed by the scene and yet be unchanged. But the preaching of the Gospel cannot leave you indifferent. This Word must bring about not only a true love for Christ but also a sincere desire to serve Him as Lord and King.

For is His dying not a priestly act of atonement? Does He by His blood not *claim* us, purchase us, oblige us to enter a new life? Who can stand by to see Christ die and not be affected? He does one of two things on Golgotha: He saves us or curses us. Yes, it true for us also; either "it is finished" or it is not!

We concentrate now on these last words of Christ as recorded in the Gospel of John: "It is finished." I know that after this He also said yet, "Father, into Thy hands I commit my spirit." But those words are not recorded in John 19. Here the emphasis is fully on the completion of Christ's work of atonement. The Lamb of God, identified in John 1, brings the ultimate sacrifice of atonement. In looking at these last words, we will give attention to the necessary preparation for this proclamation, to its careful formulation, and to its definite confirmation.

VINEGAR OR WINE?

The text begins with the fact that Jesus received some "vinegar." Now there has been a lot of discussion about this "vinegar," about why it was given and whether it was a deepening of Christ's suffering or not. It is clear from verse 25 that our Lord Himself asked for this vinegar.

He said: I thirst. A bowl of vinegar happened to be standing nearby, and so they dipped a sponge in the vinegar and lifted it up so that He could take some of the liquid. A sponge was in that situation more suitable than a cup.

From Psalm 69, "They also gave me gall as food to eat and vinegar as drink when I was thirsty," it appears that indeed this type of drink was not pleasant. Just as "gall" is unbearably bitter, so vinegar is awfully sour. However, the word used here for "vinegar" is perhaps better to be understood as a very common and cheap wine which the soldiers and the people drank: very dry and sour like vinegar, but nevertheless a form of wine.

Then it may be said: it is sad that there is no cool and refreshing water, only this sour liquid, but at least it is some fluid, which may be of help to Christ. The fact that a sponge and hyssop were available suggests that all this was purposely provided for the benefit of the crucified, and the Lord makes use of this possibility.

WHY DRINK NOW?

We have to ask ourselves this question: why did the Lord Jesus avail Himself of the possibility to drink this sour wine? Why did He actually request something to drink? For it is clear that Christ earlier, just before the crucifixion itself, refused to drink any wine. We can read in Matthew 27: 34, ". . .they offered Him wine to drink, mixed with gall, but when He tasted it, He would not drink it." Then He wouldn't drink, now He wants to drink! What is the reason?

The explainers are quite unified in their answer to this question. This wine mixed with gall was not refused by Christ because it tasted so awful, but because it contained a drug which would soften the pain of the crucifixion, some kind of anaesthetic. It was probably also offered to the others who were crucified with Him.

But the Lord did not in any way want His suffering softened through the administering of a pain killer. He would not have His senses dulled. He wanted to undergo the agony of the cross with a clear mind, in full consciousness, in order to experience fully in body and soul the wrath of God against the sin of the whole human race. So when He had tasted what was offered to Him, and knew that it contained a powerful sedative, He refused to drink it. He would bear everything in His own strength and with a clear mind so that He might fully deliver us from the wrath of God.

That was three hours earlier. Christ has suffered in silence throughout these hours in the darkness of Golgotha. These were the hours that He underwent the agony of hell and was left by all, even by His heavenly Father. Then His heart was utterly broken, and in His inexpressible anguish He summoned all His energy and called out with a loud voice: My God, My God, why hast Thou forsaken Me?

Those words were spoken through parched lips. One of the greatest torments of a crucified person was *thirst*. The wounds had begun to fester during those hours. There was loss of blood. There was the rise of fever. The thirst was unbearable. Can you understand that wine was brought along to relieve some of the agony of those crucified?

FOR OUR BENEFIT

But we already saw that Christ does not in any way want His personal agony relieved. When He therefore asks for something to drink, it is not for His benefit, but for our benefit. This receiving of the "vinegar" leads immediately to a statement, yes, to a royal proclamation!

So we must conclude that Christ asked for something to drink only so that His final proclamation would be clearly heard by all. He wanted everyone to hear what He had to say before He died. He prepared Himself for His final proclamation as Saviour of His people. So unto the very end He was not busy with Himself, but focused on His Father and His people.

Christ wanted to speak out loudly and clearly. He would not die with a soft moan, with some unintelligible last words on His lips, but with a clear proclamation for all around to hear, a word that would from then on echo through the ages in the churches until the great day of His glorious return.

Often people die unprepared, and without having said what they might have wanted to say. Important last words are left unspoken. But this is not the case here. What must be said, will be said, loudly and clearly! For Christ remains to the very end the *chief prophet* of His church, and He consciously prepares Himself for the ultimate proclamation for our benefit today, so that we may know that in His suffering and death He has perfectly fulfilled the work of atonement.

FINISHED

We come, then, to the question: what exactly did Christ say as His final words? He said: it is finished. The Greek original has only one word: finished. Actually, it is a very simple word which at first glance does not even have such a deep ring to it. Just a statement of fact: it is finished. It even sounds somewhat abstract: *it* is finished, but what is "it"?

I would like you to notice the obvious fact that Jesus does not say "I have finished," but "It is finished." In other words, as one explainer suggests, there is here at the end of Christ's life no self-justification, no self-glorifying, no speaking about Himself as if He is so important. Christ here formulates carefully, for in His speaking as the chief prophet He remains to the end the humble Servant of the LORD.

His last song is not one of self-exaltation. He does not shout: the record shows that I took the blow and did it my way. He says: I did it God's way! He wants us to know that He did not in any way leave the path of obedience, not even in His last hours of agony on the cross, but that He stayed on the path which His Father had set out for Him. The record shows: He did it God's way.

For that is what it means: it is finished. What is "it"? Well, the work of atonement, as prescribed in the Scriptures. Throughout the suffering of Christ on the cross, the Bible emphasizes that Christ did this or that in order to fulfill the Scriptures. "It is finished" refers to the divine counsel of redemption that in the suffering of the Son of God, through His hellish agony, He would complete and perfect the work of atonement.

Christ tells us now: it is done. I have, according to God's will, according to His righteous law of atonement, satisfied His wrath and paid the price, I have gone through hell for you. He formulates this carefully and precisely, without any self-praise: it is done.

A NOTE OF TRIUMPH

Our Lord comes out of the agony and darkness of hell and may proclaim to us that the work of atonement has been perfectly completed. The price for sin has been paid in full. He pronounces this in all clarity and without any possibility of misunderstanding. Here already a note of triumph begins to ring. Here already the rays of Easter begin to filter through. No one can ever turn back the clock. Now there is forever a new situation. Now there is a legal basis, a final and eternal basis under the proclamation of the forgiveness of sins.

Before Jesus dies, He wants us all to know: it is finished, and therefore, have no more fear. Do not dwell on your sins anymore. Now you may draw out of the waters of God's unending grace, in unending faith, for the work of atonement is completed. It was done according to the Scriptures, in conformity to God's law. It is official and legal, binding and unchangeable. It is finished. It is an unmistakable and clear proclamation.

Now someone might say: yes, but does not Christ's dying and burial also belong to His work of atonement and humiliation? How can He say that it is finished when He still has to die? Is it not too soon to say that it is done? Well, indeed, in a strict sense, the dying of the Lord belongs to the work of atonement. It is the concluding act, indeed, and it will follow immediately.

But the point is that all that had to be done before He could die, was now done: His active work of obedience, His fulfilling of the law, His undergoing of the penalty of the law, His hellish agony. All that had to come first, before He could even think of dying. After undergoing spiritual death, He could enter into physical death. The rest was *done* unto Him by others. He took no active part in His burial. His last act was one of dying in the knowledge that all His work was finished.

NEVER FINISHED

Many people die before they feel that their earthly work is done. Christ was only a young man in His early thirties. People might have said: what a pity. What an unfulfilled life! So young, so un-finished. So much potential gone to waste. He could have done so much more.

Indeed, we can never say of ourselves that all our work is done. We do not determine this, the Lord God does. He calls us when He considers that we have completed our earthly task. We would have liked to continue, perhaps. Or maybe we become tired of life, old and worn-out, and would rather die. But we know that only God can say about our life's work that "it is finished."

But here Christ says of His own work: finished. For He knows, with perfect divine and messianic clarity, that it *is* finished. Never was a task so well-done. Never was a job so perfectly finished. Even though people may stand around and scoff: what a failure, what an unfinished symphony, Christ says: no, it is finished, perfectly. And that means: now I can die, and I will die. With that proclamation and in that knowledge, He indeed does die, and thereby confirms that the work of atonement is finished.

CHRIST'S ACTUAL DYING

For let us look at how John then in this context describes Jesus' actual dying. He writes: and He bowed His head and gave up His spirit. Do you know what this implies? Our Lord Himself chose the exact moment and manner of His dying. No one killed Him, He Himself died by laying down His life. And by laying down His life at that moment, He confirmed that the work of atonement was done. There was no more reason to live, no more reason to suffer. So now He may die at this precise moment.

The other two who were crucified along with Him could not make this choice, could not perform this act of dying when they wanted. They had to wait until all life slowly drained from them in the ensuing hours. Their legs had to be broken, so that they could no longer fight off suffocation and would have to give up the struggle.

But Christ had then already been dead for some time. We read in Mark 15: 44 that Pilate was surprised, when Joseph of Arimathea came to ask him if he was allowed to bury Jesus, that Jesus had died so soon. Pilate even asked the centurion to verify the death of the Lord.

Christ died when He wanted to, when He was ready for it. His dying was a royal act of completion. His earthly work was finished, and after He had proclaimed this, precisely at that moment, He died. Not one minute earlier, not one minute later. He died at the time which He chose.

That is how we may understand the words: He bowed His head. He physically gave up the struggle. He gave up His spirit. He let His life go from Him. He did this voluntarily, in obedience to the counsel of God. No one forced Him. No one took His life, He gave it Himself.

He had said this ahead of time. When He spoke of Himself as the Good Shepherd who would give His life for the sheep (John 10), He stated plainly, "No one takes [my life] from Me, but I lay it down of my own accord. I have power to lay it down, and I have power to take it again. . . ." No one takes it, but I give it, freely, voluntarily, when the moment has come.

His dying at that specific moment definitely confirmed the proclamation that His work was done. Christ suffered much. Christ suffered deeply, more so than any one of us will ever know. But He did not suffer needlessly. His suffering was not cruelly prolonged without necessity. When His work was done, He died. He Himself laid down His life, to take it again on the appointed time, according to the Scriptures. He Himself put the finishing touch on His work, crowning it with His death.

Here you can see that He is also in His dying indeed the Son of God, our Mediator. No one took anything from Him, not even His life. He gave it all Himself. And so He confirmed the completion of God's counsel of redemption.

NO EULOGY REQUIRED

We can try to wax eloquent. We can try to eulogize with sweeping emotion. We can dramatize and sensationalize. But we can never come closer to the cross than through this text. Christ does not seek our eloquence or eulogies. He would be offended at our attempt to re-enact His incomprehensible suffering. All we must do is believe. And go on our way rejoicing, resolving to do what we must do in His service.

Now I may believe that my earthly task, too, will one day be finished perfectly, whether I die at a younger or older age. My work, my trials, my efforts are not vain in Christ. The unfinished symphony of my life finds its completion in Christ. So that one day, whenever God calls me, I can go to the Father in His Name, and say: He finished it, also for me, and in Him I am presented to God in holiness. Now I can live life and not fear death, for I know: it is finished in Him.

Thou Saviour, Thou hast ransomed us,
Hence we will honour and adore Thee
And cast in gratitude before Thee,
The crowns by grace bestowed on us (Hymn 22, *Book of Praise*).

The Resurrection of Jesus Christ

Easter

Christ has Really Risen from the Dead

"Then Simon Peter came, following him, and went into the tomb; and he saw the linen cloths lying, and the napkin which had been on His head, not lying with the linen cloths but rolled up in a place by itself. Then the other disciple who reached the tomb first also went in, and he saw and believed; for as yet they did not know the scripture, that He must rise from the dead".

(John 20: 6-9)

If there is anything striking about the history of the resurrection of our Lord as described in the Bible, it is that it takes such a long time before the disciples are fully convinced that Jesus has truly risen from the dead. The Word of God is very honest about this. There was no public profession of faith on that first Easter Sunday morning near Jerusalem. Instead of great certainty, there was confusion. Instead of tremendous joy, there were tears.

We read about Mary Magdalene who goes to the tomb early, sees the stone rolled away, and immediately concludes that Jesus' body has been taken by enemies, perhaps dumped somewhere else. She does not even consider the possibility of a resurrection.

We read about Peter and John who rush to the grave, find it empty, and come away puzzled and confused. Perhaps at that point there is the beginning of an idea that Jesus could have risen from the dead, but it is all still vague and undefined.

It is only on the evening of that day that Christ appears to all His disciples – except Thomas – and assures them of His resurrection. Even then there is much uncertainty and an inability to accept what is true. Later He upbraids many of them because of their outright unbelief.

FAITH TAKES TIME

It takes time to come to discerning faith. People can see certain things, but this seeing does not mean understanding or believing. The disciples can see the empty tomb, they can see the risen Lord in person, but they must come to understand all this in the light of the Scriptures. For that alone is the basis on which faith is built. So Christ gradually leads His church to realize and confess that He has truly risen from the dead and to know what this means for Him and for them.

We see in this passage of Scripture how the Lord does this. The disciples are brought to the empty tomb. The evidence in the tomb leads to the initial conclusion that Jesus has risen, but it is only the knowledge of the Word that leads to the certain confession that Jesus has truly risen from the dead.

TWO RUNNERS

It is not hard to understand the consternation which comes over Peter and John when Mary Magdalene comes rushing in with this emotional message, "They have taken the Lord out of the tomb, and we do not know where they have laid Him." This calls for action.

Immediately Peter and John rush out to the grave site to ascertain what can possibly have happened. The passage which we read gives us some interesting details. Both apostles, it says, *ran* to the tomb. But John outruns Peter and reaches the tomb first. Notice, however, that he does not go into the tomb. He stops at the entrance to look in, and he does see "the linen cloths lying there." But he cannot clearly discern what may have happened inside. I presume that the tomb was at least semi-dark, so John had only a limited vision.

He does not go in. The text does not say why he hesitates. We do know that Peter was usually the bravest among the apostles, the one who took the initiative, and when he arrives he indeed enters the tomb. It says in verse 6: "Then Simon Peter came, following him, and went into the tomb. . . ". This encourages John, who follows Peter.

INSIDE THE TOMB

The result of all this is that we now have two apostles inside the tomb. This is an important biblical fact that is sometimes overlooked. Christ has brought these two eye-witnesses through Mary Magdalene's alarm right into the tomb, so that they may see and report first-hand what has happened. The purpose of this is that all false reports will be repudiated by the evidence found in the tomb. The church will not live by wild stories, but by the results of a careful investigation of the facts.

Notice how the apostle John – and he writes many years after the event – still vividly remembers and carefully registers what they saw in the tomb. He saw "the linen cloths lying, and the napkin, which had been on his head, not lying with the linen cloths, but rolled up in a place by itself."

These are intriguing words. What do they tell us? What conclusions may we draw here? For we understand that the Holy Spirit gives us this elaborate description for a purpose. This is made known to us so that our faith may be strengthened.

In the first place, it is significant that the linen cloths – in which Christ's body had been dressed – are even present in the tomb. For if some unknown persons – either common thieves or sworn enemies of the Lord – had wanted to steal the body of Christ, they would not first undress the body and leave the linen cloths behind, but would take the body, cloths and all.

This is especially true in the case of the Jews, who could not touch a dead body without becoming unclean. And in any event, why would anyone take the body without the cloths? John and Peter will have been faced with that question.

In the second place, as the Greek text literally says, the linen cloths were *lying.* This word usually indicates an orderly and neat situation. The cloths are obviously not strewn all over the tomb in a reckless and chaotic fashion, which would be the case if someone had ransacked and looted the place. They are lying (and you may add) together, in one place, as if someone had taken ample time and care to arrange them orderly.

We read the same about the napkin, which had covered the face of the deceased. It was not hastily flung aside in a forgotten corner, but was "rolled up in a place by itself." That even receives some emphasis in the text.

OPEN AND ORDERLY

These are clues as to what happened in the tomb. The place was not ransacked. This was not the work of Roman soldiers, Jewish police, or common thieves. This was not a disturbed grave but a deserted tomb!

No one has *taken* the Lord, as Mary Magdalene had assumed; something different has happened. Whatever is neatly folded or rolled up has served its purpose and is no longer necessary. The linen cloths and the napkin, burial elements necessary for a dead body, are laid aside because the body does not need them anymore. This body has risen from the dead.

We must ask another question, and that is: who laid these cloths down in this fashion? And why, indeed, are the linen cloths lying in one spot while the napkin is at a different spot? That is a detail which cannot escape the attentive reader: the cloths and the napkin should have been lying together as part of one outfit, why are they in separate places? There must be a reason behind this fact.

In my understanding there is only one explanation which really satisfies. There must have been movement in the tomb. And who would have moved there in those early hours, except Jesus Himself? Could it have been anyone but our Lord who folded up these linen cloths, laid them neatly on one spot, and then as He walked on, rolled up the napkin, the head turban, and laid it elsewhere as He progressed? He did away with the burial vestments as He entered into the light of a new day!

Here we are shown how Christ completely does away with death and its attributes. He had been dressed by others for His funeral, but He strips Himself of the shroud of death, and leaves the tomb behind. He puts these cloths down, and majestically He steps out. This is the second great sign of Easter morning. The first was: the tomb is open. The second is: the tomb is in order.

The evidence presents a clear case and is calling out to Peter and John: don't you see it, Jesus has risen from the dead, He has moved on to greater things. This is the new order of Easter: death is conquered on its own terrain.

They never forgot, the two disciples, this scene in the tomb. Years later when John writes about it he sees it all again, the empty tomb, the neatly stacked cloths, the rolled-up napkin, all telling one message: Christ has risen. Instead of the linen cloths, He went to be dressed in a royal robe. Instead of the napkin, He received a golden crown. And instead of the musty tomb, He went on to the glorious throne.

A BEGINNING OF FAITH

The evidence in the tomb is so overwhelming that it leads to an initial conclusion. John says as much in verse 8: then the other disciple (namely, John himself) who reached the tomb first, also went in, and he saw and believed. Something began to dawn in his mind. Oh, it was only an initial conclusion. They had a long way to go. But it had to start somewhere, and here is where it began, the faith of the church in the resurrected Lord. Faith started in the twilight zone of the musty sepulchre, and soon it broke out into the full sunshine of the new day.

John is quite candid. He writes, ". . .the other disciple, who reached the tomb first, also went in and saw and believed. . .," and then comes verse 9, "for as yet they did not know the Scripture that He must rise from the dead."

Peter and John saw the open tomb. But an open grave is still a gaping hole. They face some very clear signs. But these signs must now be understood in the light of the Scriptures. John and Peter are on the way to a better understanding, but they are not yet so far that they can make a full confession that Jesus has truly risen from the dead. They have begun to see but they have not yet reached the stage that they can shout it from the rooftops.

It is a slow process, but it is a learning process. Again we must read carefully what it says in our text. John writes that he saw and believed (verse 8). Literally it says in the original: he began to believe. The wall of scepticism and doubt which John and the others had erected began to crumble. True, it was only a beginning, but it was also a turning point, the first break-through. Someone began to believe. Someone said to himself: could it be true. . .Yes it must be true; Jesus said He would rise. Therefore, He may be alive!

NOT KNOWING YET

John is not yet very vocal about it. He's not about to make a public profession of faith at this point. Later on, as he writes these words, he adds something very significant: verse 9, "for as yet they did not know the Scripture, that He must rise from the dead." It is at first glance almost like an excuse. As if he says: well, that is when I started to believe, but I did not really come right away to the full understanding of what had happened, for, you see, we did not yet know the Scripture that He had to rise.

It is not an excuse. Peter and John and the others had heard Jesus say that on the third day He would rise again. Christ had even beforehand showed them from Scripture that it had to be so. John does not deny that at all. He is saying that they had never really understood this. If I may use an expensive expression, they had not internalized it. They did not really know the what and the why!

Peter and John are faced with some very clear signs. And John recalls that for him personally there was something like a turning point. But he admits: it was only a small beginning for him and Peter. Only the knowledge of the Word would lead them to the full confession: Christ has risen from the dead. From the open tomb, they had to progress to the open Bible.

He says it honestly: they did not know the Scripture that Jesus must rise from the dead. They did not know that His resurrection was necessary and inevitable. They did not know that His resurrection was an indispensable part of God's great work of redemption. They did not know that Christ through His resurrection would grant them the righteousness which he had earned for them by His death on the cross. Indeed, they did not know why He had to die, much less why He had to rise from the dead.

THE LIGHT OF THE SCRIPTURES

If they were surprised and filled with awe at that moment, they would be amazed many more times. They would come to understand these signs in the light of the Scriptures. They would see why He had to die, to rise, to ascend, to fulfill the counsel of God. They would see things which they had never ever seen before. And it would transform their whole lives; it would change their thinking and conduct forever.

The risen Christ would give them that knowledge. He would gather them and open to them the Scriptures, and show them how in the facts of Good Friday and Easter the Word of God was fulfilled. So Jesus would bring them to a deeper understanding and a full confession.

It is, on the one hand, an honest statement of poverty: we did not know the Scriptures. At that moment, John says, as Peter and I walked home, we were filled with many questions, but also with new hope. Something had begun to dawn! But, wow, how little did we know then, compared to later, the time when the Gospel was written. For then John knew the whole story in the light of the entire Scripture.

THE SAME PROCESS TODAY

Here is where we come into the picture. We did not see the evidence in the open tomb, but also, we did not have to go through the process of learning as the disciples. We have received the whole story, the rest of the story, the full revelation. The knowledge of the Word has led us to the confession, based on the testimony of the prophets and the apostles, supported by clear evidence: Christ has risen! Everyone who believes in Jesus Christ, risen from the dead, has had his own process of learning. All have had their own questions which needed to be answered. Who can say when the turning point came in our lives? There may still be questions that need further resolution.

Our situation is indeed different from that of the disciples. Nevertheless, Christ today still uses essentially the same careful process as He did then: He leads us to the Scriptures, and by His Spirit He enables us to understand and accept the Scriptures. We are born again only by the imperishable seed of the Word of God. When we come to faith, it is because (Psalm 138) God has magnified His Word so holy.

It is quite evident from this text: our faith, the full profession of faith in Christ Who died and rose from the dead, is based on the Scriptures. The Holy Spirit works faith by the preaching of the Gospel. Whoever does not know the Scriptures cannot really know Christ. And whoever still has questions must go to the Scripture, and receive knowledge from God's Word in the communion of the saints. Who refuses to do so will never come to faith, or will destroy what little faith he has.

Many people go to church at Easter. For some it is their once-a-year religious experience. They may marvel at the empty tomb. What a beautiful, inspiring story! But they will never know what it truly and really means for them unless they know the riches of the Scriptures and seek the Word every day.

Do you see how Easter obliges us to search the Scriptures? To dig deeper? To see the glory of the risen Christ from the Word and so to experience His power? To open our lives to the ministry of the Word, and in this way to come to the full confession? And even then we must continue to seek the Word and to grow in the knowledge of faith.

That is why at baptism we promise to instruct our children and have them instructed in the truth of God's Word. That's the rule of Easter. Otherwise our children cannot come to the rich profession of the apostolic faith. That is why we will give to our children the example of attending church, and of opening our lives to the Scriptures, at home and in the communion of saints.That is why those who despise God's Word and the sacraments and who do not attend church are subject to church discipline. It is the only means to save them, to lead them back to the Lord. All this belongs to the reality of Easter.

LIVING BY THE BIBLE

John admits it honestly: those signs in the tomb were no more than a stimulus. Only Scripture gave the real answers. You see here the true character of the Christian church: it accepts the apostolic testimony – the eye-witness account – and so lives by the Scriptures. The facts are understood in their full scriptural setting and meaning. This is the purpose of all Christian upbringing, preaching, teaching, and catechism. It is that we may come to the full confession: Jesus Christ is our perfect Saviour, our risen Lord, our glorious King; a confession which fills our life with joy, gives us solid direction and eternal hope.

Let us rejoice in all that we have received in the risen Lord! Rejoice that He leads us to profess His Name. Rejoice in His assurances in baptism that we are God's children. Commit yourselves also for the future to a life that is filled by the Spirit with the true Word of God. And pray that

> . . . By Thy Spirit guided
> Clearly I Thy paths may see
> In Thy truth wilt Thou me guide (Psalm 25, *Book of Praise*)

Christ's Assurance that Many will Confess Him as Risen Lord

"Blessed are those who have not seen and yet believe."

(John 20: 29B)

In most of the churches which I have served as pastor it is the custom that on Easter Sunday morning young people make public profession of faith. I am convinced that this is a good custom. The resurrection of Christ and the profession of the Christians truly belong together. The first is connected unmistakably to the second: I believe that Jesus is the Christ, the first-born of the dead, the Son of the living God! Had Christ not risen that day, there would be from our side no public profession of faith.

Resurrection and profession. On the first Easter it was not so apparent. As we noted earlier, there was much unbelief, hesitation, doubt and even fear. Things happened so quickly and so unexpectedly. It took some time before the disciples could profess in true faith: Christ is risen, Hallelujah, Christ is risen from the dead!

HOW WILL WE EVER BELIEVE?

The Lord Jesus had to follow a careful process of appearances to His disciples, convincing them step by step that He was indeed the risen Lord. And it is not without reason that we read in the Scriptures the story of Thomas, how at first he was unbelieving when he heard his fellow-disciples testify that they had seen the Lord.

The question may come up: if it took *them* so long, even though they saw in person the risen Lord, how will others ever come to faith? If Thomas did not believe the apostolic testimony – and he was one of the disciples – how shall we ever believe? We have never seen Jesus, neither before nor after His death. Will we be able to confess Him truly and to stand firm in that confession?

What the Lord Jesus does in our text is use this encounter with Thomas and the disciples to demonstrate an important point, to teach them and us a vital lesson. He teaches the disciples who must go out with the Word about the powerful effect of that Word. He comforts the church and its members about their ministry: to sow the seed in tears and then to reap the abundant harvest with gladness. He assures us that there will be faith in the risen Christ, worked through the Spirit by the Word. We may see the visible proof thereof whenever people come to profess Jesus Christ as their Saviour. In brief, we read in this passage how Christ assures His disciples that by the power of the apostolic Word many will come to confess Jesus as their Lord and Saviour. Our Lord speaks of the miracle of this confession and the blessing through this confession.

A DOUBTING THOMAS

We all know the story of Thomas and his proverbial doubt. We speak sometimes about a person being "a doubting Thomas." And we may think: Thomas really blew it, what a poor showing! Indeed, how awful of him not to believe the women, his fellow disciples, and those two who travelled to Emmaus. There were so many witnesses whose testimony agreed, yet Thomas refused to believe. He insisted: unless I see visible proof, I will not believe.

Some explainers point out that this reaction was in accordance with Thomas' personality. He was probably the "sceptic" among the disciples, the one who always saw things from their darker side. He expected the worst and was therefore also prepared to accept the worst.

Let me give you an example. When Jesus hears that Lazarus has died, He says to His disciples, "Let us go to him." Now it was quite dangerous for Jesus to go to Judea at that time, for the Jewish leaders were looking for a way to kill Him. They were all aware of the dangers, but Thomas immediately expected the worst and said, "Let us all go that we may die with Him" (John 11: 16). Thomas is the pessimist, who says: Okay, we're in this together, let's go and get killed together. Notice that Thomas is not afraid to go and fight, but he is sure that the worst will happen. They will all die.

DEATH IS THE END

And death is indeed the end. When Jesus was condemned and executed, Thomas considered the matter finished. His worst fears had come true. Well, they had not all died, but Jesus was dead. The sad thing was that Thomas, too, had really believed in Jesus and despite his scepticism had expected great things from Him. Now it is over. My trust has been betrayed and my dreams appear to have been just that, dreams. Must I now believe that Jesus has risen from the dead? First I have to see it!

Some people are sceptical; others are gullible. Some will believe everything they hear; others believe nothing. Some are cynical; others naive. Is that the level on which we must judge things here? Is Thomas' reaction so much different from that of the other disciples? Is it a matter of personality or character?

No, Thomas' reaction is not really all that different. They all thought: dead is dead, it is over. No one really expected a resurrection. They all had to see first, before they would believe. And even then, it took them time to digest in faith what they had seen. We read earlier in John 20: 8 that when John entered the empty tomb and saw its orderly state, ". . . he saw and believed," but it means literally that he only *began* to believe. Something awoke in John at that moment, but it was not yet the full scriptural understanding and deep faith which is required. Yes, they all had to see, not only Thomas, but all of them.

A LEADER IN FAITH?

Thomas' reaction is wrong, but understandable. Therefore the Lord does not rebuke him severely. It is more a gentle reprimand: "Have you believed because you have seen Me?" (Verse 29). For in the end Thomas did come to full acceptance of the fact of the resurrection. He even made a wonderful confession, one which the others had perhaps not yet made up to that moment. He said: my Lord and my God!

Thomas gave the greatest recognition and worship which could be given: you are indeed God of God, Lord of Lords. This was for an Israelite quite a thing to say. What a giant leap of faith! The Sanhedrin had condemned Jesus on the charge of blasphemy, because He had made Himself equal to God. It is indeed the key issue, and Thomas appears to be the first one to say it outright: my Lord and my God! Had any other disciple come so far and been so outspoken?

You see here the wondrous way in which the Lord uses even our weakness and sins to promote His cause. The sceptic is turned into a believer. He who lagged behind in unbelief becomes a leader in faith. From cynic to professor, what a step ahead. Now the church has heard that Jesus is not only Lord but also God, and that He has risen from the dead by the power of His divinity!

MANY WILL BELIEVE

And Christ accepts this confession. What is more, He lets it be known at that specific moment that not just Thomas and the disciples will make this profession of faith, but that there will be many others. "Blessed are those who have not seen and yet believe." Which implies only one thing: there will be those who believe, although they have not seen, but only heard. Many people will be able to go by only one thing: the testimony of others, that is, of the apostles.

Yes, we will go one step further and say that this will be the rule: not seeing, but hearing, and so coming to faith. Our text is, as it were, a beatitude, and it gives us a ground-rule for the kingdom of heaven. Blessed are those who have not seen and yet believed.

Christ does not say these words to make Thomas look or feel bad, or to make the other disciples feel guilty because of their unbelief. The Lord is never out to make His servants look bad. He says these words in order to encourage and comfort them. They had to see, before they would believe. Yes, indeed, they are and must be *eye-witnesses,* eye-witnesses of the resurrected One, for that is their apostolic calling. They must testify of what they have *seen.* They must also come one step further: they must testify that what they have seen is in full accord with the Scriptures of old. He rose according to the Scriptures.

But lest they think that their testimony will be fruitless, the Lord Jesus assures them that many will come to believe through the apostolic Word in the glory of the risen Christ. Many will come to this profession of faith: Jesus is my Lord and my God!

FAITH REMAINS A MIRACLE

It will be a miracle. Just as Thomas was unwilling of himself to believe the testimony of his fellow disciples, so everyone who hears the Gospel will never accept it of himself. As a matter of fact, many will reject the apostolic Word. The general rule in the world is: first I have to see it, and then I'll believe it. And even then sometimes people say: did I really see what I think I saw? Seeing can also be deceptive. The eyes are easily subject to illusion. And seeing alone does not lead to faith. All the signs and wonders which Jesus did, did not bring the Pharisees to faith.

Faith remains a great miracle, a powerful work of the Holy Spirit, and it is always a response to the working of the Word of God in the lives of people. That

Word does what God wants it to do. That Word alone can convict of sin and assure of redemption. That Word brings about faith and public profession of faith.

At Easter time the Lord told His disciples: I will not be making personal appearances to everyone. I will not give special signs to everyone. I am going to my heavenly Father, and one day every eye shall see Me, also those that pierced Me. But until that day it will be: blessed are those who have not seen but do believe! It will be faith worked by the power of the apostolic Word through the Spirit who has been poured out over the church. That is the rule in the Kingdom of heaven.

FAITH THROUGH HEARING

Now we understand key passages in the Bible: faith is through hearing and hearing comes through preaching (Romans 10). What is faith? "Faith is the assurance of things hoped for, *the conviction of things not seen,*" Hebrews 11:1. Is it not as Peter wrote later, "Without having seen [Christ] you love Him, though you do not now see Him, you believe in Him. . ." (I Peter 1: 8)?

Thomas said: I have to see it to believe it. And Christ said: I'll let you see, because I want you to be an eye-witness, but I tell you all that many will believe without seeing. For believing is: accepting the testimony of the prophets and the apostles, receiving the Word of God concerning the life, death and resurrection of Jesus as the whole truth. True faith is saying with the heart: Jesus is my Lord and my Saviour, and this I know because the Bible tells me so!

And this is the power of the resurrection which is evident throughout history and still is evident today. It is an outright miracle every time someone comes to faith and profession of faith. It goes against every grain of our sinful human nature. The carnal mind does not of itself think spiritually. The striving of the flesh is enmity against God. But Christ has risen, hallelujah, and He is alive and well, living in heaven, and by the power of His Word He has worked this faith. And today He receives this confession: Jesus, my Lord and my God. The miracle is still happening, the miracle of regeneration, of confession of sin and profession of faith. Despite all contrary indications and all diabolic temptations, people say: I believe in Jesus Christ, my Lord and Saviour.

MIRACLES AND MEANS

True, miracles do not exclude specific means. Christ uses the upbringing by parents, the teaching at the schools, the catechism classes, the worship services, the study societies, the communion of saints, to bring us to profession of faith. If you don't want the miracle to happen, just shun the means. If you don't use the Word and let it work, then you will never believe. Stay away from church, close the Bible and you'll always doubt, a skeptic for life, a skeptic unto death. You will stay in the worldly way of looking at things: first see and then believe. And since you will not see Christ until He comes in judgment, when you do see Him it will be too late. The miracle of salvation must happen now, in this life, because when you see Christ it is too late. Now you must believe the Word and if you do, then you will see Him in great joy.

I want to stress this: miracles do not occur except in the manner ordained by God. The miracle of faith is by hearing the Word. Whoever has not come to the profession of faith, or whoever is really struggling with the profession he or she once made, must continue to tie the miracle to the means. Whoever professes his faith must remember, "I must be guided always by the Word and Spirit of Christ." Continue to use the means given to the church, for only then will the miracle continue in your lives; only then, having come to faith in Christ will you abide in Him. Satan will test your profession, will try to destroy the miracle by making you scorn the means, the Word, the sacraments, the fellowship of the saints. Don't let him! Resist him fiercely! You know what brought you to faith, and you know also what will keep you in the faith. If we remain faithful in this way, we shall experience more and more the *blessing* of our profession of faith.

BLESSED ARE THE BELIEVERS

For Christ says: "Blessed are those who have not seen and yet believe." This does not mean that Thomas and the other disciples are not blessed. Or that those who believe through the Word are more blessed than those who believed through seeing. The disciples were blessed as well. They had a different task, but the same blessing.

What Christ says is this: all who come to faith through the apostolic Word are truly blessed. The same word is used here as in the beatitudes, in the Sermon on the Mount, and it must therefore also have the same basic sense.

In the beatitudes the word "blessed" is always in sharp contrast to what the world thinks. The world says: the poor in spirit are lost. Christ says: no way, blessed are the poor in spirit. The world says: the meek are pitiable, for they get nothing. Christ says: blessed are the meek, for they shall inherit the earth. The world says: believers are crazy, believing some story about a resurrected Lord they've never seen. How can you believe such nonsense? But Christ says: blessed are the believers. Blessed are those who have not seen and yet believe! You see? Whom the world calls foolish, the Lord declares blessed. There is no greater antithesis than this!

What does this word "blessed" mean? Well, whenever we speak of blessing, we know that the *curse* has been taken away. The curse is always first of all: the curse of sin, the wage of sin which is death. To be blessed means to live in the embrace of the love of God, to stand in His fellowship, to be His child, and so to share in all the gifts of Christ. Blessed means: to be congratulated with a very special situation. Blessed; indeed, congratulations to those who have not seen but do believe.

BLESSING AND BLOOD

The original English word for "blessing" comes from a word that has to do with blood. Blessing comes from "bloedsian," to consecrate with blood. You are blessed, for indeed, the blood has been poured out for you; you have been washed clean by the blood of Golgotha. Is that not the essence of Psalm 32, blest is the man whose trespass is forgiven, blest is the man against whom thou wilt not count all his iniquity and guilt! The great blessing is to be cleansed of sin, and so to receive eternal life.

The apostle Peter also spoke in this vein: as the outcome of your faith you receive the salvation of your souls. Your life is saved in Christ. That is the foremost blessing of faith.

Still there is more here. The word "bless" may also be connected to the word "bliss." The original Greek has a word that includes the notion of happiness. Bliss means indeed happiness, great joy. Did not Peter write: though you do not now see Him, you believe in Him and rejoice with unutterable and exalted joy? Blessed are the believers. Blissful are the believers! The happiness of the believer is not something that can always be expressed properly or explained adequately. It is unutterable and exalted. It is a rejoicing in heavenly matters. It is a spiritual joy.

Those who believe experience already in this life a special joy that comes from faith, from the fellowship with the Father through Christ. You who believe, do you know what we are talking about? We are talking about the firm basis, the quiet certainty, the deep joy in the Lord. Yes, how blest is the man and, it says, how happy! Blessed people are happy people, whose joy rests in Christ and His perfect work.

NO MORE PROBLEMS?

Does this mean that when we profess Christ, we never have any more problems? That it is all bliss from then on? No, it doesn't. Jesus warned His disciples for false expectations. He said: you will have many trials! Satan will try to undo your confession. And Peter wrote, "now for a little while you may have to suffer various trials. . . ."

To be blessed does not mean that we will never feel depressed and never wonder about our faith and faithfulness. There will be times when, because of our sins and lack of prayer, by not exercising the power of faith, we will not feel the effects of God's grace in ourselves. There may be times when we "greatly offend God, grievously wound our consciences, and sometimes for a while lose the sense of God's favour." I just quoted from the beautiful Canons of Dort. Yes, we do make it so very difficult for ourselves and for others by our lack of proper exercising our faith. Be on guard that you do not harm your faith. Still, God will not rob us of the blessing of our profession of faith. He will cause us to experience again the favour of a reconciled God so that we adore anew His mercy and faithfulness.

Oh Thomas, it is a miracle when someone professes faith in Christ as the risen Lord. But what a blessing, what bliss comes with it and through it. Blessed are those who believe the apostolic testimony, blessed in this life and in all eternity. In all the trials, through all the valleys, God will keep their faith and give them true joy. How blest are those whose strength Thou art, yes, O LORD of hosts, how blest is he who puts his hope and trust in Thee! (Psalm 84). So we will go on, through all the valleys, until the journey ends in the New Jerusalem where we shall see Christ with our own eyes, face to face, and He will say: see, I told you!

WE WILL SEE HIM

Those who believe and confess His Name will see Christ with their own eyes, and with great joy. Those who do not believe will see Him with great fear. But see Him we shall!

Christ faced that little group of disciples with Thomas and He said: you believe because you have seen? Do you know what I see? I see my holy catholic church, I see the great multitude of those who believe in the apostolic Word, the miracle multitude, the blessed multitude with the songs of joy, the multitude gathered by the Word which I gave.

Blessed are you who have not seen Christ but do believe and profess your faith in Him. Never forget: it is based not on seeing, but on hearing, on the solid rock of the apostolic Word. And by faith you begin to see what others refuse to see. You always have a different point of view from the world. Remember this: you walk by faith and not by sight. You hope for what is not seen. Hang on to this blessing with all your might. Begin every day by saying: blessed are the believers, blissful are the believers, for they do see and shall see God.They do live and shall live with God. For the curse has been removed. Easter means that death has been overcome. New life has begun.

Let us enjoy the miracle of faith by the power of Him Who died and was buried, but lives! And let us rejoice in our eternal heritage. The lines have fallen in most pleasant places. Let us believe and confess, today and always:

"With Thee full joy and bliss are ever present!" (Psalm 16, *Book of Praise*)

Blessed are those who have not seen and yet believe that Christ has risen from the dead and that He is coming to judge the living and the dead; blessed are those who through Him acclaim the Father, the Son, and the Spirit.

The Jewish Leaders Confronted with the Truth of Christ's Resurrection

"While they were going, behold, some of the guard went into the city and told the chief priests all that had taken place. And when they had assembled with the elders and taken counsel, they gave a sum of money to the soldiers and said: tell people, His disciples came by night and stole Him away while we were asleep. And if this comes to the governor's ears, we will satisfy him and keep you out of trouble. So they took the money and did as they were directed; and this story has been spread among the Jews to this day".

(Matthew 28: 11-15)

On the first Easter Sunday there were two very important meetings. One took place on the evening of that day, and involved most of the disciples of the Lord Jesus. They gathered that evening because it had finally begun to dawn on them that the Lord had truly risen.

The other meeting took place much sooner, in the early morning. It involved the Sanhedrin, the council of priests, scribes, and elders. They gathered that morning because they had to deal with reports that Jesus had indeed risen from the dead.

Two meetings. One where the Lord Jesus Himself appeared to confirm the facts. The other where action was taken to deny the facts. Both meetings involved the greatest truth of history: the resurrection of the Lord Jesus.

TRUTH OPPOSED, NOT OVERLOOKED

Usually on Easter Sunday morning we concentrate on what the women and the disciples did and saw. Let us, however, also pay attention to that other meeting, the emergency session of the Jewish Sanhedrin. We will do this not with a certain glee as we see the Jewish leaders squirming to get away from under the weight of the facts. We take no pleasure in the outcome of that meeting. It was a sad affair.

We will look at their meeting only in order to be confirmed in our faith that the Lord has truly risen from the dead and that we today, therefore, have to do with a living Lord and Saviour. We notice in this passage that the truth can only be repressed at great cost, at the expense of personal integrity and credibility. At the meeting of the Sanhedrin the truth was not accidentally "overlooked," but wilfully opposed.

Our theme is: the Lord God confronts the Jewish leaders with the truth of the resurrection of Jesus Christ. There is a precise accounting of the facts, a wilful suppression of the truth, and a widespread acceptance of the lie.

SEALING THE TOMB

You know that the Jewish leaders had spared time nor effort to have the grave of the Lord Jesus sealed and guarded. Why were they so concerned about what might happen at this tomb? The answer is given in Matthew 27: 63. They remembered the statement of the Lord that after three days He would rise again.

This is remarkable indeed. The women and the disciples had apparently completely forgotten this saying of the Lord. At least, they did not take it very seriously, even though they had heard it more than once. But the Jewish leaders had not forgotten.

Did they really believe Jesus' words? Of course, they would never admit to the possible truth of Christ's saying that He would rise again. But still, there was the nagging doubt. They knew of the mighty power of this Jesus of Nazareth. They knew how He had raised the dead: think of Lazarus, the daughter of Jairus, and the young man of Nain. With this Jesus,they knew, you can never be quite sure! So even after He had died, Jesus occupied their fearful minds.

HIS DISCIPLES?

But they cannot admit to any of this doubt before Pilate. They call Jesus "this imposter." And they suggest: perhaps his disciples – who may want to make use of Christ's prophecy that He will rise again – will come to steal His body and claim that He has risen. That deception would be worse than all the previous ones. A Jesus who was believed to be alive posed a serious threat to their rule and power.

So they ask Pontius Pilate for a guard to secure the sepulchre. Pilate gives in easily; he is tired of the whole affair. He says: you have a guard of soldiers; go and make it as secure as you can. The explainers differ on the exact meaning of Pilate's words. Did he say: you have your own guard, the temple police, use them? Or did he give them a Roman guard? Most explainers choose for the latter, because these soldiers are later afraid of what Pilate, the Roman commander in chief, might think of their efforts. So, let's say it was a guard comprised of Roman legionnaires, hardened veterans, professional soldiers. We do not know how many men there were in this contingent (the traditional guard consisted of four soldiers), but it will have been a sizeable number, perhaps more than the usual. The Jewish leaders really want to make certain.

LIKE DEAD MEN

The guard is posted. The sepulchre is sealed. No one can come out, no one can go in! Finally the Jewish leaders can sit back and relax. The matter is definitely closed. But we have read how in the early hours, before dawn, an angel of the Lord comes down from heaven, and with mighty power rolls away the stone, breaking the seals, opening the grave. It also says specifically that he went and triumphantly *sat* on the stone. That indicates: try and roll it back, if you dare!

The soldiers are shaken with fear; it says that "they became like dead men." They are petrified and immobilized. And when they finally come to their senses, they flee in all directions, wandering in a daze through the hill country around Jerusalem.

Meanwhile, the women have come to the grave and left it again. And we read in verse 11, "While they [the women] were going, behold, some of the guard went into the city and told the chief priests all that had taken place." Only some went. The others stayed away, out of fear or uncertainty. But somehow a report must be made to the authorities. So they decided: some of us will have to go and tell the story.

TELLING THE FACTS

Why do these soldiers go to the chief priests and not to Pilate, their commander? The answer is probably two-fold. The soldiers had been placed under the direct command of the Sanhedrin, and to them they therefore report. Secondly, Pilate might not be as receptive to their story as the Jewish leaders, who know more about Jesus and His claims. So they go to the chief priests.

What did they tell the priests? Matthew formulates it very carefully and precisely, "...they told the chief priests *all that had taken place.*" These men do not come with some incoherent story about apparitions and ghosts – even though they are in a state of shock and confusion – but they give the facts. It even says: they told *all* that had taken place. They did not omit a single detail. They did not come with part of the story, but they told the truth, the whole truth, and nothing but the truth!

They said: look, we were standing on guard, as commanded, when there was suddenly an earthquake, and this person, with a face like lightning and raiment like snow, came and rolled away the stone and sat upon it. There was nothing we could do to prevent it! One explainer even suggests that these soldiers, who were closest to the actual event of the resurrection, may have seen Jesus come walking out of the sepulchre, after the angel rolled the stone away. The Bible doesn't tell us that, so we may not state it as a certainty, but indeed these soldiers were the only witnesses of what really occurred at that sepulchre. And their conclusion can only be: something miraculous happened, the grave was powerfully opened, and that means that this Jesus has somehow come back from the dead.

A PRECISE ACCOUNTING

Do you think that these chief priests doubted the story of the soldiers? Do you think that they – who knew the Scriptures – could not identify a person in white raiment? They realized that they were faced here with the appearance of an angel of God and that the words of Christ were proving true in a manner which they never would have expected.

The chief priests are given a precise accounting of the facts. The first to hear about what happened at the grave are not the disciples, but the priests and elders. The fact of the resurrection does not pass them by unnoticed. In this way the Lord causes the resurrection of Christ to be made known to the Jewish leaders in precise terms.

No, Christ does not appear to them Himself. He had said to the priests: you will see Me no more until the day of judgment. He will appear later that day, on that second meeting, only to His disciples. But the chief priests are confronted with the facts just the same. In this way God makes another appeal to the Jews to come to grips with the facts and to confess the truth. The chief priests indeed see that the matter is of great importance: they call a full meeting of the Sanhedrin together.

A HASTY MEETING

In the early morning hours, the messengers go out to gather the elders. Imagine all these men being awakened, dressing quickly, and hastening with all their early morning dignity to the meeting.

The chief priests assemble, it says, with the elders. We have here another official meeting of the Sanhedrin, the Jewish council. It does not say specifically whether the scribes, the theologians, were called in, but we can safely assume that as many members of the council as possible were present.

It must be noted that we have here the most authoritative church court in Israel. These are the men who must be the shepherds of the flock and lead the sheep in all truth. As they gather, and hear what happened, they have the opportunity to recognize the facts and make the truth known. They could have said to one another: this proves that we have unjustly dealt with a true Servant of the Lord, and we must now change our position. Let us tell the people what happened at the sepulchre.

VERY FEW OPTIONS

It says in the text that they took counsel. This means that they debated and discussed how to deal with the issue. Usually their debates were quite lengthy, but here there was very little time to lose. Actually the debate did not have to be lengthy at all, for there were few options. If they refused to change their stand – and they did – they could do one of two things: discredit and deny the soldiers' story or bribe the soldiers to change their story.

The Jewish leaders sensed that the real story was not easily discredited. The people were still impressed with what Jesus had said and done and how He had died. Therefore the story would have to be altered. Let us not deny that the tomb is empty, for it obviously is, they argued, but let the guards say that they fell asleep and that Christ's disciples came and took the body away.

This is nothing but purposeful and wilful suppression of the truth. The Jewish leaders know that they are now causing a lie to be spread. It would have been one thing to have said nothing or to have left the interpretation of what the soldiers experienced up to the people; it is quite another thing to change the story and knowingly suppress the truth.

THE SANHEDRIN'S PROBLEM

Meanwhile, the Sanhedrin is faced with a problem. These soldiers will not agree to present this as a version of what happened. It simply is not true. Besides, the story is self-incriminating. To fall asleep while on guard is the greatest shirking of a soldier's duty. To admit it is to admit great failure. A soldier does have his code of honour. And if they tell this story and Pilate hears of it, will he not take measures against them? The penalty for falling asleep while on guard was severe. Do you remember what king Herod did to the sentries who had to guard Peter but were unable to do so? Herod had them put to death (Acts 12: 19). Would Pilate take a different stand? It's bad for morale when soldiers who shirk their duty get away with it.

And so they *bribe* the soldiers to tell a false tale. It is clear from the original text that they paid them a large sum of money. Just as in the case of paying off Judas, the money will have come from the temple treasury. Think of the irony: the money given by God's people to maintain the sacrificial service in the temple is now used to deny the reality of the greatest sacrifice ever made!

And what about Pilate's possible disciplinary measures? The soldiers are assured that the Sanhedrin will intervene on their behalf. Verse 14: "And if this comes to the governor's ears, we will satisfy him and keep you out of trouble." The Jewish leaders a few days earlier pleaded with the hated Roman governor. Now they must plead with his soldiers. But they will do anything to suppress the truth about Jesus. This is how deeply they have fallen.

AN UNBELIEVABLE STORY

Meanwhile, do you see how the quickly concocted story is one that holds no water? Anyone can see that. If the soldiers were sleeping, how do they know that it was Christ's disciples who took away the body? Sleeping guards cannot identify the so-called grave robbers. Secondly, would not the moving away of the sealed stone have made enough noise to awaken the soldiers?

How could the Sanhedrin ever believe that the people would accept this tale? How could they themselves dismiss the soldiers' testimony? Well, it is easy to believe what you desperately want to believe. The greatest deception of all is self-deception. And if you repeat a lie often enough, people will believe it. You can fool the crowd most of the time.

Let us realize, however, that the Lord in His mercy *sought* Israel to the end, even after the crucifixion. He gave to the leaders the facts. But they rejected them, and conspired to have the truth twisted. So the people were robbed of their rights. How terrible when officebearers withhold the truth from God's people!

CHRIST STILL ON THE AGENDA

Meanwhile, Christ is vindicated. He occupies the Sanhedrin's agenda even after He has been pronounced dead. And He never will get off that agenda either. The Jewish people will always be faced with the claim of the risen Lord and Saviour, Jesus Christ! Yes, the whole world will be faced with this claim.

It is written so that we would know for sure: Jesus has truly risen from the dead. The facts bear it out. The meeting of the Sanhedrin, early on Easter morning, could not avoid the risen Christ. He forced them to make a decision. The sad part is that the Sanhedrin's false version has been widely accepted. For Matthew adds that the soldiers took the money and did as they were directed. He writes, "And this story has been spread among the Jews until this very day."

The soldiers *immediately* went out to tell the people of Jerusalem their version of the events of that morning, and the story spread like wild-fire: the disciples of Jesus have stolen His body. Satan is quick to have his own version of things in place before the disciples even get a chance to accept and proclaim the truth.

TO THIS VERY DAY

When Matthew writes that the soldiers' story has been spread among the Jews " to this day," he may well be referring to a time span of some forty years. Meanwhile many other things had happened to bear out the truth of the resurrection. Think of the outpouring of the Holy Spirit on Pentecost, the signs and wonders done by the apostles in Jesus' Name, and the establishment of Christian churches in many parts of the Roman empire.

Matthew does not say that all the Jews accepted the false version. Thank God that many of them did accept the true account. But on the whole, as also Paul testifies in his letter to the Romans, the people of the Old Covenant have by and large rejected the risen Lord Jesus Christ. It is for Paul, as it should be for us, a matter of great grief and sorrow.

As you may know, Matthew's main purpose in writing this Gospel was to convince the Jews that Jesus of Nazareth was indeed the Messiah. Therefore he had to show how the false story about what happened at Easter came into the world. Jews everywhere had to read it and know how their own leaders falsified the facts. And in writing these words, Matthew again appealed to the people of Israel as yet to consider the truth. The Lord has confronted the Jewish people also at Easter with the reality of the resurrection.

NO PHYSICAL RESURRECTION?

The lie finds widespread acceptance. This is true also today, and not just among the Jews, but also in many so-called Christian churches. The resurrection is theologically a much disputed fact. It is made into a *symbol*, an expression of the church's hope for a better future. Jesus lives on, people are told, in our hearts. His ideals, His teaching, His selfless example are still with us. In that sense many will say: yes, His grave is empty. But a physical resurrection? A living Lord who rules supreme in heaven? No, that cannot be true. Easter is only symbolic of new hope, of spring, of the undying human spirit!

You know why so many are misled. It is because they do not acquaint themselves with the real facts, which means, in our time, because they do not know the Scriptures. They have no way of checking and unmasking the lies of their leaders. They simply accept that a physical resurrection can not have taken place.

Can a church which promotes such teaching against the testimony of Scripture still be called a "church"? Someone who left the United Church of Canada – where such views are tolerated and even propagated – said: I became a Christian *after* I left the United Church. The situation may not be the same among all members of that church, but the statement is a telling one.

THE EVENING MEETING

The system of lies about the resurrection of Christ has become more refined since the first Easter. But the truth remains clear as well: Christ has truly risen from the dead. Remember, there was also that other meeting on Easter Sunday, in the evening. Christ appeared there to declare His peace to all who love Him, and to send out the witnesses of the truth to proclaim the Gospel of salvation! That evening meeting proved to be of greater consequence than the morning meeting of the Sanhedrin. For the Gospel is still being preached.

There is widespread acceptance of the lie, and the self-deception of people will only grow. But, praise God, there is also widespread acceptance of the truth, the truth that sets us free in Christ.

The message of Easter is that we must live by the apostolic Word which Christ gave to us.

> Praised be the Son
> For His redeeming work is done!
> He died, was buried, but He lives,
> And to His ransomed people gives
> His blessed Word to guide us! (Hymn 29)

This is the Word which has been proclaimed to you, so that you may rejoice in Him Who has risen from the dead and Who will return again, the Saviour, God incarnate.

The Definitive Appearance of the Risen Lord to His Church

"Now the eleven disciples went to Galilee, to the mountain to which Jesus directed them. And when they saw Him they worshiped Him; but some doubted. And Jesus came and said to them: all authority in heaven and on earth has been given to Me. Go therefore and make disciples of all nations, baptizing them in the name of the Father and of the Son and of the Holy Spirit, teaching them to observe all that I have commanded you; and lo, I am with you always, to the close of the age".

(Matthew 28: 16-20)

We find in this well-known passage of Scripture the "grand conclusion" of the Gospel of Jesus Christ, as described by Matthew; that is, the "grand conclusion" of Christ's ministry on earth after His resurrection and before His glorious ascension. It is yet to be followed, of course, by Christ's return on the clouds of heaven. But here is the conclusion of what Christ did on earth for our salvation and justification.

It is indeed a *grand* conclusion. Christ here opens a mighty perspective to His disciples, His small church. I'd like you to notice in this passage the pervading and dominant use of the word "all": all authority, all nations, all commandments, always. There is here no limited view of things but a catholic, universal, all-inclusive scheme. At the end of His earthly ministry, having risen from the dead in glory, Christ sets His goals high and His scope wide.

This is in keeping with the significance of Easter. The resurrection of Christ means His victory over sin and death. Christ begins to receive the homage and worship that is His due. And this victory of Easter has a forward thrust and momentum: we now may await the great and final victory, the full gathering of the Church and the perfection of the age. We even have our own specific calling in this gathering as members of the Church, also as officebearers in the Church.

CONCLUSION AND BEGINNING

The "grand conclusion" of Matthew is also an impressive beginning. Now it really starts. The worship of the Church. The true confession that Jesus is the Christ, the Son of the living God. The apostolic ministry of the Church. The work of the apostles, and when they fall away, that of elders and deacons. All is done under the authority of the glorious Head of the Church, who has conquered sin and death.

These are the elements which the text mentions. They are the elements on which we should focus each Easter. The passage deals with the definitive appearance of the risen Lord Jesus Christ to His New Testament Church. We read about the christian confession of the Church, the royal assurance for the Church, and the apostolic mandate to the Church.

BACK TO GALILEE

The Gospels give us various accounts of meetings between the risen Lord and His disciples. There is the meeting described in verse 9, which took place on Easter Sunday itself, on the evening of that remarkable day. There is the meeting which took place exactly one week later, where Thomas was confronted with the truth of the resurrection, as described in John 20. There is the meeting at the Sea of Tiberias, where the apostle Peter is restored to his office, described in John 21. And there undoubtedly have been many more meetings between Christ and His disciples, meetings at which He convinced them of the truth and certainty of His resurrection and also opened to them the Scriptures, so that they would understand the meaning and purpose of what had happened.

Matthew does not mention any of these meetings, except the first one on Easter Sunday. He takes us from Jerusalem right to Galilee. There Christ began the instruction of His disciples, and there He also finalized it.

We do not know exactly when the appearance mentioned in our text took place. Presumably it was shortly after Easter itself, for Christ already on that day directed them to Galilee (verse 10). The disciples listened to this directive, and went to Galilee to await further instruction. We read: "Now the eleven disciples went to Galilee, to the mountain to which Jesus had directed them." Although it was not the first meeting in Galilee which Matthew describes here (the meeting at the Sea of Tiberias which John mentions as the third meeting between Christ and His disciples will have preceded this one – see John 21:14), it certainly was a definitive appearance of Christ. Definitive means: bringing the matter to an end, for here Christ provides conclusive instruction. The text gives us this instruction in a nutshell. It is, as it were, a summary of Christ's teaching after His resurrection.

WORSHIPING THE RISEN LORD

The disciples are waiting for Christ. When Matthew speaks here of disciples, he specifically means the eleven, for they are addressed first of all, although this manner of speaking does not necessarily exclude others. Christ is primarily concerned here with His eleven disciples, but in them He addresses the entire Church. So the eleven were on this occasion waiting for the Lord, perhaps with some of the other brethren (see verse 10).

And we read, "And when they saw Him they worshiped Him, but some doubted" (verse 17). By now it has pretty well become established that Easter is a tremendous reality: Christ has risen from the dead! And therefore the most obvious reaction to Christ's appearing is worship. Christ already received this worship on Easter Sunday; see verse 9, "And they came up and took hold of His feet and worshiped Him." He received it in Jerusalem, and He receives it also now in Galilee.

Here it means that they fall down before Him, thus recognizing Him as their Lord and their God. It was the Jewish way of giving the highest honour to God. The disciples so recognize, yes confess Christ to be the Son of the living God, the Messiah, the King of kings.

There is after the resurrection a deeper recognition of the mystery of the Messiah: that He is fully the Son of God, worthy of divine honour. The Christian confession, "You are the Christ, the Son of the living God," finds new depth and meaning on Easter Sunday and thereafter. And this will be the first task of the New Testament Church: to confess Christ as the true Messiah, as the only-begotten Son of God, as the only and complete Redeemer. So what characterizes this meeting in Galilee first of all is a profession of faith that Christ is risen Lord and Saviour.

BUT SOME STILL DOUBTED

We also read that some doubted. The Word of God is quite honest in this respect. We are told that not everyone believed right away. The four evangelists all make mention of this doubting attitude. We read in Mark 16: 4 that Christ "upbraided" His disciples for their unbelief and hardness of heart. We know from Luke that the disciples were frightened at His appearance, as if they saw a ghost. We know from John that the apostle Thomas publicly disbelieved Christ's resurrection. And here, too, we read about doubt.

Some explainers see this doubt not as the outright unbelief in the resurrected Lord, as was shown at the beginning, but more as uncertainty as to whether this person on the mountain is really the Lord. Some, not sure that it was really Jesus, sort of "hung back," took a "wait-and-see" attitude. In any case, they are not all equally convinced. The power of unbelief and doubt is always strong. The confession that Jesus is the Christ does not come as spontaneously as we would like. It takes time to come to this confession, as I remarked earlier. It takes a lot of convincing. The disciples have to *see the facts,* and be absolutely convinced that Christ has risen bodily from the grave. They must also learn to see these facts in the light of the Scriptures, otherwise they will begin to doubt again. They have to be led deeper and deeper into the Word so that doubt is replaced by awe and wonder.

DOUBT IS NOT THE NORM

We today, in our worship services, do not see Christ. He does not appear to us physically. We are not called to stand on a mountain in Galilee. But we do have the apostolic testimony. We have the full revelation of God, the entire Scriptures. The Lord Jesus Himself said to Thomas: blessed are those who have not seen and yet believe; those who believe and confess that Jesus is the Christ, the Lord and Master.

This is the confession which Christ expects and receives, on Easter and since Easter. It is the result of much work and much growth. With some of us it takes longer than with others. Everyone has his own personal history in coming to public profession of faith. And even then doubt has to be overcome day after day. The Holy Spirit must work constantly in us with the Word of God. Parents, teachers, officebearers have their task and concerns here, so that all our youth may come to this confession, and so that all members may persevere in this confession.

They worshiped but some doubted. It is said in all honesty. These are the facts; but this is not the norm. The norm is that all members of the Church believe and confess that Jesus Christ is their risen Lord and Saviour. They must all grow in this confession, in faith and in obedience.

This requires the constant watchfulness of the Church and of the office bearers. We may rejoice greatly whenever someone professes the Lord Jesus as the risen Lord and Saviour. But we also know that this profession will be sorely tested by our arch-enemies, Satan, the world, and our own flesh. Making profession of faith is not the end of spiritual growth, but the beginning. Having confessed your faith, you cannot let down your guard as if you had reached the final destination. Now all the more you must fight against doubt and unbelief, temptation and sin. Now all the more you need the assurance that the risen Christ rules and governs your life and that through him you will persevere.

ROYAL ASSURANCE

We do not read here that our Lord admonished those who doubted on that mountain in Galilee. He did that earlier, in Jerusalem. There He admonished them severely. They had no reason, no right to doubt, for He had always spoken clearly to them. Perhaps He spoke here also words of admonition as well as encouragement, but we do not read of it. We do read of the royal assurance which He gives to His disciples.

It says in verse 18, "And Jesus came and said to them: all authority in heaven and on earth has been given to me." Jesus came, it says, and this means that He drew near to them and bridged the gap that was there, physically, so that all could see that He was really the Jesus of Nazareth whom they knew. He again established that closeness, that communion which characterized His appearances as risen Lord.

Christ gives His disciples a royal assurance: all authority in heaven and on earth has been given to Me. This is the declaration of a true King. It is not simply the authority which Christ always had as Son of God, but it is the power of the resurrection, the authority which He received through His perfect obedience.

COMPLETE CONTROL

Christ says: I have absolute authority. Complete control. It is not just restricted to the earth, it is also manifest in heaven. His is a kingship which combines heaven and earth and makes them one.

The word authority here means especially the *lawful right* to govern. With that right comes also the ability, the power to govern, but first the absolute right of Christ is established. It is a right which has been given to Him, by God the Father, as a fruit of His obedience and humiliation. He has now been given a Name above every name!

You may remember how Satan pretended that he had control over all the kingdoms of the earth. He offered to give Christ authority on earth, if only Christ would worship him. Christ would then not rule in heaven, but certainly over all the earth. But Satan does not even have the right to make such an offer. He is a rebel, a revolutionary, who has *taken* the kingdom by force. Christ *receives* the authority through obedience, directly from God.

The Church receives this royal assurance that Christ alone has full authority. Whether He always demonstrates this in the world is a different matter. But He alone has it: all things lie in His almighty hand.

ALL AUTHORITY

It is of great importance to the Church to know that He is in charge of heaven and earth, and also of our own lives. That He has the kingdom and the power, lawfully, together with the Father and the Holy Spirit, in perfect unity. This is our certainty and comfort.

Christ wants His Church to know this before He ascends to heaven. For if we did not know it, how could we stand in the faith?

To have all authority means that Christ will work out His victory over sin and death, bring it to completion, in the world and also in our lives. No one can stop Him or withstand Him. And this is said in order that we would not fear but fulfill our tasks as church, as believers, as office bearers.

THE GREAT COMMISSION

For the church has a task to fulfil. At this definitive appearance, Christ gives to His Church a mighty mandate, often called the great commission: "Go therefore and make disciples of all nations, baptizing them in the Name of the Father and the Son and the Holy Spirit, teaching them to observe all that I have commanded you" (verses 19 and 20).

It is from our vantage-point an impossible task. How could such a small and weak group of men ever undertake such a great mission? But Christ gives it anyway. He says: Go *therefore.* Because *He* has all authority, the disciples can approach all nations. The world that lies under the authority of Christ lies open to the preaching and teaching of the Church. That is the great connection in the great commission! Not just "Go", but "Go therefore."

Christ gives to His Church the apostolic mandate. And we do not have the space to deal with these words in depth, but we must make some general observations. The mandate is to preach the Gospel, to all people, and to do it in a certain manner.

THE MARKS OF THE CHURCH

We find the expression: make disciples. Disciples are not just people who learn about Christ, but people who *submit* to Christ. See the connection with the words: teach them to observe all that I have commanded you. Discipleship of Christ, membership in the Church is a commitment, a total commitment.

The mission of the Church is an urgent mission, and her teaching an urgent teaching. The eleven disciples here become apostles to make more disciples, whose lives will be completely subjected to Christ the Lord.

We sometimes restrict the apostolic mandate, the so-called "great commission," to mission and to preaching. But notice all the elements: make disciples through the preaching of the Gospel. Baptize them, that is, seal the Word through the administration of the sacraments. Teach them to observe, that is, exercise the proper discipline of the Word. Preaching, sacraments, and discipline are the three marks of the Church of Christ, and they are contained in this apostolic mandate. To do these three things is the task of the Church, and here lies the challenge for the officebearers of the Church.

A CLEAR MANDATE

It is the Church's mandate to go out with the Word so that people may submit to Christ. They are called out of the world by the Word. They are distinguished from unbelievers through Holy Baptism. And they are brought to a new life of obedience, keeping the commandments of the Lord.

In Christ's definitive Easter appearance to His Church He makes clear what He expects of His apostles. So it becomes also clear what He expects of the officebearers and other church members in our time. We are not apostles, but we are called to see to it that the ministry of the Church, evident in the preaching of the true Gospel, the pure administration of the sacraments, and the faithful exercising of Church discipline, continues today in the Church of Christ, so that God's people may be a salting salt and a city on a hill. You are called to see to it that the love of Christ, working in His Church, is evident to all around.

I AM WITH YOU ALWAYS

It can be done. Is it not remarkable that this small group of disciples, standing on that mountain in Galilee so shortly after the resurrection, did go out and made a beginning with this apostolic mandate? And that beginning resulted in the world-wide preaching of the Gospel. Against all human odds it became clear that Christ indeed has all authority in heaven and on earth.

The Church experienced what Christ here adds, "And lo, I am with you always to the close of the age." Christ knew that He was placing a very tall order on the shoulders of these simple men. The office is always too great for the office bearers. But they do not have to do it in their own strength. Emphatically, Christ says: lo! That is, see, believe, that I am with you. Always. Under all circumstances. At all times. Whether there is peace and prosperity or persecution and adversity, I am with you. And He will be with His church until the close of the age, when He returns on the clouds of heaven. Until the perfection comes, when sin and Satan shall be no more.

The promise of Easter is that the Lord who rose from the dead will never be absent from His Church, but will always enable her to live in this world and fulfill her ministry. That He will never be absent from us in our personal lives, but remains IMMANUEL, God with us.

We see here how Christ, King of the nations and King of the Church, shows us His Church moving to the great Day of Christ; His Church, which is being gathered by the Gospel and shows forth new life in communion with Christ under the discipline of the Holy Spirit.

We are taken up in this wonderful work of Christ and see its glorious fruits.

Ye servants of God, your Master proclaim
And publish abroad His wonderful Name. . .

God ruleth on high, Almighty to save,
And still He is nigh, *His presence we have.*

Then let us adore and give Him His right. (Hymn 64, *Book of Praise*)

The Mandate to Preach the Gospel of Christ's Great Victory

"And He said to them: go into the world and preach the Gospel to the whole creation. He who believes and is baptized will be saved; but he who does not believe will be condemned".

(Mark 16: 15, 16)

I wrote about the fact that it took time for the disciples to come to the full understanding and the firm faith that Jesus Christ had risen from the dead. Here in Mark 16 we read again about their persistent unbelief. It says that Christ even upbraided them "for their unbelief and hardness of heart" (verse 14). It was difficult to convince them that He had indeed risen in glory from the bonds of hell and death.

Can the Lord still use such unfaithful men in His service? Can these wavering men ever be stalwart apostles? Should the Lord not say, "I had better find some others who will go out an preach with more conviction than you"? Well, it is remarkable that in all four accounts of the Gospel there is mention of the missionary mandate immediately after Christ's appearance to His disciples.

Let us take a look at the other instances. Matthew 28: 19, "Go therefore and make disciples of all nations." Mark 16: 15, "Go into all the world. . . ." Luke 24: 47, ". . .that repentance and forgiveness should be preached in His Name to all nations, beginning from Jerusalem." John 20:28, "As the Father has sent Me, even so I send you." It is clear and convincing: the risen Lord maintains the disciples' initial appointment, despite their fear and unbelief. Which means: the Church is not absolved of her missionary task but confirmed in it. The work of mission is not dependent on the faith and ability of the workers in the harvest but on the truth and power of the Master of the harvest.

CHRIST'S DETERMINATION

It often is difficult for a church to place a missionary on the field. There are human factors which play a role; there is also the sovereign and wise providence of God. But lest our commitment waver and our zeal fail, let us look once again at the command which the Lord gave to His disciples and in them to His Church. Our theme is: Easter means for the Church an expressly renewed missionary mandate to preach the Gospel of Christ's great victory. We will give special attention to the catholic extent and the serious intent of this preaching.

We must see in this passage first of all the determination of our Lord Jesus Christ. It is the determination of love, which does not give up. Christ's appearances to His disciples after His resurrection have this main purpose: to prepare and equip them for their missionary task, for this will be their actual work. For forty days they get an intensive course in missiology, so to speak.

They must go out! Yes, if ever there was reason to go, it is now. Now they have the complete picture, the whole story about the death and the resurrection of the Lord. Now they can tell about the great and true victory of Christ: how He went from the cross to the tomb and from the tomb to the throne. During these days Christ teaches them the true depth of the Scriptures and shows how the facts accord with the Word of God. He gives them a solid and clear message to proclaim.

CATHOLIC AND ECUMENICAL

The first thing which we notice about this renewed missionary mandate is that it is from the very beginning emphatically catholic and truly ecumenical. It says: go into all the world and preach to the whole creation. This means that in an ever-expanding circle the apostles and those who come after them will have to preach the Gospel. "Catholic" means: all over the world. Ecumenical means: containing the entire (known) world.

We may look at these words a bit more closely. It says literally: go through the whole world (=kosmos, the totality and unity of the created world) and preach the Gospel to every creature (= all people, every human being on earth). That is, go everywhere and speak to everyone. There are no limits, there are no boundaries. This is a far-reaching mandate. It is also a very tall order for a little church. It does not mean that all persons head for head must be reached, but it does imply that in all regions and places the Gospel must be proclaimed so that as many as possible may hear.

HIT THE ROAD

The word that is translated by "go" actually means to travel or to *trek*. It implies that one hits the road and goes to faraway places. And this, of course, means that one is subject to danger and must make sacrifices. You cannot travel without exposing yourself to the dangers of the road. You come to live in distant lands and in an unknown culture, and this brings with it specific problems. It is obvious that not everyone is able to do this work and that personal and family circumstances play a role.

But travel into the whole world they must. Missionaries are the real globetrotters, not from Harlem but from Jerusalem. They must go from Jerusalem, to Judea, to Samaria and to the ends of the earth, the Lord said in Acts 1.

In this connection I want to make a few remarks about the distinction between mission and evangelism. They are the same activity: making the Gospel known. But they take place in a different setting and are performed by different people. We see evangelism as the testimony of the church in its immediate vicinity, in its own community. And there is obviously a calling here for us as individual members and for the congregation as a whole. The Lord Jesus told us to be a light on a candlestick and a city on a hill, to which people around us can and will come.

But we see *mission* as the preaching of the Gospel by ordained missionaries in places where there is no church of Christ, where people have never heard of His glory. Mission implies going out, far and wide, to distant lands and isles, moving on whenever a church has been established, so that the Word of Christ may come to the ends (the farthest corners) of the earth.

I do not want to make it sound romantic, but typical mission work takes place on the frontiers where the pioneers are, where new trails are blazed. Wherever people are found and cultures are discovered, there the Gospel must be preached. Mission seeks the outlying areas, and focuses on nations where the Gospel is not really known.

IN THE WHOLE WORLD

We must have an eye for the catholic nature of the mission mandate. Preaching the Gospel throughout the world is a prime calling of the church. It was, of course, a command first directed to the apostles. They had to struggle with the fact that the Gospel was not only for the Jew but also for the Greek. When they realized this, they went out far and wide indeed.

"The whole world" was for them the then known world of the Roman empire. Paul went from Jerusalem to Rome, to the heart of the empire. So he can write at a certain moment (to the Colossians): in the whole world [the Gospel] is bearing fruit and growing (1:6). Indeed, how quickly, how far did the Gospel spread in those early apostolic years.

But this command was given also to the entire New Testament Church. The apostles covered a lot of territory, but they couldn't cover the whole earth. Whenever new territories are discovered and new peoples found, the Gospel must go to them. It is not without divine providence that the Gospel was first preached in Europe, for it was from this continent that the discovery of and the voyages to the new world were made, and in the wake of the explorers came the preachers.

We must understand that we do not have things in our hands. In the Canons of Dort we confess that God sends preachers to whom He will and when He will. It is God who opens doors and who determines times and opportunities. We must be diligent and patient. We must do what He commands and wait for His blessing, also when we are disappointed. We must adapt and change when necessary, but we may never surrender the task. For it is not our Gospel, but His; not our glory but Christ's.

Christ says to His disciples: now it is the time to go out. In an ever-expanding circle, covering more ground all the time, so that my salvation reaches the ends of the earth. Now that I have risen from the dead the Gospel must go from Israel to the Gentiles, from Jerusalem to the farthest land. And although the disciples had to get used to this catholicity they did go, often despite themselves, and the church still today sees it as a prime task to equip and send missionaries abroad. We have a part in that task, and we must see it as both a great privilege and a serious calling, one that may not be neglected, despite the costs and the sacrifices. The Gospel must be preached everywhere with serious intent.

A CRISIS

This preaching brings about a great crisis, a great decision. The Lord Jesus makes no bones about the intent of the preaching: "He who believes and is baptized, will be saved; but he who does not believe will be condemned" (verse 16).

The preaching is first of all a bringing of "glad tidings." The mandate is: preach the Gospel, and Gospel means: the good message. Missionaries are not prophets of gloom and doom who come to tell the natives that the sky is falling in. It is a message of joy and therefore the content and tone must be jubilant. Let this be very clear. On the home front and on the mission field preaching is always a bringing of glad tidings.

At the same time, the preaching places people before a decision with eternal consequences: believe and be saved; do not believe and be condemned! There is no in-between stage, no neutral area; it is always one or the other. The preaching separates grain from chaff, sifts tares from wheat. Wherever the Word is heard, the great decision falls: heaven or hell, eternal life or eternal death.

WITH EARNEST INTENT

We must understand that whenever the Gospel is preached, it is preached with earnest intent. That is, God really means it. Christ is really "offered by the Gospel," the Canons of Dort say. In the preaching the saving grace of the Lord Jesus Christ is truly offered. Those who believe, will be saved. This is without any doubt. Those who do not believe, will be condemned, as sure as day is light and night is dark.

Those who believe will be saved. That is the first intent of the preaching of the Gospel. The missionaries are to make known that God does not desire the death of the sinner, but rather that he repents and lives. God desires that those who hear be saved by faith in Christ. This is His express command to all who hear: repent, believe, and be saved. It is the authoritative declaration of the risen Christ. Therefore it is also the express responsibility of all who hear: they must respond in faith! God does not give people a free choice, but He says (Psalm 2): Now kiss the Son, lest He in fury scorn you, lest in His wrath the LORD cause you to perish!

A GENERAL OFFER OF GRACE?

May we therefore say that in the preaching of the Gospel there is a general offer of grace? Perhaps some readers remember that this was a point of dispute with the Protestant Reformed Churches in the fifties, and continues to be a point of dispute today. They said: we cannot speak of a general offer of grace; that is Arminian. And they did not hesitate to calls us crypto-Arminians. They said: if you speak of a general offer of grace, you make salvation subject to the free choice of man.

We are aware of that danger. A "general offer" does not mean that all people come to faith. Still we must maintain that when God causes the Gospel to be preached, it comes with a earnest promise and a command to all who hear. There is a real promise and a real command. This is how we confess it in the Canons of Dort, "But as many as are called by the Gospel are earnestly called, for God earnestly and most sincerely reveals in His Word what is most pleasing to Him, namely that those who are called should come to Him. He also promises rest of soul and eternal life to all who come to Him and believe" (Chapter III/IV, Article 8).

The preaching of the Gospel is earnest and sincere. People who hear the Word, who believe it, and apply it to their lives, will have peace with God. In this sense the Gospel applies in the same way to all who hear it. The reactions to the preaching, however, differ greatly. Some believe, some do not believe. Indeed, the natural reaction is to reject the Gospel. And many will reject it from the start. Were it not for God's sovereign grace, no one would come to faith. And whoever does come to faith will confess this as an act of God's great and unmerited mercy.

We do not know how people will respond and who will believe or not. But that is God's business. Our business is to preach indiscriminately to all wherever and whenever we can and so put forward the earnest intent of the Gospel.

FAITH AND BAPTISM

Believe and be baptized. It says: all who believe and are baptized will be saved. Wherever the Gospel is preached and people come to faith, baptism follows as sign and seal of God's promises. Baptism is the special mark and distinguishing feature by which God confirms that we are His children. By baptism we are separated from the world and ingrafted into the Christian Church. Therefore the Church must preach and baptize. And in Matthew the Lord adds: teaching them to observe all that I have commanded. This refers to church discipline. Preaching, sacraments and discipline, the marks of the true Church apply, as we saw earlier, also on the mission field.

Now here we must be careful. Christ does not say here that only adults may be baptized. Perhaps you know that some people insist, on the basis of this text, that faith always comes before baptism, and that since infants cannot believe, they may not be baptized, see Mark 16: 16. It doesn't say this here, however.

Indeed, faith precedes baptism. There is no adult who is baptized without showing repentance of sin and making profession of faith. There is a connection between faith and baptism. For we are justified by faith, and that is signed and sealed by Holy Baptism.

AND TO YOUR CHILDREN

But the Scriptures also teach that the promise of salvation is given to believers and their children. To you is the promise, said Peter on Pentecost, and to your children. Therefore the children, as members of Christ's Church and as belonging to the covenant in Christ's blood, shall be baptized. That too is clear in the teaching of Christ. The children of the true people of Israel are heirs of the covenant, heirs of the Kingdom.

Therefore believers are baptized with their household, as we read in the Bible. This is done also today, on the mission field and on the home front. And when those who are baptized grow up – being nurtured in the Christian faith – they have to duty to confess their Lord and Saviour.

THE SERIOUS WARNING

So people everywhere are set apart from this world and grafted into the body of Christ. But the warning remains: whoever does not believe, will be condemned. And the word means: utterly condemned. Elsewhere the Bible says: those who do not believe, are condemned already. The Canons of Dort state very clearly that the wrath of God remains upon those who do not believe the Gospel. We are all by nature children of wrath, subject to all kinds of misery, yes condemnation itself. But God lifts His wrath from those who believe in Christ, and He will definitely acquit them on the day of judgment.

The hearts of people, their deepest motives and intentions, will be made known. And so, in the gathering of the Church out of all places and lands, Christ's glory will become manifest. The power of His resurrection will be apparent: small church, few workers, eleven apostles and those who come after them, but a great harvest, a mighty multitude.

We today are still called to work with Christ in presenting the earnest call of the Gospel wherever we can, at home and abroad, so that it may be true of us what was already confessed in Israel: declare His glory to the nations, make known to all their populations His marvellous works! (Psalm 96:2).

Now is the time to call the world to repentance and faith. Now is the time for mission, far and near. Soon it will be the time for judgment. Now is the time for sowing. Soon it will be time for harvest. If the church loses its evangelical zeal and forgets its missionary calling, it destroys its reason for being, cuts out the heart of its mandate, and becomes a dead body. But the church that lives by the Gospel, under the blessing of the risen Christ, will always seek to pass that Gospel on to others.

The Ascension of Jesus Christ

Ascension

The Promise of the Baptism with the Holy Spirit

"for John baptized with water, but before many days you shall be baptized with the Holy Spirit".

(Acts 1: 5)

During the forty days that our Lord was still on earth after His resurrection and before His ascension, He spoke to His disciples about many things. For example, He opened to them the Scriptures, so that they would understand the reasons for His suffering, death, and resurrection. He also spoke to them about the kingdom of heaven, what it meant and how it would come.

During these same days, as we can find in this passage, He prepared them for the day of Pentecost, the outpouring of the Holy Spirit. He did this already on the first day of His resurrection, when He breathed on them and said, "Receive the Holy Spirit," and we find the same element again in our text: "before many days you shall be baptized with the Holy Spirit." Before we deal with the ascension itself, it is important to reflect on Christ's teaching which preceded the ascension.

Our Lord refers to what John the Baptist had said some years before, "I have baptized you with water, but He will baptize you with the Holy Spirit" (Mark 1: 8).

It is quite clear that in these texts the baptism with the Holy Spirit is in a sense contrasted with the baptism with water. The question is: how are we to understand this contrast? And also, how are the two, the baptism with water and the baptism with the Holy Spirit, related?

This is an important issue today, especially in our discussions with assorted Pentecostal groups, but also generally with charismatic Baptist movements. What is this "baptism with the Holy Spirit"?

WATER VERSUS SPIRIT?

When you contrast these two very strongly, as Pentecostal groups are inclined to do, you get this kind of approach: the baptism with water (or "water-baptism") is only an outward and formal happening which doesn't mean very much. It is called "the first blessing," but it is really of a lower order. The baptism with the Holy Spirit (or "Spirit-baptism") is the real thing, the inward evidence of being a child of God. It is called "the second blessing", and it is of a much higher order.

Therefore, Pentecostals will ask you: have you been baptized with the Holy Spirit? And they mean: have you consciously experienced the descending of the Holy Spirit into your heart, an experience accompanied by various spiritual manifestations like speaking in tongues and seeing visions? If you say "no," you are considered to be a Christian of inferior rank, if you are a Christian at all! For the water-baptism cannot measure up to the Spirit-baptism. And you will understand, in this scheme of thinking baptizing an infant really has little or no meaning at all. Pentecostals will also make it a condition for attending the Lord's Supper whether or not you have you received Spirit-baptism.

So Spirit-baptism becomes the end and purpose of religious experience. And when we are confronted with this kind of reasoning, we are not always properly equipped to deal with it. Sometimes some of our people, who perhaps are not too happy in the church or with their own lives, meet Pentecostal people, who seem so bubbly in faith and are so vocal about Jesus. They then learn that they must undergo

"Spirit-baptism," something which the established church represses. So they suddenly find "the missing ingredient" and are won over to the Pentecostal way. They may tell you later that they've found the missing link. The church only baptized with water, but now they have been baptized with the Holy Spirit.

Is this how we must understand the words of the Lord Jesus Christ, and contrast the two? What is the meaning of this expression "being baptized with the Holy Spirit"?

PREPARATION FOR PENTECOST

The expression "Spirit-baptism" may have become a common dogmatical term through the theology of the Pentecostal movement, but is that term understood properly within its context or is it isolated from its context, and given a meaning which it originally did not have? This is an important question for all of us.

What do we see the Lord Jesus doing here in this text? Well, He is preparing His disciples for the day of Pentecost. He does not say in general: you must be baptized with the Holy Spirit, but He says: before many days – and that means very soon and at a *specific* time – you *shall* be baptized with the Holy Spirit. And then follows in Acts 2 the day on which Christ's promise of baptism with the Holy Spirit is fulfilled.

So from a *particular promise*, directed to specific people, at a given time, we should not make an unspecified *general command*, directed to all people, all the time. At least, we should not do it in the sense in which the Pentecostal theologians like to do it. The context simply does not allow it. It's like lifting a text, or rather a phrase, out of the Bible "you shall be baptized with the Holy Spirit," turning that promise into a question (have you been baptized with the Holy Spirit?), pasting it on the wall, and conveniently forgetting the setting in which it belongs. Such texts start to lead a life of their own, and no longer function in a responsible Scriptural sense.

COMMAND OR PROMISE?

The Lord Jesus in our text does not give a command (you must be baptized with the Holy Spirit) but He repeats a promise: in a few days you shall be baptized with the Holy Spirit. And that promise was indeed fulfilled on the day, the exact and precise day, of Pentecost. This must be our starting-point when we try to understand these words.

Now the question may legitimately be asked whether this promise of being baptized with the Holy Spirit is in the Bible restricted to a one-time event at Pentecost, or whether this kind of baptism also takes place today. If we try to explain the issue in this manner then we do not isolate the text *from* the Bible, but we are examining it within the various contexts wherein it appears *in* the Bible.

Then you should note that the expression "being baptized with the Holy Spirit" is used in the Bible only – as also here in Acts 1 – in five specific passages, and in each one the significance of John the Baptist and Jesus Christ is compared and contrasted. The other five are: Matthew 3: 11, Mark 1:8, Luke 3: 16, John 1:33, and Acts 11: 16.

There are many other texts which speak about the work of the Holy Spirit and how we are to receive Him, but the expression "*baptism* with the Holy Spirit" is used only in those six passages. And here indeed a contrast is being made between the work of John the Baptist and of Jesus Christ. And the inference in each text is the same: that the work of Jesus Christ is greater than that of John the Baptist, because He builds on and completes the work of John. Jesus does what John the Baptist could not do: He has cleansed His church by His blood and has poured out over His church the Holy Spirit.

THE TIME IS NEAR

With this understanding we go to the text in Acts 1. In verse 4 we read that Jesus tells His disciples to stay in Jerusalem, and to wait there for the promise of the Father, which, He said, "you heard from Me." Christ had spoken to His disciples before about the coming of the Holy Spirit. He had done so in the prophecies of old, think of Joel 2. John the Baptist had spoken of the fulfillment of this promise in his preaching at the Jordan. Christ again spoke of the coming Holy Spirit just before His death, at the Lord's Supper, when He promised His disciples the Comforter, the Counsellor (John 14-16). He did so again immediately after His resurrection, when He appeared to them (John 20:22).

So the promise of the coming of the Holy Spirit had been clearly given and had been amply repeated. Now the time had come for this promise to be fulfilled. Stay in Jerusalem, says the Lord, for the time is drawing near.

And then comes the reference in our text to John the Baptist: "for John baptized with water, but before many days you shall be baptized with the Holy Spirit." Now comes the moment about which John the Baptist spoke in his day: the baptism with the Holy Spirit. The Lord does not so much contrast water-baptism with Spirit-baptism as He points out the great progress which has been made since John the Baptist, namely the death and resurrection of Christ. Christ can do what John could not do, namely, grant in fullness the renewing power of the Holy Spirit.

What was the meaning of the water baptism administered by John the Baptist? We read in Mark 1: 4 that it was "the baptism of repentance for the forgiveness of sins." John the Baptist announced the coming of the Messiah, and called Israel to repent, and so to prepare for the Messiah. They had to repent in order to be washed from their sins through the work of the coming Messiah. And only when they were thus washed, as signified in water-baptism, by the blood of the Lamb of God, would they receive the baptism with the Holy Spirit, that is, the renewal through the Spirit of God. In this way, through the redeeming and renewing work of Jesus Christ, they would be saved from the wrath to come.

JOHN AND JESUS

Now John could only proclaim the necessity of, and preach the promise of, redemption and renewal, as signified in the baptism with water. Only Jesus would *bring about* that redemption and renewal. John had already admitted this when he said, "After me comes He who is mightier than I. . . ." I am only a herald who proclaims and promises, but He is coming who will bring it all about. When He comes, He will cleanse you with His own blood, and He will renew you through the power of His Spirit. Yes, said John, I have baptized you with water – and water is a clear sign and a sure seal – but after me comes He who will, by baptizing you with the Holy Spirit, give you the matter that is signified and sealed in my baptism with water.

Therefore, now that Christ has shed His blood on Golgotha, He also may announce the day that His Spirit will be poured out. For the outpouring of the blood has opened the way for the outpouring of the Spirit.

So the expression "being baptized with the Holy Spirit," understood in its precise biblical context, specifically denotes the promised event that occurred on the day of Pentecost, an event and a day that cannot and need not be repeated.

REPEATED?

Now someone will say: but this "baptism with the Holy Spirit" *was* repeated, in Acts 11, where we read about Peter's account of the Holy Spirit falling upon the gentile believers in Cornelius' house. As you remember, Peter went to the house of Cornelius, a Roman centurion, and preached the word there, and as he was speaking the Holy Spirit fell upon all who heard, and they spoke in tongues, and then Peter says, "Can anyone forbid water for baptizing these people who have received the Holy Spirit, just as we have?"

And when Peter must later explain his actions to his fellow apostles in Jerusalem – that he allowed Gentiles to be baptized with water – he explains it with a reference to the manifestation of the Spirit (11: 16), "And I remembered the word of the Lord how He said, John baptized with water, but you shall be baptized with the Holy Spirit." Peter is saying: how could I refuse these converted heathen the baptism with water, when they clearly received the baptism with the Holy Spirit! If they received the greater gift (the Spirit), how could I refuse the lesser sign (the water)?

Does this passage in Acts 11 demonstrate that the baptism with the Holy Spirit was not a one-time event at Pentecost, but can be repeated, in any event was repeated, and therefore could possibly be repeated today? No, it doesn't. For again, we must consider the context. What happened in the house of Cornelius is a very specific, ground-breaking event, namely the beginning of the inclusion of the Gentiles into the Christian Church. The apostles had not (yet) ventured into preaching the Gospel to non-Jews, to the uncircumcised. This would prove to be a major step, not without controversy. Peter himself had to be prepared for it by a special vision, the one of the sheet with the unclean animals, to learn that what God has declared clean or cleansed (think again of washing and baptism) Peter may not call "common" or unclean. Three times this vision occurred, and then three men stood at Peter's door, asking him to come to the house of Cornelius, a Gentile.

CONFIRMED

Peter understood the vision, for he says to Cornelius (10:34): "Truly, I perceive that God shows no partiality." And when he then preaches the Gospel to these Gentiles, the Holy Spirit falls upon them, and they begin to show the gifts of the Spirit. Notice how here "Spirit-baptism" even precedes "water-baptism," if I may use those terms, to demonstrate that this is indeed a new initiative of God.

And when Peter later is called to account by the Jewish Christians in Jerusalem (note how it says in 11: 2 that he was criticized by the circumcision party), he refers to what happened at Pentecost. Peter says: I know that this is a new development, but, brothers, it was just like what happened at Pentecost. Remember how the Lord Himself promised that we would be "baptized with the Holy Spirit"? The same thing happened to the Gentiles, and how could I then refuse them the baptism with water? Peter says: God gave the same gift to them as He gave to us, when we believed in the Lord Jesus Christ.

The point here is not that Pentecost is repeated, but that it is mightily confirmed! The effect of Pentecost is extended, according to the prophesies of old, also to non-Jewish believers. They, too, may share visibly in the gifts of the Holy Spirit, and therefore they have the right to the sacrament of baptism as well.

So Acts 11 does not tell is that this "baptism with the holy Spirit" is constantly repeated. It tells us that at this pivotal point in the history of the New Testament Church, namely the beginning of the mission to the heathens, the church is reminded of the great promise of Christ. That promise, fulfilled at Pentecost, is that all who believe in Him will share in the gifts of the Spirit and belong to that Church over which the Spirit was poured out at Pentecost.

A NEW SITUATION

So we must conclude that the term "being baptized with the Holy Spirit" refers to the event that took place at Pentecost, and also that a new situation has come about, the indwelling of the Holy Spirit in the church and in the believers. It is a reality in which the entire Christian Church of the latter days may share: the gifts of the Holy Spirit are for all, Jew and Gentile, who believe in the Lord Jesus Christ. There are two phases, Acts 2 and Acts 10, the mission to the Jews and the mission to the Gentiles, and both find their root in that one baptism with the Holy Spirit on the day of Pentecost.

When you look at it this way, you leave those texts within their biblical setting and you explain Scripture with Scripture. Then we also understand that we today do not require a special "baptism with the Holy Spirit." Nowhere in the New Testament do you read of this requirement in these terms.

We do read everywhere that we must constantly draw on that great spiritual gift of the outpouring which took place that day! The Spirit came to the Church to stay there, to work there, in all the members, and we must now live through and in the Spirit, who has come. Pentecost means the indwelling of the Spirit, and that is the new element of Acts 2, confirmed in Acts 11. That is the repeated emphasis of New Testament teaching. Do not repeat Pentecost, but draw on that great reality, every day, all your life. As the Holy Spirit is given to the Church, so He is given to all members, to each individually, and we may all, together and as individuals, live by that Spirit, whom Christ gave to His Church on that day as a fruit of His work of atonement and resurrection.

NO FALSE DILEMMA

Therefore we do not make any false dilemma between "water-baptism" and "Spirit-baptism," as if water-baptism is relatively unimportant. For the one is inseparably connected to the other! It is remarkable that the Lord Jesus did not abolish the baptism with water in favour of the baptism with the Holy Spirit. In the line of Pentecostal thinking, He should have said: water-baptism belongs to the time of John the Baptist, but we're past that stage now, only Spirit-baptism is important today! No, He said, "Go therefore, and make disciples of all nations, baptizing them in the Name of the Father, the Son, and the Holy Spirit." The reality is now Pentecost, the indwelling of the Holy Spirit, the sign is still Holy Baptism, the baptism with water.

And the baptism with water is not of a "lesser" order at all. For what do we confess with respect to this baptism and the Holy Spirit? The Form for Baptism says it clearly: when we are baptized into the Name of the Holy Spirit, God the Holy Spirit assures us by this sacrament that He will dwell in us, and make us living members of Christ, imparting to us what we have in Christ, namely the cleansing of our sins and the daily renewal of our lives, till we shall finally be presented without blemish in the assembly of God's elect in life eternal.

THE LASTING INDWELLING OF THE HOLY SPIRIT

The water of baptism still – even more clearly now than in John's days – speaks to us of the indwelling of the Holy Spirit, in which we share with all God's covenant children. And as we must come to live out of our baptism, so we must come to live through the Spirit! It's not a "second" blessing, it is all part of that one blessing which we have in the salvation in Christ Jesus.

Pentecost – described as the baptism with the Holy Spirit – was a one-time event. I will return to this point later, when dealing with Acts 2. But we note already now that its power and effects are received and felt by every generation anew. Once baptized, the church will feel it always. While the outpouring of the Spirit took place on one historic day, the omnipotent and unrestricted presence and power of the Spirit are felt by us every day. So we can speak indeed – with

Scripture – also today of being filled by the Spirit, guided by the Spirit, comforted by the Spirit, walking in the Spirit. As long as we do not isolate this from the saving work of Christ and elevate it to something "extra," an added requirement for salvation, we are on solid biblical ground.

If we have to accede any point to Pentecostal theology, it may be this: that we must learn, not to repeat Pentecost and its miraculous signs, even though acknowledging that the Spirit is able to do so, but to live more out of the blessed reality of Pentecost, signified also to us in our baptism, that the Spirit is here with us, to stay. That He "dwells within our hearts" (Hymn 36) and that we may yield to Him, learn from Him, receive from Him, day by day, gifts unimagined and inexpressible. The outpouring, as historical event, is not repeated, but "the life-giving Spirit," obtained for us by Christ, as the Form for the Lord's Supper so beautifully says, does certainly impart to us day by day what we have in Christ.

In that sense we should not restrict the word "outpouring" to a one-time event,for the Spirit constantly pours out over us the gifts of Christ. The more we see this, the more we may live in it and reflect it in our lives.

The baptism with water today signifies to us and our children that we through faith in Christ are connected to Him as members of His body, and *therefore* also receive the gifts of the Holy Spirit so that our faith is made fruitful and productive. For these gifts we may pray and with these gifts we are filled and must work to the glory of God and the edification of our neighbour.

In that sense, we are with the church "baptized with the Holy Spirit," immersed in Him, and overflowing through Him. This is part of what we have in Christ Jesus, our Lord, so that we can sing, in the fullest sense of the word,

> Blest be the LORD, who on our way
> Provides for us, and day by day
> Upholds us by His power (Psalm 68: 8)

The Great Task after Christ's Ascension

"So when they had come together, they asked Him: Lord, will you at this time restore the kingdom to Israel? He said to them: it is not for you to know times or seasons which the Father has fixed by His own authority. But you shall receive power, when the Holy Spirit has come upon you; and you shall be my witnesses in Jerusalem, and in all Judea and Samaria and to the end of the earth".

(Acts 1: 6-8)

In the next chapter we will look more closely at the biblical account of Christ's ascension. We will see how the Gospel concerning the ascension shows us Christ going on with His work. Before we move on to that event, I want to pay some attention to Christ's last words on earth, spoken shortly before He ascended.

Do "last words" have a special meaning? Often when someone we love has left for a long time or permanently, and also when someone has been taken from us through death, we try to remember the last words that were spoken to us by this person. Someone coined the phrase: famous last words. The last words of many important people have been meticulously recorded.

But often "last words" do not mean very much. Believe me, it's not so important what you say when you leave; it is more important how you communicate when you are still together. In the case of our text, however, the "last words" of the Lord Jesus Christ are of great significance, not just for the disciples, but for the entire church of the latter days.

For in these last recorded words, the Lord Jesus gives a mild rebuke and also a mighty mandate. He tells us very clearly what we should and should not be busy with until He comes again. We therefore have a proper orientation, direction, and purpose in life. Our theme is: the Lord Jesus directs His disciples to their great task in the time after His ascension. While they ask about the definite end, He speaks about the decisive beginning.

A QUESTION AND A RESPONSE

You have noticed, of course, that Christ's last words are in fact a response to a question asked by the disciples. I do not want to get into all the exegetical detail surrounding the time and the tone of that question, for that would take up too much of our time, but I do want to analyze the question briefly with you, so that we can better appreciate the Lord's answer.

The disciples ask Jesus, "Lord, will you at this time restore the kingdom to Israel?" There are explainers who suggest that this was a wrong question, which shows an impatient and worldly outlook. The disciples were not be prepared, they say, to wait and work until it pleased Christ to return. Some even suggest that this question was actually a rejection of Christ's teaching about His impending ascension and the intermediate time. But I do not think that we have to draw such conclusions.

It is really a very logical question. Luke tells us in Acts 1:3 that Christ during the forty days in which He appeared to the disciples was "speaking to them of the kingdom of God." The "kingdom of God" was Christ's main topic of instruction and discussion during the time between resurrection and ascension. What a glorious topic!

What does it mean that Christ spoke to His disciples about the kingdom of God? It is the very same theme which Christ preached at the beginning of His ministry on earth. It was already the theme of the preaching of John the Baptist, who said, "Repent, for the kingdom of heaven is at hand" (Matthew 3:2). And of the Lord

Jesus, Matthew writes (4:17), "From that time (namely after John's arrest) Jesus began to preach saying, 'Repent for the kingdom of heaven is at hand'." The Lord simply took up the early theme of John the Baptist about the kingdom of heaven.

And how many times, for example in the parables, did the Lord Jesus not elaborate on the theme of the kingdom? It is no wonder, then, that after His resurrection the same "kingdom" teaching plays a key role in His instruction, and that the disciples ask a question about it. This kingdom, which continues without end, when will it come in fullness?

THE BREAKTHROUGH OF THE KINGDOM

Christ will have explained clearly to His disciples that the kingdom of God had its decisive breakthrough and victory in His own death and resurrection. The kingdom of God was eternally secure on the foundation of Golgotha, where the devil was defeated, where the atonement was made. The kingdom of God, the kingdom of the life and the resurrection, would never be defeated; instead it would grow and be victorious everywhere.

Jesus spoke to His disciples about how they could live again as servants, yes as children of God, in His kingdom, protected by Him always, to His glory and praise. Certainly, He will have told them also that the kingdom had not yet come in fullness or perfection. It was and is still: Thy kingdom come! Much still had to be "restored" (to use the words of our text), but the final reality would be that the kingdom of God would be perfected.

And that is where the question, the difficulty of the disciples comes in. It is not that they doubted the restoration of the kingdom. On the contrary, they had seen so much that they fully believed it. They did not ask, as many people do today, "Will the kingdom be restored?" Many people today say or think that the kingdom of God, with its promises of joy and peace, is a hoax, because life is only what you make of it. But the disciples are filled with the idea of the kingdom of God! Except, they ask: will you *at this time* restore the kingdom to Israel?

I'll leave those words "to Israel" out for a moment and concentrate on "at this time." For there lies, also in view of Christ's answer, the weight of the question. Thy kingdom come, yes, Lord, that's fine, but will you restore it at this time, now?

AT THIS TIME?

At this time, they say. That means: in our time, during our life time. The disciples know that the history of the world is going to a specific end. They ask about that end. Will it come about in their days? Will they see not just the beginning of that process but also its progression and conclusion? Jesus, will we in our life experience and witness the end of the ages, the coming in glory of the Holy One of God? Will we see the completion of the work to which you have called us as your disciples? Will we, who have stood at the beginning, witness the unfolding and the ending of the coming of the kingdom?

It is not unbelief which is expressed in this question. It is not mere curiosity, either. There is a certain longing, a yearning for the swift restoration of the kingdom of God. The disciples already had been through so much with the Lord, will they now also see the restoration of the kingdom? Therefore: how long yet, Lord? When will the final curtain fall on the ever-unfolding drama of history in which also our personal lives are taken up?

A GENTLE REBUKE

It is a question which must be properly appreciated. Sometimes we, too, say: Lord, is the end near? Is it not enough now? Sometimes, when great calamities befall us and God's people, we can yearn for the restoration of all things, the perfection of the kingdom of God. It is unfortunate that often adversity must bring us to experience and express this longing, but that is how it goes. And it is then important to know that our Lord Jesus Christ *understands* this yearning.

Christ's response to the question is in a sense a rebuke, a reprimand. But notice that it is a gentle rebuke, for Jesus understands the deep feelings in and behind our probing questions. But although gentle, the answer is also very clear and resolute, "It is not for you to know the times and seasons which the Father has fixed by His own authority." To paraphrase that simply, the Lord says: it is none of your business; leave that to the Father in heaven.

Literally it says: it is not *of you,* it does not belong to your realm. You have no say in that matter whatsoever. It is even so that the times and seasons do not belong to the *revelation* of God. Whatever God has revealed in His good pleasure – and He has revealed much – He has not made known to us the times and seasons.

Not that the times and seasons haven't been set. They have been.Christ does not want us to think that there is no time-limit. For the duration has been determined up to the day, the hour, and the minute. The Lord says that the times and seasons have been set by the Father's own authority. God in His sovereign decree, as the supreme authority, has *fixed* the times, that is, He has set them unchangeably.

Notice also how the Lord Jesus here speaks about times and seasons. The words essentially denote the same thing: the period between Christ's ascension and return. Yet there is a subtle variance in meaning. *Times* denotes the various periods of time, the total length, the duration. *Seasons* denotes more the developments during that time, the events in their sequence and relation, the situations and opportunities.

This is important. The Father has not just determined the duration of the time between ascension and return, but also what will happen in that time. He grants the opportunities and governs the situations. There will be times of prosperity and progress for the church, of much opportunity. There will also be times of adversity for the church, of much disappointment. But no events, whether in church history or in our personal lives, fall outside the authority of the Father.

NOT FOR US TO KNOW

It is not for us to know the times and seasons. This is a truth by which we must live. We like to know exactly what time it is. We want to be able to predict what opportunities might come our way. Yes, we'd even like to know how close we are to the return of the Lord. But all this has not been revealed to us.And any speculation on this is not only doomed to fail but is an outright insult to the Father.

You know that even Christ did not presume to have that knowledge. There is a well-known text in Mark 13: 32, where the Lord Jesus says that of that day no one knows, not even the angels, nor the Son, but only the Father. Nor the Son! Many explainers have struggled with those words, but Christ simply says that even He, in His capacity as Mediator, having come in the flesh and humbled Himself for our sake, does not presume to know of the day.We see here something of the great humility of the Son, who bides the Father's time and the Father's hour. If Christ showed such humility in leaving the times and seasons to the Father, how much more humility should we show in this respect?

It lies in the Father's own authority, it says. "Own" in the sense of unique and special, belonging only to God. No one else has this sovereignty. We have to learn never to argue with God about times and seasons, whether they be in our estimation too early or too late, for God alone has fixed these. And everything He does is always right on time, right on schedule, leading to the final trumpet and the appearing of the Son of man.

DO NOT WASTE TIME

It's not for us to know the times and seasons. Why not? So that we will make the most of the time that we do receive by God's grace and providence, and not waste one day. So that every single day we will walk by faith alone. So that we do not make our own little schedules and times which neatly interact and even compete with God's sovereign schedule, but live by faith, always. So that we trust in Him alone, in whose hands lies all time, also our times, up to the last second of the history of this world.

Whenever you know exactly how much time is left, it is tempting to misuse it. Instead of worrying about the time, we must concentrate on using the time well, and fulfilling our task as long as God grants the seasons. We who do not know the duration of the time must see to the proper usage of the time. And that is where the Lord directs His disciples and us. Not: how long yet? but: we will work, Lord, as long as you give the times and seasons, and when you return, you will find us faithfully labouring in your vineyard.

FOCUS ON YOUR TASK

I want to make a few remarks yet about verse 8. Notice the contrast, "*But* you shall receive power when the Holy Spirit has come upon you; and you shall be my witnesses in Jerusalem, and in all Judea, and Samaria, and to the end of the earth."

The "times and seasons" are not your business, but I will tell you what you must fully realize: your task, your business. Do not ask me about the definite end, for we stand only at the decisive beginning. Indeed, it's not over, it has only just begun!

I refer you back now to the words mentioned earlier: will you restore the kingdom *to Israel?* The disciples obviously still had a rather limited view of the extent of the kingdom and the kingdom-work. They saw it primarily – if not exclusively – as a matter of Israel, of the Jews. Their vision was restricted to the land and people of Israel. At least, from Christ's answer we notice a very clear broadening of the circle: Jerusalem, yes, Judea, but also Samaria, and even the end of the earth!

The disciples are given a tremendous mandate: preach the Gospel to all creation, first to the Jews, but also to the Greeks, the Romans, yes, wherever people live, let the message of the Lord be heard, let the facts of salvation be proclaimed.

BEYOND ISRAEL

What a contrast. "In our time?" How will the disciples ever in one life-time be able to reach the ends of the earth? Restore the kingdom to Israel? No, extend the kingdom to the ends of the earth! For this, time will be needed, and it will be given by God. Opportunities will be created. Don't think the end is near, for the task is still too great. Concentrate on your task.

The disciples could never do this monumental work on their own. They would not be able to witness in Jerusalem, let alone to the ends of the earth. But Christ promises them for this monumental task also the accompanying and enabling power of the Holy Spirit. "You will receive power," it says, and this word means the ability to do what is asked. Jesus asks nothing of us except what He also enables us to do. He does not hand out impossible mandates. Difficult tasks, yes, but not impossible ones. You will receive power, clearly not from yourselves, but from above, from Me, "when the Holy Spirit has come upon you." So that you can go and do what I command, and a decisive beginning can be made with this great task that will affect all creation, every tongue, tribe, and nation.

Don't ask about the end, but see what opportunities I will give from the beginning, from Pentecost on, until the Gospel has been preached throughout the world.

The Lord Jesus fulfilled this promise. He gave power to these simple men to begin this monumental task. These people did things they never dreamt of before. They were enabled to stand up to kings and princes, to soldiers and emperors. They travelled far and wide, and they spoke as witnesses of what they had seen and heard in Christ. They did not worry about the times and seasons, for they were too involved with their work. They did not look at the clock, for they saw fields that were ripe for the harvest. As any farmer will tell you, when you have to bring in a harvest, you have no time to look at the clock. The exact time is unimportant when there is so much to do, every day.

OUR FIRST CONCERN

Now the question may be asked: does this mandate, given to the disciples, count for the whole church of the latter days, for us today? We cannot be, as the disciples were, eye-witnesses. The office of the apostles was unique. It must also be said that we are not all called to be ministers and missionaries. But it is still true for all of us that our foremost concern must be the proclamation of the apostolic doctrine, which is, salvation in Jesus Christ and Him crucified. We must see to it today that this work continues, with our prayers and gifts. We must "witness," that is "testify" of Christ in our daily life, through our walk and talk. That is why we are here on this earth: to live and work for the coming of the kingdom of God, about which Christ gave us such wonderful promises.

That must be the focus of our daily work, no matter what our vocation is. In this respect, I refer you briefly to what we read in II Thessalonians. Some of the Thessalonians had come to believe that the return of Christ was imminent. They started to look at the clock. You know what happened? Some gave up their jobs and ceased their normal routine. I mean, why bother and work when Jesus can return any day? What sense is this life when the new life is about to begin?

Paul admonished the Thessalonians in the same way that Christ gently rebuked the disciples. Paul also stressed: much must happen before Christ returns, for example, the coming of the man of lawlessness! In any case, we must never cease our daily work because we are looking at the clock. As far as the times and seasons are concerned (I Thessalonians 5: 1), the Thessalonians should know that this is God's realm. They are to continue their work. Paul strongly emphasizes this: if anyone will not work, he will not eat. And he exhorts all people living in idleness: do your work in quietness and earn your own living, and do not be weary in well-doing.

DO NOT BE WEARY

Do not be weary, says Paul, in well-doing. Sometimes the burdens of life, also the life of Christians, can be utterly wearisome. Why not just quit, and wait for Christ to return? What sense do this life and all our efforts have, also in view of all the trials? Well, you may pray, "Come, Lord Jesus," for the Bride and the Spirit say "Come," but at the same time you must continue your life and your work, for the glory of God and the benefit of your neighbour. Just go about your business, quietly, faithfully.

Intense and wrong expectations can be very paralyzing. False expectations can lead to idleness. But we are exhorted in the Lord Jesus Christ to live our lives faithfully, as God's children, to do our work, and to leave the times and seasons in His hands.

Christ is coming. I hope He will come today so that we may be united with all the saints who have preceded us. But until He comes, as long as we are here, until He relieves us of our earthly task, despite all the weariness which sometimes comes over us, we shall each one of us continue to work for the coming of the kingdom. We shall do so not in our own strength, but empowered by the Holy Spirit we shall continue to glorify God in our lives from day to day, each in our place. Our vision will be far and wide: the Moor, with the Philistine and the Tyrian, on the roll of nations He will count all these as born on Zion's holy mount, in many tongues, one God, one faith confessing (Psalm 87). Yes, keep your vision far and wide for the day when the decisive beginning of Ascension and Pentecost becomes the definite end of the history of this world. Then will the eternal marriage feast of the Lamb begin.

For, Lord, when Thou again in glory on the clouds of heaven shalt shine, we Thy flock shall stand before Thee. And until then, you will find us working, so busy with our task that the times passes quickly. And before we know it, Jesus has come.

Christ's Last Earthly Ministry to His Church

"Then He led them out as far as Bethany, and lifting up His hands, He blessed them. While He blessed them, He parted from them, and was carried up into heaven. And they returned to Jerusalem with great joy, and were continually in the temple blessing God".

(Luke 24: 50-53)

We come now to the biblical description of the ascension of Christ. The moment of the ascension was a very important moment for Christ and for the church. We might even draw a direct line from the moment of the ascension to the closing of every church service every Sunday.

Let me explain this. What happens when we conclude the worship services? Two main things, really. We praise the Name of the Lord in our closing song, and we receive the blessing of the Lord via the servant who is authorized to do so. Blessing and praise form the final acts of the service in which the preaching of *reconciliation* is central.

Do we not find the same elements in this text from Luke, which describes the ascension of our Lord? Christ has brought His congregation together in Bethany, on the mount of Olives, united now in the wonderful reality of reconciliation. It is well after Golgotha and Easter. Christ has performed the highest priestly service in His one sacrifice on the cross. He has gathered His disciples around Him again and proclaimed to them grace and life.

Now the time has come to part. Christ must enter into the glory of heaven; the church must take up its earthly task. And at this very moving moment in the history of the church, we read of *blessing and praise!* It is a fitting conclusion of Christ's earthly ministry.

After the one high-priestly sacrifice on the cross comes the full priestly blessing. The church will live on earth under that blessing. And this blessing will activate the church and call it to continuous praise and worship, until He comes again to judge the living and the dead. Our theme is, then, that Christ in His ascension as the only High Priest performs His last earthly service to His church. In doing so, He places His church under His continuous blessing and He incites His church to His continuous praise.

A SOBER DESCRIPTION

It is striking that the ascension is described in such simple and sober terms, even though it is actually one of the greatest moments in the life of the Lord Jesus Christ and in the history of the church. There is no extensive report, no elaborate description or documentation. Luke devotes only four verses to the event, of which just one actually records the fact of the ascension, namely verse 51. That's all. We will notice the same sobriety in Acts 1, where the event of the ascension is also described.

This brevity stands in marked contrast to the broad and expansive description of Christ's suffering. While Christ's suffering on the cross is extensively documented, his moments of glory are soberly described. His suffering *had* to be described broadly, fully and clearly, for on the cross He performed his foremost priestly deed. There He gave the one perfect sacrifice of body and soul. But even if the fact of the ascension is described in sober terms, it is still a moving account. Luke brings out Christ's final act as a simple, yet stirring priestly act.

TO THE MOUNT OF OLIVES

We read that the Lord has led His disciples out as far as Bethany. Luke does not say that they arrived in Bethany, but that they went in that direction. They went out of Jerusalem, most likely through the so-called "golden gate" in the temple wall, and then through the Garden of Gethsemane to the Mount of Olives, in the direction of Bethany.

There Christ will ascend to heaven, in the midst of His disciples. Christ was crucified *outside* Jerusalem. There He performed His greatest priestly task and there He will also perform His last priestly act on earth. It is now no longer a matter between Him and the Jews, but between Him and His Bride, between the Lord and His church.

There they stand, the Lord Jesus and His church, His disciples and (according to Acts 1) possibly some of the women and a few relatives of the Lord. It is a relatively small group of people, the first of the Lord's great "harvest." They stand there together, sharing in the wonder of the risen Christ, in the wealth of the new covenant, yet also isolated from the rest of Israel. Apart from Christ and each other, they are "on their own."

SAYING GOODBYE

Are they "impressed" with what is going to happen? They know that the Lord will depart, because He spoke about it many times before, even before His crucifixion. The moment of "farewell" is always a difficult moment, and here, after so many emotional events, it will have been particularly difficult.

It is hard to say "goodbye." In such a situation you usually see one of two reactions: one person becomes quiet and looks at the floor, not knowing really what to do or say, while another person, doing exactly the opposite, loses himself in a torrent of words and hides the pain under a cloak of frantic activity. To say "goodbye" is indeed a difficult matter.

And what about Christ Himself? How does He react to this situation? Is He going to give the disciples one last stirring speech? Will He make one last round, and shake their hands, one by one, with a last personal message? "Peter, tend my lambs." "John, remember my love." "Thomas, stand firm." "Mary, be courageous!" Is there a final admonition and a word of comfort? Some people tarry long when they have to go away.

But we do not read of any of these things. I rather have the impression that everything has now been said. Christ approaches His followers not one by one but as a body. They are all in the same situation now, and all are in need of the same thing. Christ does what they may not have expected – or did they? We read, "and lifting up His hands, He blessed them" (verse 50b).

THE FULL BENEDICTION

The blessing with the uplifted hands! This was the well-known priestly blessing given in the temple *after the sacrifice was brought!* When the people were gathered outside on the temple square, and the smoke of the altar with the incense was still drifting towards heaven, the priest would come out, lift up his hands and say, "The LORD bless you and keep you, the LORD lift up His countenance over you. . .and give you peace." And the people would say, "Amen."

We should note that Christ has never before given such a priestly blessing. We read elsewhere that He laid His hands upon children to bless them, but that was of a different nature than this blessing. But now He gives the full priestly blessing. Because now He has, as the only high priest, brought the perfect sacrifice and the one atonement for the sins of His people and reconciled them to the LORD.

Our Lord may now, *must* now, before He parts from His people, lift up His hands to give them the priestly blessing. And now for the first time this blessing is truly based on the one given sacrifice, not on the blood of oxen or sheep or bulls, but on the blood of the Lamb of God! Now the blessing of God comes to the church with full effect and in true force. This is the ultimate goal of the priestly office: to let the people of God go to their homes reconciled and blessed.

SAYING GOOD WORDS

Is this simple priestly act not richer than a thousand words? For this is something to hold fast to. With this blessing you can go out into the world and live your life. Christ departs for the glory of heaven, but He leaves His church behind under the full blessing of achieved reconciliation. He places His church under His outstretched arms; the church *is* under His blessing, officially and permanently. This is the most beautiful "going away" gift or "farewell present" anyone could give or receive!

"He blessed them." Literally it says, "He spoke good words." That is what "blessing" really is: saying good things to someone, wishing them the best. The best to you every day. The same Greek word is later used for "praising."

Saying good things. When God does that, it is called "blessing." When we do that, it is called "praising." But Christ's blessing is more than just a matter of a few words: it is the blessing of the covenant, of the new covenant. It implies great spiritual gifts, such as the forgiveness of sins and the life everlasting, and from there on all that is needed to live a joyful and meaningful life before the Lord. To be blessed means: to stand in the communion of the living God in Christ and through the Spirit, day and night. Blessed also means: to stand in the communion of faith with one another, even after Christ has ascended into heaven.

THE PERMANENT BLESSING

Christ may go, but the blessing is permanent. See verse 51, "*While* He blessed them, He parted from them, and was carried into heaven." Christ's hands stay outstretched as He ascends! It is another contrast with the priest in the temple. The priest had to lower his hands again between each sacrifice. But now the last sacrifice has been brought, and the arms remain extended, for the blessing is continuous, permanent and never-ending.

Christ departs, and the disciples see Him go with outstretched arms and open hands, arms which never drop and hands that never close! Also after He arrives in heaven, and is seated on the throne of God, the blessing does not cease. A rich stream of unending covenant blessings is poured out over the church. This last priestly act on earth finds a mighty progression from heaven.

This means that the church will never be poor, in the sense of being robbed of Christ's blessing. Here is the triumphant crowning of the cross of Golgotha: "that He might fill us with His blessing" (Form for Celebration of the Lord's Supper).

That is what we celebrate in remembering the ascension of our Lord. We stand today under the same outstretched arms and in the flow of the same blessing. That blessing, based on the reconciliation of Golgotha, is laid upon the congregation every Sunday again, and is with you every day, every week. That incites us to praise Him. He says "good words" to us; we say "good words" to Him.

NO REAL FAREWELL

This "farewell" is not really a farewell anymore, is it? This blessed departure has a beautiful result. The disciples are not broken-hearted; on the contrary, we read, "And they returned to Jerusalem with great joy" (verse 52). The ascension has not diminished, rather increased the joy of the church. Certainly, the disciples will have felt the pain of farewell and they will have missed the Lord's personal presence. But there is no sorrow, only great elation.

Great joy. That means: they have understood the blessing. They have gladly accepted the high-priestly blessing of Christ. They know that they have not gone a step backwards, but a great stride ahead. They have not been cut off from their Lord, but are eternally united with Him.

So they go back to Jerusalem with increased joy. When we read the words "great joy," we should not think that they were jumping up and down in ecstasy all the way back to Jerusalem. Some interpret this to mean an outpouring of outward emotions. But the word used means more a deep inward joy, and it has a close relation to the Greek word for "grace." It is God's grace in Christ which gives such deep joy and overcomes even the pain of Christ's departure. The disciples return to the same old city of Jerusalem, but life will never be the same again. Their hearts are filled with the grace of God and the joy of knowing the glory of the Lord.

WITH HEART AND MOUTH

And when the heart is thus filled with joy, the mouth pours forth praise! Christ's priestly blessing leads to prophetic praise by the church. The blessing of Christ activates and incites the church to praise.

This is an important matter. The blessing of Christ becomes evident in congregational activity. Christ speaks "good words" to His people; the action always originates with Him. But the church cannot remain without reaction or response; the church must then also speak "good words," must bless God and praise the Lord. So the Christ who blesses and the congregation which praises are united in the service of the Father.

CONTINUALLY IN THE TEMPLE

For we read, ". . .and [they] were continually in the temple blessing [praising] God" (verse 53). Christ does not bring His church to tears on Ascension day but leads His church to praise, even continuous praise.

They were continually in the temple praising God. Please do not misunderstand this. Luke does not mean that they were there day and night, twenty-four hours. Of course not, for they had to go home, to eat, drink and sleep. The service of the Lord does not do away with the normal pattern of every day living. But Luke means "continually" in the sense of regularly, at set times, and also often.

The small congregation at Jerusalem is making itself known publicly. At set times they come together in the temple to praise the Lord for His grace in Christ. For a blessed church cannot hide its life but is a prophetic church, revealing its life in its worship and praise.

They do this in the temple. Is that not a bit strange? They received the blessing outside the temple, separate from the temple, why do they still sing their songs of praise inside the temple? Has the temple not become outdated and is its use now not obsolete?

It is indeed remarkable and therefore also important that the disciples are still at this time involved in the temple. The Old Testament temple is being filled with New Testament praise. Here we see the antithesis emerging between Judaism and Christianity. For it is Christ who demands and receives praise also in that old temple.

And this "continually." Which implies: this congregation is not bound anymore to the temple liturgy. It does not have to wait for the daily sacrifice to be brought or for the priest of the day to come out and give the blessing. They are still in the temple, but they are already loose from the temple liturgy, and they may introduce a new liturgy, free from the altars, sacrifices, and priests. For this congregation is sanctified by the one great sacrifice and stands under the full blessing of the only High Priest, Jesus Christ.

They are still in the temple, indeed, for they still seek the unity with old Israel. But they worship in the style of the new Israel. And it will become more and more apparent that the praise of this church is not bound to places, times, offerings, or priests, but may be heard freely, everywhere and always.

A BEAUTIFUL CONCLUSION

Is this not a beautiful conclusion to a rich Gospel? Christ ascends to heaven, blessing His church, and the disciples return to Jerusalem to turn the old temple into a real house of God. It had to end this way. A blessed church is a prophetic church. A blessed church is a praising community. Out of a new heart rise the new songs of praise to God who made it all possible in Christ Jesus.

It has to be so, I say. Otherwise we lose the blessing. If the church is not active in praise and prophecy, the blessing is forfeited. Let us be a joyous, worshipping church. Our whole life is contained within the blessing of Christ, and our whole life must be geared to the praise of His glory. This is even more true for us today than it was on the day of ascension. For now the Spirit has been poured out and the revelation of God has been completed. We have come much further in the history of the church. The old temple in Jerusalem no longer exists. We worship in spirit and in truth, wherever the Lord calls us.

Now the blessing of Christ must be fully visible among us, in our worship, our psalms and praise, and also in our whole walk of life. It must become apparent that we live under the outstretched arms and open hands of the ascended Lord, that we expect and receive from Him all things, and that we give to Him all honour and praise. For through the ascension of Christ we are directed towards heaven, where Christ is, seated at the right hand of God.

He blesses us from heaven, every day.

We praise God for it, every day. Continually. Now and forever. The congregation that lives under the constant blessing of Christ is always active in the service of the Lord.

Christ in His Ascension Greater than Elijah

"And when He had said this, as they were looking on, He was lifted up, and a cloud took Him out of their sight. And while they were gazing into heaven as He went, behold, two men stood by them in white robes, and said: men of Galilee, why do you stand looking into heaven? This Jesus who was taken up from you into heaven, will come in the same way as you saw Him go into heaven".

(Acts 1: 9-11)

As we turn now to the account in Acts concerning the ascension of our Lord, we may be reminded that the Bible also at another occasion speaks of an ascension. In II Kings 2 we read about the ascension of Elijah, a dramatic and traumatic occurrence. And the question can be asked, what is the relation and difference between these two events?

Just for the record, some Bible scholars also see a reference to an ascension in Genesis 5: 24, about Enoch, "[who] walked with God; and he was not, for God took him." The refrain "and he died" was not applicable to Enoch. God took him home in another way than all the others described in Genesis 5. In Hebrews 11: 5 we read, "By faith Enoch was taken up so that he should not see death; and he was not found because God had taken him."

Since we do not receive any further particulars concerning the manner of Enoch's "ascension," it is best to restrict ourselves to comparing the ascension of Christ with that of Elijah. And we note that there is a vast difference between the two, which we may indicate as follows. Elijah's ascension shows us the great distance between heaven and earth, but Christ's ascension shows us their unity.

TARRY HERE

In the account of II Kings 2 we find Elijah and Elisha going from Gilgal to the river Jordan. It is remarkable how Elijah time and again, at Gilgal, Bethel, and Jericho, tells Elisha to stay behind, "Tarry here. . . ." Some see this as a testing of Elisha's resolve whether he will follow Elijah to the end, but we may also conclude that Elijah wished to spare his successor the trauma of the impending departure.

Elisha, meanwhile, does get the message, also via the sons of the prophets in Jericho, that Elijah will be taken away from him. Nevertheless, he perseveres in following his master even across the Jordan.

The situation is much different in Acts 1. Our Lord does not at all seek to discourage His disciples from being with Him for this important event. In Luke 24: 50 we read that Jesus even leads His disciples as far as Bethany. The Lord wants them to be in the fullest sense witnesses of His ascension into heaven.

Moreover, whereas only one man, Elisha, witnessed the ascension of Elijah, several men witnessed the ascension of Christ. Also in this respect we may conclude that Christ is greater than Elijah. And while the "sons of the prophets" stood at a distance and were left behind when Elijah and Elisha crossed the Jordan, there was no distance between Christ and His disciples.

EVERYTHING SAID?

There is another difference which merits our attention. The ascension of Elijah takes place rather abruptly. We read in II Kings 2: 11, "And as they still went on and talked, behold a chariot of fire and horses separated the two of them." Their conversation was cut short. Right in the middle of a sentence, perhaps, came an interruption from heaven. Suddenly, the fellowship of these two men came to and end.

Elisha may have had many things to ask. From his reaction, "My father, my father!" we may conclude that he experienced the sudden separation as traumatic. They were separated while still talking. The connection was broken and the line went dead.

In Acts 1, we find a completely different scene. In verse 9 we read, "And when He had said this, He was lifted up. . ." Christ had just given His final instructions. The disciples knew exactly what they must do. The conversation was not interrupted, but was finished. Christ had said everything that He wanted and needed to say. There were no loose ends that still needed to be tied up.

Christ had completed His work on earth and achieved all that He had set out to do. Whereas Elijah left behind much unfinished business and needed a successor, Christ's work was finished, and no one on earth needed to continue the work that He completed.

CHARIOT OF FIRE

Perhaps the greatest difference between the two ascensions lies in the fact that Elijah was taken up in a chariot of fire and horses of fire, while Christ was simply "lifted up". In II Kings 2: 1 we also read that the LORD was about to take Elijah up to heaven by a whirlwind. So Elijah's ascent takes place through wind and fire; he is almost violently pulled away from this earth.

We therefore find also in II Kings 11 the word "separation." There is an instant division between Elijah and Elisha. The wind and the fire stand between them. There is a gap that can not be bridged, and this leads Elisha to cry out with anguish.

The fact that Elijah is taken up by a chariot and horses has further significance. Chariots and horses were used in battle. The negro spiritual may speak of a "sweet chariot," but there really was nothing sweet about it. The chariot and the horses make clear that there is still a feud between God and this world, also between God and His apostate covenant people.

God comes down in power and majesty, with heavenly wind and fire, and snatches Elijah away from this earth. And the only witness, Elisha, must stand back, shaken, shattered, stunned. Elisha feels the great distance which there is between God and man, between heaven and earth. No one can go where Elijah has gone.

There are explainers who see in the appearing of "fire" (and the wind mentioned in II Kings 2: 1) the necessity of purification. Elijah must be renewed by the Holy Spirit ("wind") and purified by fire before he can enter the glory of heaven. He can not appear before God as he is, but must undergo a transformation. The force of the wind and the heat of the fire are then seen as symbolic of the change which Elijah must undergo as He enters the presence of a holy and sovereign God.

And indeed, a transformation was required. We cannot appear before God in our sinful and mortal bodies. We are reminded of Paul's words in I Corinthians 15: 50, "I tell you this, brethren: flesh and blood cannot inherit the kingdom of God, nor does the perishable inherit the imperishable." Elijah cannot ascend as he is. The fire and wind not only lift him up but also transform him so that he can stand before the throne of God. In that sense, also, there is an immediate separation between Elijah and Elisha. The two men are no longer alike.

BEFORE THE EYES OF HIS DISCIPLES

The ascension of our Lord, on the other hand, takes place in calmness and peace. There are no fiery chariot and horses. Christ is not suddenly swept away, but lifted up. His ascent is gradual and clearly visible. The disciples can see Him, as He ascends with outstretched arms, blessing them (Luke 24: 51). Luke notes particularly that it happened "as they were looking on" (verse 9). The Heidelberg Catechism therefore correctly states in Lord's Day 18 that Christ "before the eyes of His disciples was taken up from earth into heaven." The disciples have a different function than the prophet: they must see clearly what happens in order to give an exact eyewitness account.

It says, "and a cloud took Him out of their sight." This can be taken in various ways. Some suggest that Christ was visible in His ascent until He reached the clouds high above the earth. But others are of the opinion that from the beginning of the ascension a cloud appeared, so that Jesus gradually disappeared.

The truth is probably that in the process of Christ's ascension a cloud gradually appeared around Him. We may see this "cloud" as the presence of God. The disciples realize, when this cloud appears, that Christ is enveloped by the dimensions of heaven, taken into the glory of the Father, and so disappears from their view.

Again we are struck by the simplicity and peacefulness of the entire event. Christ ascends in His own right and glory, unassisted by chariots and horses, and so enters in the glory of the Father.

WHY THIS DIFFERENCE?

When we seek an answer to the question why these two events are so different from each other, there can really be only the one answer: whereas in Elijah's ascension we still see the distance which exists between heaven and earth, in Christ's ascension we may see their unity.

Christ enters into heaven in our flesh, and this is described as an almost natural course of events. The reason is that God's great fury now has passed. For Christ has brought the one sacrifice for sin. He has broken down the wall of hostility which existed between God and men. This ascension, therefore, speaks of reconciliation.

Christ enters heaven as man. It is now for the first time that a human being, perfectly righteous and holy, enters into the presence of God. Never before has any man appeared in this manner before God. Never before has the unity between heaven and earth become so apparent as at this occasion.

God is now reconciled with His people. We may enter heaven freely. Fire and wind are no longer necessary, for we have been cleansed by the blood and Spirit of our Lord. His ascension demonstrates that the gap between heaven and earth has been bridged on Golgotha.

Therefore the Heidelberg Catechism can rightly state in Lord's Day 18 that Christ's ascension means that "we have our flesh in heaven as a sure pledge that He, our head, will also take us, His members, up to Himself."

THE COMFORT OF THE ASCENSION

This is the basis of the comfort given in Hebrews 10: 19 and following verses: "Therefore, brethren, since we have confidence to enter the sanctuary by the blood of Jesus, by the new and living way which He opened for us through the curtain, that is His flesh. . .let us draw near with a true heart. . . ."

In Christ the way to heaven is opened for us. We may enter the heavenly sanctuary. We do not go through the curtain which separated the holy of holies from the other parts of the temple. We have direct access to heaven through Christ's flesh.

ANGELS APPEAR

There is another remarkable difference between the account of Elijah's ascension and that of our Lord. After Elijah has ascended, the prophet Elisha stands alone. It simply says. "And he saw him no more" (II Kings 2: 12).

We read further that he took hold of his clothes and rent them into two pieces. And then he took the fallen mantel of Elijah and went back to the Jordan. He is a man who walks and stands alone. No one comes to comfort or guide him. Heaven remains closed.

But as the disciples are gazing upward, perhaps straining to see if they can yet catch a glimpse of their beloved Lord, it says, ". . .behold, two men stood by them in white robes." Again we see how the distance between heaven and earth has been bridged. For these men in white robes can only be angels, heavenly messengers who at this point must comfort and direct the disciples. There is no fallen mantel as last piece of evidence, but a message from God.

LOOK AROUND, NOT UP

These angels come with a question and a promise. First they ask, "Men of Galilee, why do you stand looking into heaven?" The title "men of Galilee" establishes a bond of familiarity and confidentiality. These angels know the men with whom they are speaking. Angels and disciples are no longer strangers, but united in the service of the one Lord.

The question is, "Why do you stand looking into heaven?" From this we may conclude that the disciples continued to look up, also after Jesus was taken from their sight. This may indicate that they were now at a loss as to what to do. Now the angels do not severely rebuke the disciples. The question is only a mild reprimand. They come with a promise, "This Jesus, who was taken up from you into heaven, will come in the same way as you saw Him go into heaven." Jesus will return. The disciples need not think that the farewell is permanent. Christ is coming back to this earth.

This Jesus, it says, the very same man. He will not change during His time in heaven. He will not change either in His relation to His church on earth. He will return as He left, visibly and gloriously.

ON THE CLOUDS OF HEAVEN

There will be a difference, of course, between Christ's ascension and His return. This difference is indicated by the apostle John in Revelation 1: 7: "Behold, He is coming with the clouds, and every eye will see Him, every one who pierced Him. . . ."

Only the disciples saw Him go. But all people – even Christ's sworn enemies – shall see Him return in glory. He will come "with the clouds." This means that He will come visibly from above.

John actually writes that Christ is coming already. This truth dominates the entire book of Revelation. From the very moment Christ entered heaven, He has one task to fulfill: to prepare the great day of His glory.

But Christians must not waste time looking up. Instead, we must go out to do the work to which Christ has called us. For when He does come, He wants to find us busy in the work of the Kingdom.

The promise of the angels is therefore also a challenge: continue with your apostolic mission. Christ works in heaven on your behalf, and you must work on earth in His Name. And one day He will return, for all to see, and as His coming will be terrible for those who have pierced Him, so it will be joyous for those who served Him.

Such a promise was not given to Elisha, when Elijah ascended in whirlwind, fire, and smoke. Elijah cannot return on his own steam. But Christ will come in His power and glory with all the saints – also with Elijah – to judge the living and the dead.

HEAVEN AND EARTH UNITED

The ascension shows us that heaven and earth are now forever united in Christ. Christ works in heaven; His church works on the earth. Angels and men have a common task: to work for the coming of the Kingdom of heaven.

And one day it will be true that heaven and earth will fully be one. John writes in Revelation 21: 1, 2, "Then I saw a new heaven and a new earth; for the first earth had passed away, and the sea was no more. And I saw the holy city, new Jerusalem, coming down out of heaven from God as a bride adorned for her husband."

When Christ returns, God Himself will come to live with us on a new earth. The best is yet to come. In that faith the disciples went back to Jerusalem and a new era began. Heaven and earth are already one in Christ. Soon they will be fully one, on the great day of Christ's final appearing in glory.

Then we shall reap in abundant measure the riches of Christ Jesus, our Lord and King.

The Ascended Christ Gathers His Church in Preparation for Pentecost

"Then they returned to Jerusalem from the mount called Olivet, which is near Jerusalem, a sabbath's journey away; and went up to the upper room, where they were staying, Peter and John and James and Andrew, Philip and Thomas, Bartholomew and Matthew, James the son of Alphaeus and Simon the Zealot and Judas the son of James. All these with one accord devoted themselves to prayer, together with the women and Mary the mother of Jesus, and with His brothers".

(Acts 1: 12-14)

The ascension of our Lord Jesus Christ into heaven means for the church a totally new period of time. For the disciples on the day itself it meant a definite farewell: Christ would no longer be physically with them on earth. It would be quite different than before, and in certain ways much more difficult. Now, truly, the church would have to live by faith, and not by what is seen.

We have already concentrated on the ascension itself. We saw how Christ departed from His disciples while blessing them (Luke 24:50-52), and noticed how they gazed up at Him until a cloud took Him out of their sight (Acts 1: 9). This time I want to pay some attention to another question: how did the disciples react to the ascension? What was their immediate course of action? How did they deal with this definite departure, this decisive event?

We ask these questions not because we may expect from the disciples themselves anything good. They are not exemplary in themselves. When we look at the disciples, we often see the opposite of what is required of them. Remember how they all deserted Christ on the night He was betrayed and arrested? And where were they on Easter morning? They had to be gathered together and convinced at length that Christ had truly risen from the dead. At that time they did not at all remember Christ's word or heed it. No, the disciples have until now not shown much positive action.

A MOMENT OF SADNESS?

We might expect them now perhaps to linger a bit on Mount Olivet, to be again indecisive. A time of departure can be one of sad reminiscing and sorrowful reflection. They all have their combined experiences and their personal memories of the Lord, and of the wondrous things that have happened. But all that is now over, past, fini. Christ has gone home to His heavenly Father, so why do they not all go home too, back to Galilee from where they came?

We can understand it if the ascension led to a moment of sadness. It is so hard to bid farewell, and they would not again see the Lord in this life. But that moment of sadness, if it came, did not last very long. It is striking how the disciples immediately act upon the words of the two angels. They do not gaze anymore into the sky or linger longingly on the mountain. They tear themselves away from the whole scene.

BACK TO JERUSALEM

We read in verse 12, "Then they returned to Jerusalem. . . ." Then means: without delay, right after the angels spoke, as a response to their words. They act in accordance with Christ's will. They go to Jerusalem and they begin to act and live as a church, as the church of Christ. They begin to look forward to the fulfillment of the promises of the Lord, the promise of the outpouring of the Holy Spirit.

This is not the same group of people as on Easter morning. Yes, it is the same group of people, but they have come much further. They have already changed immensely. And this is nothing less than the fruit of Christ's redeeming and renewing power. That is what we are looking for. Not the initiative and obedience of the disciples, but the power of the risen and ascended Lord Jesus Christ. People do not change and cannot change unless Christ changes them. They will not assemble unless He gathers them. This is especially clear immediately after the ascension.We see here how the ascended Christ gathers His church in preparation for the day of Pentecost, and we note the unity and the ministry of this church.

UNIFIED ACTION

Although Jesus Christ, the Head of the Church, has now ascended into heaven and is no longer physically with His Church on earth, and although at this moment the Holy Spirit has not yet been poured out, still the disciples show positive and unified action. This is nothing less than a manifestation of the grace and the power of the Lord.

We see this clearly in the words which precede our text. They returned to Jerusalem, it says. This is precisely what the Lord had commanded them to do. He had emphatically charged them not to depart from Jerusalem but to wait there for the outpouring of the Spirit of God. Jerusalem is not chosen without reason, for it is the heart of Israel, the covenant people. Jerusalem is also the base of the operations of the Christian Church. Christ had said, "You shall be my witnesses [starting] in Jerusalem. . . ."

IN THE UPPER ROOM

We read that they went to "the upper room where they were staying" (verse 13). There has been a lot of debate on exactly where this "upper room" was, but it most likely was the same room where the Lord celebrated with them the Passover and instituted the holy supper. It probably belonged to the parents of Mark, the young man who fled naked the night Jesus was arrested.

Apparently the disciples had stayed there regularly, going out during the day to Olivet, coming in at night to the upper room. So it was a familiar room, filled with good memories. It was the same house to which Peter fled after he escaped from prison (Acts 12: 12). This house, then, with its upper room became a central point for the young Christian Church. It was there that they held their key meetings for counsel and prayer. By immediately going to this particular house, to this room, the disciples already indicate that they will continue as congregation of the Lord Jesus Christ in worship and prayer. The ascended Christ has on earth an assembled congregation!

And then follows the list of the names of the apostles, as we find it also elsewhere in the New Testament. This list is so important here, for it asserts immediately after the ascension who the earthly shepherds are, the lawful office bearers in the Church. The Christian Church will be from the beginning an *apostolic* Church, based on the testimony of chosen eye-witnesses.

ELEVEN DISCIPLES

I do not now want to discuss the list of names, but we do note one thing: the name of Judas Iscariot is, of course, missing. There are eleven disciples. That is an obvious fact maybe, but nevertheless a very telling and painful one.

The Church of Christ has at this early stage already experienced loss, even in its circle of office bearers. It is not a perfect Church yet. They may all be gathered in unity in that upper room, but there is one missing, one who was with them from the beginning, and who has gone from them, and even betrayed the Lord. The Christian Church will experience more often and in many ways the loss of members, of whom some even become traitors. Eleven disciples, the number is not full anymore.

But if you look at the names of those who remained, you can be amazed that they are still together. It says in our text, "All these with one accord devoted themselves to prayer. . . ." All these, namely those eleven apostles. They are mentioned first because they are the apostles, the office bearers, and they belong together as a unit, and so determine the unity. They are still together in a remarkably close and unified manner.

WITH ONE ACCORD?

Do you remember when the Lord was still with them how they always fought and bickered? Especially about who was the most important? Who would get to sit at Jesus' right hand or at Jesus' left hand? Do you remember how they disagreed on the course of action? Stay with Christ or stay in Galilee? Do you remember how they opposed the very idea of a cross and thought in terms of worldly victory? Do you remember their fears and doubts?

They were a group that was sorely divided, with much dissent and harsh treatment of each other. They have quite a past, and humanly speaking, little future. How can they still be together? Is this not a time bomb ticking away, about to explode? The fiery Peter, who has yet so much to learn, the quiet John, the pessimist Thomas, the radical Simon – not to mention the others – all these, as the text says, how will they ever stay together and be unified? Especially now that the Lord is not with them in person to keep them together, to still their storms, dissolve their disputes, and heal their hurts?

ALSO THE WOMEN

Add to this the fact that there are also some others mentioned here: the women and Mary, the mother of Jesus, and his brothers. The "women" are obviously those women who ministered unto Christ during His time on earth. I think of Mary Magdalene, for example, and the wives of some of the apostles.

Mary, the mother of the Lord, is also mentioned, but not first. I want to emphasize this for a moment. If Mary, the mother of our Lord, had taken such a prominent position in the early Christian Church as Rome would have us believe, then the order should have been: Mary, the apostles, and some of the women. But this is not the case. Mary has a place in the church, certainly, but not a prominent place.

As a matter of fact, this is the last time in the Bible that we even read of her. Nowhere do we read, as Rome claims, that Mary later ascended to heaven as queen-mother to rule with Christ.

Still, Mary will have had her input in the early Church, for she knew many things about her beloved Son and Lord. And then we also read about "his brothers." These are then blood-brothers of the Lord Jesus. Yes, they too are among those who gathered in the upper room. One of them, James, will later occupy an important place and even write a letter which has become part of the Bible. But remember how they at first disbelieved Jesus and even mocked Him? Had there perhaps been sibling rivalry or envy at first? But they, too, have come to accept the Lord Jesus Christ as their Saviour and Lord. Will they, however, be able to accept the apostles as their leaders, now that Christ has ascended? Were they, after all, not closer to him than Peter, or John, or Matthew?

We see a church with a lot of family relations, some influential women, a group of varied leaders. Is this the church of Christ? Can this fragile congregation withstand the wiles of the devil and truly be moulded into a unity? Indeed, there will still be many stormy waters and many rivers to cross, but the unity of the Church is unmistakably there: all these were *with one accord.* The ascension does not split up the Church or lead to division on which course of action to take. They are united.

THE SAME SPIRIT

With one accord, it says. I want to use a stronger term yet. It says literally: *with the same spirit.* Actually the word denotes strong feeling and passion. They felt very strongly about the matter. They were completely united. They were not listlessly hanging together, but they worked together with conviction; they assembled with purpose and common zeal. They were all believers. They were all fully and intensely committed to Christ Jesus.

Why is this so? Well, this is the unity of faith. They have now come to see and to accept Jesus Christ for what He really is. They have, in those forty days that Christ was with them after His resurrection, come to understand the facts in the light of the Scriptures. Therefore they can cope with the fact of the ascension. They know exactly why He had to ascend. They see it as a step in His glorification. They know what He will do there in heaven, namely prepare a place for them and gather the Church out of all places. They know what they, in the meantime, have to do.

ALREADY THE BODY OF CHRIST

And they cannot wait to get started. They have one common desire and purpose. This is because Christ has already moulded them into a body, His body, and because even in His ascension He does not cease to govern them by His

Word and Spirit. It is at this moment still ten days from Pentecost, but do not think that the Holy Spirit is completely absent from the church. Do not think that the Word does not function among them. Do you believe that they ever were for one moment orphans without a Father, without a Head and Master?

What we learn here is that the ascended Jesus Christ immediately asserts His authority and power in the unity of His Church. It is the unity of obedience to the Word, the unity of faith and of the zeal of faith. And if that is how it is between Ascension and Pentecost, how must it then be after Pentecost? Or how must it be today?

The Church is characterized as a communion of faith, as a body with one soul, one mind, one spirit, a common purpose and a common zeal. This is the norm which Christ maintains from heaven, and this is the work of the Holy Spirit on earth. It is in this unity that the Church shows that it is governed by one Head and one Lord, Jesus Christ.

The Church did not become fragmented, splintered, and divided because of the ascension, because the binding factor was now gone, or because now so many people competed to govern it. No, the Church became divided because people did not obey the Word. Because they lost their zeal for Christ, sought their own glory, and so forgot the glory of God. Because they began to fight for their own name, and no longer saw the need for the edification of the congregation. But this was not the case after the Ascension and before Pentecost. The Church was united in common zeal and immediately began to fulfill its important ministry.

LINKED WITH CHRIST

We read that with one accord all these people "devoted themselves to prayer." This is an important piece of information. For now we see what a living *link* the New Testament Church still has with heaven and with Christ.

When Christ ascended into heaven, the contact between Him and His Church was not broken. You would almost expect that to be the case. You might think: Christ has ascended high above the clouds into the heavens, and He is now, until He returns, unreachable. There is no more contact, and the church is left to paddle around on its own steam without any contact with its heavenly Head. It sits around, sorrowful and grieving: "O my soul, why are you grieving, why disquieted in me?" (Psalm 42).

But this is obviously not the case. They say: Hope in God. The church immediately resorts to prayer, and so,"in prayer transcending distance," lifts up its heart to heaven, where Christ Jesus is, seated at the right hand of God. It is not without reason that we may sing from Hymn 31, the hymn about the ascension, "We lift our hearts to Christ on high." Or from Hymn 32: "seek the things that are above." The contact is never really broken. The eye-contact is broken, yes, on Mount Olivet, but the spiritual contact is not. The communion remains intact from day one.

DIRECT ACCESS

This is important. Romanists try to make us believe that the church now needed time to get used to the new situation. They could no longer call directly upon the Lord Jesus Christ, for He was glorified. They had to go via Mary and the saints. But Mary and the saints – the apostles – are all sitting in the upper room in Jerusalem, and they call directly and immediately upon the Name of the Lord. The ministry of the Church is not to place all kinds of mediators between itself and the Lord, but instead, through lawful office bearers, to lead the congregation in calling upon its heavenly Head and Saviour. Oh, the importance and wealth of knowing the Scriptures!

It says here that they devoted themselves to prayer. A word is used that means doing something constantly. Devotion is something that goes on all the time and not just from time to time. It also means doing something with conscious perseverance. They put their mind and soul in it and they would not quit. There was an open channel with heaven and they would not allow that channel to get clogged up through inactivity. The Church from the day of ascension understood: the way is open through Christ, who as our High Priest has gone into the inner heavens, the heavenly sanctuary, and we must go that way. They came to the upper room and they said, "Let us then boldly seek God's face, There to find mercy, help and grace. Our great High Priest will intercede, Come to our aid in time of need" (Hymn 33: 6).

EVERYTHING FROM HEAVEN

They devoted themselves to prayer, it says, and a word is used that specifically means petitioning, beseeching God. They put themselves in the hands of the Lord. They knew that especially now they had to expect everything from heaven. That was always the case for God's people, but it was never brought home so clearly as on the day of the ascension. There is no help coming from among men. He who descended, and who was one of us, our only Saviour, has now ascended, and therefore we must until He returns look upward, look forward, expecting from the heavenly throne alone all blessing and help.

But prayer never stands on its own. We read, for example in Acts 6, how the apostles speak about their specific duties as being prayer and the ministry of the Word. The assembled congregation in the upper room began immediately to seek the Word of God, and to be edified by the apostolic preaching. The Church began to live by the Word and to preserve the Word through the apostolic testimony. And that Word, in turn, gave content and meaning to prayer and praise.

So we see the ministry of the Church appearing already on the day of the ascension. They went back to the upper room to remember the Word of Christ and to call upon God in His Name. They too ascended, that is, they lifted up their hearts in faith to heaven, where Christ Jesus is.

ACTIVITY STILL CONFINED

It is not yet Pentecost. This activity is still confined within the perimeters of the congregation. But soon the Spirit will be poured out. And the Word will go out to all Jerusalem, to Judea and Samaria, and to the ends of the earth. The whole world will be called to prayer and praise, to recognize the mighty saving work of God in Christ Jesus. The whole world will be called to submit to the authority of the ascended Christ, the first-born of the dead and the Ruler of kings on earth.

It is a world-wide ministry indeed. But the first task remains as well: it is also an in-depth ministry. It is the ministry of the Church to preach the Word to its members, to lead in prayer and to urge to prayer, so that everyone will go the way of the open channel to heaven, so that we all may ascend in faith to where Christ Jesus is, and in prayer transcending distance seek the God of our existence.

Christ opened the line to heaven. The Church must through its ministry seek to keep that line open. That is what Christ teaches us through the little "upper room" congregation on the day of His ascension. He said: see, I am not far away. For the Word is near you, in your hearts and on your lips, and you may lift up your hearts to heaven, where I am, from where I am coming on my great day of descending in glory.

CHRIST GATHERS HIS CHURCH

So we know what we have to do today and how we are to live today. The Church that hears the gospel of the ascension knows the way to God, shares the flame of faith, and is unending in devotion.

And there is a great comfort here. If Christ already then kept His little Church together in this way and directed them to heaven, will He by His outpoured Spirit and completed Word not do so all the more today? He will assemble His Church today in preparation for the great day of His return. In His hands this gathering is safe and secure and will be completed. From the ascension to the great return it is clear: the Church is the gathering of Christ, and He alone will complete what He started. For this we will pray with great devotion today.

The Outpouring of the Spirit of Jesus Christ

Pentecost

Pentecost: The Feast of Fulfillment

"When the day of Pentecost had come. . . ."

(Acts 2: 1A)

On Pentecost the church particularly commemorates Christ's outpouring of the Holy Spirit. Unfortunately, many people today do not know much about Pentecost. Did you ever notice that many calendars indicate Christmas, Good Friday and Easter, but omit Pentecost? Apparently, Pentecost does not generally speak to the human imagination as much as Christmas and Easter. We have Christmas poinsettia's and Easter lilies, but who ever heard of Pentecost pansies?

There is, to be sure, also a good number of people who see precisely this day as the highlight of the ecclesiastical year. They even have named themselves after this day. I refer, of course, to the Pentecostal assemblies, one of the largest and fastest-growing denominations in North America. They say: to be really a church of Christ, you must be a pentecostal church. And their repeated and vehement complaint is that the "mainstream" churches have completely ignored Pentecost or suppressed its truth and reality.

Our concern is not primarily with the teachings of the Pentecostals, although reference will be made to them in this and following chapters, either implicitly or explicitly. In this chapter our concern is first of all with the question why the outpouring of the Holy Spirit took place on the Jewish feast of Pentecost, fifty days after Easter. Why was it not fifteen, or forty-five, or sixty days? Does the fact that it happened on the *day* of Pentecost have a special meaning?

That question will be answered in the affirmative. It was not without reason that the Holy Spirit was poured out on the first Pentecost after Easter. For Pentecost was already of old the feast of fulfillment, when the people of God received and enjoyed the blessing of God's covenant grace. And we also, as New Testament Church, may see Pentecost as the feast of fulfillment. For on that day we received the abiding presence of the Holy Spirit as the fruit of Christ's completed work of atonement. As such, its occurrence is unique and its blessings are constant.

THEY DID NOT KNOW

We should realize that the disciples did not know that the Holy Spirit would be poured out on Pentecost. Yes, they knew that He would come, witness Christ's own promise: "before many days you shall be baptized with the Holy Spirit." They knew it would happen soon, but not exactly when.

They also knew that they had to stay and wait in Jerusalem. And that is what they did. As we have seen earlier, they returned after the ascension of the Lord Jesus to "the upper room," where they had been staying. There they prayerfully awaited the fulfillment of the promise. So it continued until the day of Pentecost. We read in Acts 2: 1 that when the day of Pentecost came, they were together in one place, possibly the same house where also "the upper room" was located.

I said: the disciples did not know that on that particular day the Spirit would be poured out. At least, we have no indication of any prior knowledge on their part. But, perhaps, in view of the character of that day, they should have expected something to happen.

AN IMPORTANT DAY

For Pentecost was certainly one of the most important festive days of the Jewish calendar. It was a day when Jerusalem was filled with many pilgrims who came to worship in the temple. What better day to expect a work of God than this one?

It has been assumed that the Lord Jesus chose this day precisely because so many people would be gathered in Jerusalem. If you want a "crowd" to witness what will happen, certainly one of the feast days makes for an excellent opportunity. People everywhere, from all over, come especially for the occasion: what an excellent opportunity to reach a large audience. And Pentecost is the first official feast after Easter.

But that is not the reason why the Lord Jesus chose the day of Pentecost for the outpouring of the Holy Spirit. Our text actually lays a much stronger connection. In the English translation of the Revised Standard Version it just says, "And when the day of Pentecost had come. . . ." The King James Version, a bit more accurate, but not accurate enough, has: when the day of Pentecost had fully come. The New International Version (NIV) simply states: when the day of Pentecost came, a rather bland translation. The North American Standard Bible informs us by means of a footnote that it literally says: when the day of Pentecost *was being fulfilled.* The original text indeed has that verb. That is why the old King James Version added the word *fully.*

A DAY OF FULFILLMENT

Why do we bother to enter into such detail? Because it is important. The Lord Jesus chose the day of Pentecost for the outpouring because of its *redemptive-historical* significance. The outpouring on that specific day was nothing less than a fulfillment of a covenant promise made long before, a blessing foreshadowed in the ceremonies of the old covenant.

The expression that a time or a day is being fulfilled means in the Bible that a prescribed period (of waiting, or of purification) has now officially and legally passed. The time set by the Law of God has arrived. And that time is measured from the event that precedes it.

Let me explain further by going back with you to Leviticus 23, where we read about the feast days prescribed to Israel. Israel's first and foremost, ever-returning feast day was, of course, the sabbath, the weekly day of rest. We find that in Leviticus 23: 1-3. In verse 4 we read about the appointed (special) feasts of the LORD, the holy convocations. The first one of these holy feasts was in the first month, starting on the fourteenth day, the feast of the Passover and Unleavened Bread. This Passover feast, we read in verse 10, coincides with the gathering of the first fruits, the beginning of the harvest season.

So first: the Passover. And the Passover, as you know, is the feast of the deliverance out of the land of Egypt, out of the house of bondage. Israel was always to mark that event of liberation by the Passover and the offering of the first fruits.

But then comes the second feast, about which we read in Leviticus 23: 15, "And you shall count from the morrow after the sabbath, from the day that you brought the sheaf of the wave offering (the first fruits): seven full weeks shall they be, counting fifty days to the morrow after the seventh sabbath. . . ." Pentecost means literally the fiftieth day, an exactly prescribed time from the day of the Passover.

THE COMPLETION OF THE HARVEST

And what was the meaning of this "fiftieth-day feast," this Pentecost? It was the feast which marked the *completion* of the harvest, the harvest in all its fullness and richness. Pentecost was therefore the feast day on which Israel celebrated the many blessings of the LORD which He had given them in the promised land, after delivering them out of slavery.

In the history of salvation, then, Pentecost is a feast which celebrated the rich blessings which flowed forth out of God's work of deliverance. He not only led them *out of bondage*, but He also led them *into freedom!* He not only made them *free*, but also made them *rich!* Pentecost, therefore, is the wonderful and gracious consequence of the Passover feast. That is why the two are always connected; it can only be Pentecost-feast of blessings in Canaan after it has been Passover-feast of deliverance from Egypt. Do you see the redemptive-historical connection?

Seven full weeks, forty-nine days, had to be completed after the Passover. And on the morrow of the next day, the fiftieth day, the time was fulfilled, the harvest was gathered, and Israel was called together to rejoice in the rich blessings of God. Why seven weeks? Because the number "seven" is the number of the fullness of God, the fullness of His glory and His grace, the fullness of His power and His blessings, which he has poured out over His people. I could not help thinking here also of the expression: the seven spirits which are before His throne, the fullness of the Holy Spirit with all His power and majesty.

The feast of Pentecost, of the full harvest, flows out of the feast of the Passover, of the first fruits. Israel was to remember always that the many blessings poured out by God were a direct result of His mighty work of deliverance. The blessings were given to a people that was passed over in God's judgment and whose sins had been reconciled by the blood of the passover lamb.

BEGINNING AND RESULT

Do you not see that the words of our text, "When the day of Pentecost was fulfilled" have a special meaning?

For we may see it now in a deeper light. The passover found its fulfillment at Golgotha. The first fruits are evident in the resurrection of Christ. There *we* were liberated from the bondage of sin and death in Christ Jesus. Then the great paschal lamb, Jesus Christ, sacrificed Himself for our sins. There the way was opened for all the heavenly blessings of God to be poured out over us.

Is it then such a wonder that on the day of Pentecost, when according to the law the required time of waiting had been fulfilled, the Holy Spirit was poured out? The Holy Spirit is the One who imparts to us all the riches of Christ Jesus. He fills us from above with every spiritual blessing in Christ. If Pentecost follows Passover, shall then not the outpouring of the Holy Spirit follow Golgotha and Easter? Do the death and resurrection of Christ not open the way for the greatest and richest of all heavenly blessings: the presence and indwelling of the Holy Spirit? Now the people of God will be filled with riches even greater than under the old covenant.

That is why Luke puts it this way: the day of Pentecost was *fulfilled,* because on that day the church officially and lawfully reaped the full benefit of the deliverance in Christ Jesus' death and resurrection. What was foreshadowed under the old covenant in Passover and Pentecost found its fulfillment in the redeeming work of Christ and the outpouring of the Holy Spirit. Leviticus 23: 16 finds it way right into Acts 2: 1. And it is God Himself who lays connections here which we may never ignore.

DO NOT ISOLATE PENTECOST

We may, for example, never isolate "Pentecost" from Good Friday and Easter. The Holy Spirit does not come out of the blue, all on His own, but He is the Spirit of Christ, who proceeds from the Father and the Son. He fulfills and completes the work of Christ, by pouring out over us all the riches we have through the cross and the resurrection in Christ Jesus. The Holy Spirit comes to finish and perfect the work of Good Friday and Easter, to bring in from the first fruits (Easter) the full harvest of all God's children.

What does Pentecost then mean? It means that God now through the presence and work of the Holy Spirit lets us receive and enjoy all the gifts we have in Jesus Christ our Lord. Thus the church is greatly enriched precisely on that day.

Notice also the contrast here. Most of the Jews were celebrating on that day the "old" Pentecost, the feast of the earthly , material blessings in Canaan. But the disciples may celebrate the new feast of the heavenly, spiritual blessings in Christ Jesus. For them the old Pentecost has no more meaning as such, for it is fulfilled in the outpouring of the Holy Spirit. On that day, Christ takes His Church, leads it into the full riches of the new covenant, and says: see how I make you blessed unto all eternity to enjoy forever the riches of grace.

NOT REPEATED

Now we must see the consequences also. Just as Good Friday and Easter were redemptive-historical events or occurrences, which cannot be repeated and are never repeated, so Pentecost, the outpouring of the Holy Spirit, is *not* repeated. The death and resurrection of Christ open the way to the outpouring of the Holy Spirit, and that outpouring is a unique occurrence. For us Pentecost is the official and lawful beginning of a new era in the life of the people of God. Christ died only once, yet we reap the benefits of this all the time. He rose only once, yet we enjoy the fruits of it every day. So also: the Holy Spirit is poured out only once, and yet we share in His presence and power constantly.

It's almost like – forgive me the very imperfect comparison – officially taking into use a public building. You do that once, when the building is opened, with a colourful ribbon-cutting ceremony, and then the building is open for all to enter. You don't constantly repeat the ribbon-cutting ceremony, for that would be an insult to the architect and builder.

Therefore, it is not Scriptural to speak of a "pentecostal" experience today. You can not repeat the pentecostal experience. I do not usually quote from specific sources in this book, but let me by way of exception insert a quote from a masterful little book by Professor Donald MacLoed of the Free Church of Scotland, a book called *The Spirit of Promise.*

Prof. Macloed compares Pentecost to the crossing of a threshold, from one dispensation to the other, and he adds: it is a threshold to be crossed once, and once only into the new era. He writes further, "To speak of present-day experiences as pentecostal is to overlook the unique grandeur of the event. It was one of the decisive moments in the history of redemption, comparable to the crucifixion, the resurrection, and the second advent. Luke's description of it is reminiscent of the appearance of Jehovah on Mount Sinai. . . .To speak of present-day charismatic experiences in these terms would be absurd. Pentecost was a climactic perforation of human history by the divine, a unique point of transition from the era of preparation to the era of fulfillment."

Indeed, a unique point of transition. A definite dividing line between the old and the new covenant, drawn once, after the great sacrifice and the glorious resurrection of our Lord.

A NEW SITUATION

We are now as church of the Lord Jesus Christ in a new situation. The Spirit is present among us, has made His permanent dwelling in the church. That is why we may constantly reap the blessings of Pentecost. We do not need any repetition of Pentecost to share in these blessings, for they are constantly with us. If the Spirit is now with the church, so are the blessings of Pentecost.

What are these blessings? Not necessarily those of the day of Pentecost itself. Those signs had a temporary significance. They belonged, as it were, to the ribbon-cutting ceremony. The blessings which are constant are those which we and all believers of every age and place have in Christ: the blessing of redemption from sin, renewal of life, and the hope of the life everlasting. The building is open: the way to God in Christ through the Spirit is open.

CONSTANT BLESSINGS

Constant blessings, now, because it has been Pentecost. We can speak about the lasting gifts of the Spirit: the Word of God, the offices in the church, the imparting of wisdom and knowledge in the way of salvation through the teaching of the Scriptures, the communion of saints. The Holy Spirit continues also today to guide the church and all its members in the way of Christ Jesus, our Saviour.

Constant blessings. We can speak also about the fruits of the Spirit, as they are mentioned by Paul in Galatians 5: love, joy, peace, patience, kindness, goodness, faithfulness, gentleness, and self-control. Time and again the Holy Spirit brings forth these fruits in the lives of believers everywhere.

And all these gifts and fruits, these manifold blessings, direct us to Christ Jesus, who pours them out from the throne of God by the working of the Holy Spirit. And so the church in all these things glorifies Jesus Christ as the Source and the Giver. The Holy Spirit leads us to glorify Christ as our great Lord and Saviour.

Pentecost, I said, is a unique occurrence, but indeed we still reap the constant blessings today. If it were not for Pentecost and the outpouring of the Spirit, we would not believe in the Lord Jesus. We could not come to faith nor persevere in faith. But we have received the abiding presence of the Holy Spirit as fruit of Christ's completed work of atonement.

Abiding presence. We may sing, Hymn 36 (*Book of Praise*)

> Praise the Spirit who will never
> Leave the Church by blood once bought!

Constant blessings. We may sing, Hymn 36:

> Wilt Thou with our Saviour's merit
> Fill the earth's remotest end.

The one day of Pentecost led to a never-ending flow of spiritual blessings, all merited by Christ and imparted by the Spirit, so that we may sing Israel's Pentecost-thanksgiving song, Psalm 65, in a new light:

> There in Thy holy habitation
> Thou wilt Thy saints provide
> With every blessing of salvation
> Till all are satisfied (Psalm 65: 3)

THE HOLY SPIRIT POURED OUT OVER THE CHURCH OF CHRIST

"And they were all filled with the Holy Spirit and began to speak in other tongues, as the Spirit gave them utterance".

(Acts 2: 4)

It is good and important that we remember the event of Pentecost and constantly reacquaint ourselves with its significance. Of all the christian feasts, besides Ascension perhaps, this one, as we saw in the previous chapter, is maybe the most neglected and the easiest forgotten. What really did happen on Pentecost? How are we to interpret the occurrence in the broader context of the Bible? And what does Pentecost imply for us today, who live in a much different time and age? These questions have our attention in this section.

Pentecost is the last feast on the christian calendar. The festive calendar starts with advent and Christmas, and ends with Pentecost. We may therefore say that Pentecost closes off a certain period of history (the ministry of Christ on earth) and marks the beginning of a new era, the final and concluding phase of world history until the glorious return of the Lord Jesus Christ. This makes a correct understanding of Pentecost very important for the church of Christ.

In the previous chapter we looked at the specific day on which the Holy Spirit was poured out. We now focus on the wondrous signs in, and the amazing results of this outpouring, so that we may get a more complete picture of what happened on that day.

THE HARVEST

We have seen that Pentecost is inseparably connected to the harvest of the crops. We are not going to "allegorize" or spiritualize this, but it is clear that the New Testament speaks in a special way about the harvest. Our Lord Jesus Christ in His parables spoke at various times about it as the gathering in of believers, the gathering of the church. He said, for example, that the harvest was plentiful, but that the workers were few. And we can read in the letter of James, written to Jewish Christians: "Of His own will He brought us forth by the Word of truth that we should be a kind of first fruits of His creatures" (1:18). Here the idea of "first fruits" is indeed concretely tied to believers brought forth by the Word of God.

This is the prophetic significance of the day of Pentecost. That is why the Lord waited for this day. Good Friday and Easter mark the great victory over sin and death; Pentecost marks the beginning of the great and final harvest of those who are redeemed from sin and saved from death. Here is the fulfillment of all the preceding feasts. For now, more than ever before, it is evident that the harvest is from the Lord. He will ensure that His church is gathered out of all peoples and places and times in the unity of the true faith. Because of Pentecost we can say today, "I believe a holy, catholic, Christian church."

WONDROUS SIGNS

Explainers have always been fascinated by the signs which accompanied the outpouring of the Holy Spirit on Pentecost: wind and fire (verses 2 & 3). In the next section I want to devote more attention to these signs, but let us now already take a general look at what is reported in this passage.To be sure, there was no wind and there was no fire, for the Bible says: a sound *like* the rush of a mighty wind and tongues *as of* fire.

The sound of the wind fills the entire "house" where they were sitting. It could have been the upper room where they celebrated the last passover. It could also have been a corridor in the temple. The fire appears first as a ball of fire, from which individual tongues or flames separate themselves, spread out over the gathered disciples and resting on each one of them. They all get their own tongue of fire.

So we have here an audio-visual presentation which was not only apparent to the disciples, but noticed also by outsiders. This at least was true of the sound of the wind, for it caused others to come and to see what could be the cause of these manifestations (verse 6).

SIGNS ARE MERELY INDICATIONS

Now signs are never important in themselves, they always direct us to something greater. And we need not speculate on what these signs may possibly mean, for they simply indicate the presence of the Holy Spirit. From the signs it becomes clear that the Holy Spirit has descended and stays in the midst of the church.

Our Lord Jesus Christ Himself already compared the presence and the work of the Spirit to the wind, when He said to Nicodemus, "The wind blows where it wills, and you hear the sound of it, but you do not know whence it comes or whither it goes; so it is with everyone who is born of the Spirit" (John 3:8).

The wind is symbolic of renewal. It brings the clouds that give the rain. The wind is also symbolic of separation, for it blows away the chaff that clings to the grain. The wind is free and sovereign, and goes where it wills. So the wind is here an indication of the sovereign and free work of the Holy Spirit who renews as He wills and separates believer from unbeliever. In Hebrew the same word is used for "wind" and "spirit."

Fire was already in the Old Testament a sign of the powerful presence of God. Remember the "burning bush" at which Moses first met the LORD. Think of the fiery cloud which guided the people of Israel out of Egypt. Think of the fire and smoke which filled the temple when Solomon dedicated it to the LORD. Therefore John the Baptist could speak about Christ as the one who would baptize with the Holy Spirit and with fire.

Fire is also symbolic of renewal and purification. It burns away the unfruitful branches so that the fruitful branches have more room to grow. You are either warmed or burned by it. It purifies or destroys. And nothing is able to stop its force and power.

GOD HAS COME TO STAY

These two signs convey one message: God Himself has now descended to His people. He has come in the Holy Spirit, in a sovereign and free manner, to live with His people spiritually. Wherever these signs were manifested before, the

LORD God was present, either to bless or to judge, and now on the day of Pentecost God has come to His people in order to stay. For notice how it says of the tongues of fire that they *rest* on each one of them. Rest. Stay. It denotes a position of permanence. As we sing in Hymn 36: "Praise the Spirit who will never leave the Church by blood once bought."

The signs indicate that the Holy Spirit comes in the peace and fellowship which Christ has earned on the cross. He will be a light within the believers and a fiery wall round about them. God is prepared to live with His people for Christ's sake. The distance is gone and the gap has been bridged at Golgotha. We see here the union of God and His church.

At the same time, wind and fire remain powerful, separating, purifying forces! The outpouring of the Holy Spirit brings with it a time of decision. It is the beginning of the last phase, the critical phase of world history. Now the thoughts of men throughout the world will be made manifest by the power of the Spirit. Now the last offensive of the Gospel has begun.

A TIME OF GRACE

Our Lord Jesus Christ spoke of this period of time as a time of grace, as the acceptable year of the Lord. It is the time when repentance is still possible, the time when judgment is held off until the great day of Christ's return. It is also the time when because of Christ there will be division: parents against children, children against parents, brothers against brothers. And out of a man's own family shall come his enemies, for the sake of the Gospel.

The wondrous signs in the outpouring, wind and fire, are very comforting. God dwells with us, for Christ's sake, in the Holy Spirit. We have fellowship with Him by faith. Yet the warning remains: the time of the last decision has come. We will all have to unite in the truth and submit to the true apostolic preaching which began on the day of Pentecost.

THE EFFECT OF THE OUTPOURING

Let us consider yet what is the effect of this outpouring. The immediate effect is that "they were all filled with the Holy Spirit" (verse 4). All of them, not one excluded. All the disciples experience the same gift. There is no distinction between clergy and laity, as if the one has more than the other.

The effect of the outpouring of the Holy Spirit is that the church as a body becomes a prophetic and witnessing church. Some may have a more prominent task in this respect than others, and the apostle Peter will deliver the first Pentecostal sermon, but all are involved and activated by the Spirit to witness of the great work of God.

For we read, "and [they] all began to speak in other tongues." This is the immediately audible effect of the outpouring: the disciples in the house, or now spilling out, as it were, on to the streets, begin to speak "with other tongues."

THE SPEAKING IN TONGUES

There has been much discussion about the significance of these tongues, and whether it is the same thing about which the apostle Paul speaks later in I Corinthians, the ecstatic tongue-speaking which is sought after in Pentecostal groups. I believe that the two are not the same. The tongue-speaking of the Corinthians was not intelligible; no one could follow it unless there was an interpreter. Paul therefore concluded that it was not really edifying for others and that it did not have a prophetic meaning.

But here on the day of Pentecost everybody understands. They all say: we hear them speaking in our own languages, and that means known languages, not some incomprehensible gibberish.

We cannot fully explain this. We do not know whether it lay in the speaking of the disciples or in the hearing of the multitudes that everything could be understood. But the point is: the people heard about the great works of God.

The speaking of the church begins. This means: a new and public ministry of prophecy commences. The normative proclamation of the Gospel and the authoritative apostolic preaching find their starting point on Pentecost in Jerusalem. The church, made bold in the Spirit, comes out to proclaim the Word of God.

"As the Spirit gave them utterance," it says in verse 4. Which means: the Holy Spirit determined exactly what they were going to say and how they were to say it. The speaking of the church is firmly controlled by the Holy Spirit. The disciples, so to speak, are under the quality control of the Spirit; they speak as He wishes. He binds them to the Gospel while they bind the people to the Gospel.

They hear about the great works of God. What else can this be than the work of salvation in Jesus Christ? What else than the redemption and the renewal of life? That is the message of the church since Pentecost. There is life in the Son of God. And it comes with the serious call to repent, to break with a former way of life, and to live from now on according to God's will. The apostle Peter will work these elements out in his subsequent sermon.

AN OFFICIAL BEGINNING

Pentecost then marks the official beginning of the proclamation of the apostolic doctrine. These men in Jerusalem are the first missionaries, the first labourers in the great harvest. And on that day already many are brought in, at least three thousand souls (verse 41). For the Word of God is powerful, "it is the power of God for salvation to everyone who has faith," Romans 1:16.

Do you see how on this day there is already a rich harvest for the Lord? That harvest continues, because Pentecost means an ongoing harvest, until the last has been brought in by the preaching of the Gospel through faith. Our worship, our preaching and baptizing also today are proof that the Spirit is poured out and that the harvest is being gathered.

And when the full harvest is ready, the Son of man Himself shall come and take His harvest home (Hymn 57: 3, *Book of Praise*). That is what Pentecost calls for: the final harvest feast, which is also the marriage feast of the Lamb, when death and sin have been cast away forever, and we receive perfect joy, the eternal ecstasy of full blessedness. That is the one feast which still must come and will come, the feast which will never end.

Special Pentecostal Signs

"And suddenly a sound came from heaven like the rush of a mighty wind, and it filled all the house where they were sitting. And there appeared to them tongues as of fire, distributed and resting on each one of them".

(Acts 2: 2, 3)

Pentecost has been characterized as the unknown feast. Maybe that is true to an extent also among us. What does Pentecost mean? What decisive change did it bring about? I read somewhere that the basic reaction to Pentecost today is the same as it was on the day itself. Verse 12 tells us that ". . . all were amazed and perplexed, saying to one another, What does this mean?"

Pentecost brings the church of Christ into a new situation, and in order to understand that situation, we must know what went on that day. It was the day of the outpouring of the Holy Spirit, and it is very significant for us to see how the Holy Spirit was poured out. Therefore, I want to concentrate on the signs which indicated or accompanied the outpouring. For the unique character of the outpouring of the Holy Spirit is manifested in the special Pentecostal signs. We will look at the meaning and the underlying message of these signs.

SIGNS AND SPECIAL EVENTS

We know that the major events in the history of salvation, Christmas, Good Friday, Easter, and the Ascension, were accompanied by signs. At Christmas there was a special star in the heavens, and a choir of angels sang in Ephratah's fields. On Good Friday there was an earthquake, and the curtain of the temple tore into two parts. At Easter and on the day of Ascension angels appeared to advise the disciples. These signs were not common occurrences, but happened to indicate a new situation.

That is why you do not keep seeing these signs. They are reserved for special occasions. Let this be our first conclusion: whenever we have these signs, God has brought about a new situation. That is why we do not have to have the signs repeated: they stand only at the beginning of that new situation. This is our answer to all who would like to see the special signs, like the speaking in tongues, repeated today.

SIMPLE AND CLEAR SIGNS

At the same time it must be said that when the Lord uses signs, He does not use arbitrary ones, but signs which have a clear meaning. For why use a sign that no one would understand? The signs are marked by simplicity and clarity.

Here I can immediately add: the signs that God uses to point to special occurrences are not entirely new; they have been used before, although under different circumstances. If people know the history of the church well, and if they know the Scriptures, they will immediately understand the significance of certain signs. God uses old signs to herald a new day.

The signs on the day of Pentecost are wind and fire. I will deal later with the exact description of these signs (it does not say that there *was* wind and fire, but something *like* a mighty wind and tongue *as of* fire). First, however, we will seek to determine the meaning of wind and fire in the Scriptures.

WIND AND FIRE

On the day of Pentecost the people, about 120 in all, had gathered in the house with the "upper room" or perhaps in one of the corridors of the temple. While there, they heard a sound like the rush of a mighty wind. It was a very loud and heavy noise, for it brought people running from all directions (verse 6: ". . .at this sound the multitude came together"). The word "rush" indicates the swooping in, swooping down of the noise, like that of an approaching hurricane or tornado, or a gale force suddenly hitting a house. Such winds have the tendency to develop quickly and strike swiftly. That is how we must imagine it here: the sudden, loud rushing in of the wind, a noise so heavy that it drowns out everything else. And you can imagine that people instinctively duck and cringe. No gentle breeze, but gale force one. That is the first sign.

The second is no less remarkable. The disciples see "tongues as of fire, distributed. . ." (verse 3). This description would indicate that these tongues of fire were first together as one ball of fire, which then broke up and distributed itself. It is certainly not something to gaze at without apprehension. If a ball of fire came our way, with the individual flames breaking away toward us, would we not rather step back and get out of its path? This is the second sign.

THE PRESENCE OF GOD

I am firmly convinced that the disciples who had been taught by the Lord Jesus Christ in the Scriptures, knew the meaning of these two signs. They may have been surprised by the sudden and unexpected appearance, and there may have been an initial shock, but they quickly understood what was happening.

For these two signs, wind and fire – especially in combination – clearly denote the presence of God. They can mean only one thing: God is now descending into their midst. They witnessed the *ascension* a few days ago; now they may witness – hear and see – the *descending* of God.

When God came down to His people in the Old Testament it was always with wind and fire, or in thunder and smoke, which are accompanying signs of wind and fire. Let me just give you a few examples. When the LORD God appeared to Moses in Midian, it was in a burning bush. The fire was the visible indication of God's immediate presence. And when Israel was led out of Egypt, they were guided by a "pillar of cloud" by day, and a "pillar of fire" by night. During the day the pillar was like a cloud, smoldering, but at night it glowed a fiery red, and it made clear that God was personally and visibly with them.

And when the people of Israel gathered at Mount Sinai, and the LORD descended on that mountain, we read of "thunders and lightnings and a thick cloud"; yes the whole mountain "was wrapped in smoke because the LORD descended upon it in fire, and the smoke of it went up like the smoke of a kiln. . . "(Exodus 19: 18). A ball of fire descending, leaving in its wake a trail of smoke, accompanied by thunder and storm: this is how the LORD descends!

Can you understand then why Israel so strongly associated occurrences like thunder and lightning with the almighty power and presence of God? Psalm 29 – a good Psalm to sing on Pentecost – speaks of lightning and thunder, storm and fire as signs of God showering peace upon His people. Think also of Psalm 78, where we read how God guided His people with fire and supplied them with food by means of the wind. And note Psalm 18:

> He rode upon a cherub bright and splendid, on wings of storm and wind the LORD descended. . . . Light was His crown and brightness went before Him, Red fire and hail broke through the clouds that bore Him, His thunder roared and echoed through the sky; His mighty voice shook vale and mountain high.

Wind and fire upon the earth, with an all-pervading noise, what else could the disciples think but that God was descending into their midst?

CHRIST'S OWN INSTRUCTION

These signs may have spoken even more clearly to the disciples because Christ, when referring to the Holy Spirit, had spoken of wind and fire. He said: the wind goes where it wills. . . so it is with everyone who is born of the Spirit (John 3). Wind and Spirit. He said that the disciples would be baptized with the Holy Spirit, and did not John the Baptist speak of being baptized with the Holy Spirit and with fire? The Old Testament signs had already a New Testament meaning for the disciples. They knew it on the day of Pentecost: now is being fulfilled what Christ has promised, the outpouring of the Spirit of God. For this we have been waiting ever since the ascension, and the moment has come.

There are, to be sure, secondary meanings of the signs of wind and fire. Commenters have drawn attention to the fact that the wind refreshes and fire purifies. Wind and fire are signs, then, of the regenerating power of the Spirit of God. There is also the explanation that wind and fire make a separation between true and false Israel, between the real believers and the unbelievers, between synagogue and church. They are signs of the great antithesis which has come upon the earth since Pentecost, of the critical nature of the latter days, when God will make manifest what is in the hearts of men.

All this is undoubtedly true. But the meaning of the signs is first and foremost that God comes to live with His people, in the Holy Spirit. He makes a dwelling in His Church, and so Christ Himself comes to live in the midst of His Church. We have a heavenly Head, for the ascension remains a fact, but it is equally true that our Head is now through His Spirit in our midst, to lead and to guide us, together and individually, as His people. This is the clear meaning of the signs. And when we have seen this, we also have an eye for their deeper message.

STAND BACK?

For there is something else here to which we must give attention. When in the Old Testament God descended in person to His people, these signs were meant as a warning, as a means of separation. It was the wind and the fire, the thunder and the smoke, which made Israel keep its distance.

Did not God say to Moses at the burning bush, "Do not come near. . ."(Exodus 3:5? Stay back, for you might get killed! And when the LORD was to descend on Mount Sinai, the LORD strictly charged Moses to tell the people, "Take heed that you do not go up into the mountain or touch the border of it, whoever touches the mountain shall be put to death. . ." (Exodus 19: 12 ff). The same message: stay back, or you're dead!

It was real fire and real wind, which could kill you; real fire and real wind which made you keep your distance. And why was this distance required? Because of the sinfulness of the people. No one could get near to gaze upon the LORD. Even when there was a form of consecration, still none could get through to the LORD. The holy God could not allow sinful people in His immediate vicinity. The wind and cloud were at a distance, the fire burned further away: do not come near.

We are in the Old Testament still in the dispensation of the shadows, the dispensation which symbolized the distance between God and His people, a distance that existed despite the unity in the covenant. Old Testament Israel had a tabernacle and a temple with a curtained-off area where no man could enter, except once per year the high priest. The dispensation of shadows was a dispensation of distance: pillars of smoke, walls of fire, forces of wind and thunder said that God is near and yet unapproachable, close and yet distant.

And this was true in spite of all the sacrifices, in spite of the priesthood of Aaron and his sons, in spite of all the blood of bulls and goats that flowed every day. God was near, but He kept His distance. His Spirit was present, but not in full measure. For the one sacrifice had yet to be made. The great priesthood according to Melchizedek had to be fulfilled. The blood of the Lamb of God had to flow. Then the distance would be terminated. Then the gap would be closed. And then the presence of God would be fully with His people. Then the Spirit of God would be fully poured out over the new, the spiritual Israel, the true sons of Abraham according to the faith. That was prophesied by Joel and Isaiah and others. And that is what happened at Pentecost.

NO MORE DISTANCE NOW

At Pentecost there is no real wind. Remember, I already pointed out that it says: a sound from heaven *like the rush* of a mighty wind. A real wind, a tornado, would have blown them away. If a real typhoon had filled the house, it would have collapsed and they would all have been dead.

There is also no real fire here, but tongues *as of* fire. Had it been a real fire, a burning hot ball of fire with flames leaping out, they would all have been scorched. The whole house would have gone up in flames; no one would have survived.

The same signs appear: God is present! But the signs have lost their destructive power. The signs no longer maintain a distance, but bring about a closeness and display a unity which was absent before. That is the deeper meaning of these Pentecostal signs.

Notice how indeed the noise of the rushing wind fills all the house. Not a part of the house, let's say where no one is sitting, but all the house where they were sitting. This is expressly mentioned. Not: the disciples are here, and the wind is over there. No, the disciples are here, and so is the wind. God and man are together. Notice also how it says of the fire that it was distributed and rested on each one of them. Not: here are the disciples and there is the fire. No: here are the disciples and here is also the fire. God and man are together. There is no separation now.

THE GREAT STEP FORWARD

This is the great step forward. And this was possible only because of the perfect sacrifice of Jesus Christ. Here is the union of a people with God who have been reconciled because of the death of the Son, Jesus Christ. Pentecost is possible only because of Golgotha. The outpouring of the Holy Spirit is a direct result of the outpouring of Christ's blood on the cross. See here the unity of the works of God.

We may never isolate the outpouring of the Spirit from the other great facts of salvation. Never make this the ultimate feast, one that stands on its own, as many so-called Pentecostals do. But see the line in the history of redemption. See the fulfillment of the promise that God will live forever with His people. I think here of Psalm 132, "For Zion by all men admired, the LORD has chosen and acquired, and for His resting place desired. . . For evermore I there will dwell." But this is even richer and truer for us than it was for David. David still looked toward a temple of stones. But we may see here the temple made up of living stones, the body of the Lord Jesus Christ, His Church which He acquired with His own blood. There He will dwell in the Holy Spirit. There He will shed His abundant blessings. Of this people it is really said, "Her saints will shout in happiness."

And all this directs us forward to the day when Christ will physically descend in glory with His angels. For then God will be forever in person with His people. Pentecost is already a great step in that direction, but not the final step. The last promise must yet be fulfilled.

THE SPIRIT CAME TO STAY

But see how far we have come! The tongues of fire, it says here, "rested on each one of them." Literally it says: they sat. That means: permanently. The Holy Spirit is here to stay. There is no distance anymore between the Father and us, through Christ, and in the Holy Spirit. You must understand this, for it is the essence of Pentecost. We all, who are ingrafted into Christ by faith and are living members of His Church, have the anointing of the Holy Spirit.

We do not always work with this properly, and we may even resist the Spirit, but the Spirit is here to stay in the Church. Do we not confess in Lord's Day 20 of the Heidelberg Catechism about the Holy Spirit that "He is also given to me, to make me by a true faith share in Christ and all His benefits, and to remain with me forever"? Yes, Pentecost is for real. It is for keeps. The Spirit is here to stay, to lead us through this life to the life to come, through this world to the world to come.

Let us believe this and work with it every day. Let Christ work in us by His Word and Spirit. Enjoy the reality and fruits of Pentecost daily. We do not need the signs anymore. But we must appreciate the new situation, the grand reality: we who have been reconciled to God by the blood of Christ may live close to Him, for by His Spirit He has bound us to Himself forever.

Called to Profess the Mighty Works of God

". . . we hear them telling in our own tongues the mighty works of God".

(Acts 2: 11B)

Since Pentecost, as I explained earlier, is the feast of the great harvest, it is no wonder that this day was filled with public profession of faith and the administering of holy baptism. We read in Acts 2: 41 that those who on that day received the Word of God confessed their sins, sought refuge in Christ, and were baptized. If the Holy Spirit had not been poured out that day, would we in our time still witness and experience wonderful events such as baptism? The answer is clear to all of us.

Once when I was preparing myself for a church service on Pentecost, I came across a rather interesting description of what Pentecost means. A Reformed professor of theology referred to it as "the birthday of the Christian congregation" (H. Bavinck, *Magnalia Dei*, page 374). If that is a proper qualification, and I believe it is, then we may say to each other on Pentecost: Happy birthday, congregation!

On the day of Pentecost the Christian congregation was born. Now you may say: no, that is not true. The Christian congregation existed long before that day. It existed when Christ called and sent His disciples, even before His death. It existed, in the old dispensation, in the people of Israel. Actually, if you really want to be accurate, you have to say that the Christian congregation was born in Paradise, when God gave to Adam and Eve the promise of the coming Christ.

Yes, the Christian church was born already in Paradise, where the Gospel was first revealed. I will not deny it. But still we can say with our professor that on Pentecost such a decisive step forward is taken that one can speak here also of a "birthday." For on that day the Church of Christ fully comes out of the shadows and begins its public ministry that will reach beyond Israel to the nations abroad. On that day, when the Spirit is poured out, a new life begins for the Church of Christ, a new phase is entered, a major transformation takes place which will have world-wide consequences. Therefore, indeed, Happy birthday, congregation!

For Pentecost is the fulfillment of the promises of old that the Holy Spirit will be poured out over the entire church of Christ, and that all the church will prophesy and testify of the mighty works of God to all the world. The Holy Spirit existed and worked before Pentecost. But on Pentecost it becomes clear: they were *all* filled with the Holy Spirit. This leads to a new day. Indeed, we see in this passage how the Christian Church is called and enabled by the outpouring of the Holy Spirit publicly to profess the mighty works of God. We will note the promising manner and the rich content of this profession.

A UNIQUE EVENT

I have on more than one occasion called Pentecost a one-time, unique event.The outpouring of the Holy Spirit on the day of Pentecost is special and not repeated in the history of salvation. Yes, there are passages in Scripture which speak of the congregation or of individuals being greatly moved by the Holy Spirit after Pentecost (see Acts 4). These events, however, as we will see later, are not a repetition of Pentecost but merely a confirmation that the Holy Spirit has truly come to stay with the church of Christ.

The event itself was unique. You can see that, as we noticed in the previous chapter, in the two signs indicating the outpouring: that of the sound as of a mighty rushing wind, and that of the appearance of tongues of fire which descended upon all members of the congregation. There was also a third aspect, which was as miraculous and wonderful as the first two signs. When the Holy Spirit had taken hold of all those present, these people, we read in verse 4, "began to speak in other tongues as the Spirit gave them utterance." This "speaking in other tongues" is an additional sign of the presence of the Holy Spirit.

The difficulty is how we must understand this speaking. As you know, the apostle Paul later (in his first letter to the Corinthians) discusses what he calls "speaking in tongues." From I Corinthians 14 it is clear that Paul means by this a language that is not understood by other people, unless there is an interpreter. This gift, probably a matter of ecstatic utterances, was perhaps nice for the speaker, but nonsense for the hearers. Therefore Paul's conclusion is: such "speaking in tongues" is not something that convicts unbelievers or outsiders, who will instead conclude that the Christians are mad, crazy. They don't know what you're talking about and cannot be edified.

PEOPLE DO UNDERSTAND

I mention this to demonstrate that at Pentecost something quite different happens. The point in Acts 2, evident in this text, is the opposite: people do understand, and are convicted. Therefore, the speaking in Acts 2 is not the same as what is described in I Corinthians 14.

Luke is, in fact, very careful in choosing his words. The disciples did not "speak in tongues" as such, but he says, "they spoke in other tongues." And it appears from verse 6 ("each one heard them speaking in his own language") and from our text ("we hear them telling in our own tongues") that not some unknown language is meant but concrete languages of that time. The people could hear and understand. This is where the miracle lies.

Now some explainers, who insist on identifying this speaking on Pentecost with what Paul later describes, say that the miracle lies not so much in the fact that the disciples speak in tongues, but rather in the hearing of the people. They say: the disciples spoke only in one tongue but the people heard it as if it was spoken in their own language. So they shift the emphasis from the speakers to the hearers. But this is clearly not the meaning of the passage. The text says that the disciples began to speak in other tongues (various, plural), and that the assembled people heard them speaking in these languages.

MANY NATIONALITIES

That is why we also have in this chapter a list of nationalities, each with its native language. You cannot but think here of Psalm 87: on the roll of nations He will count all these as born on Zion's holy mount, in *many* tongues one God, one faith confessing. Many tongues. One God, one faith. There lies precisely the promise of Pentecost.

People from everywhere could hear the Gospel in their native language. And there must have been quite a variety of tongues spoken by the disciples: there were people from Mesopotamia in the east, to Rome in the west, to Egypt and Libya in the south. Notice how many continents are included here in the "roll of nations": Asia, Africa, and Europe. It includes the whole expanse of the vast Roman Empire and goes even beyond it.

You cannot but ask yourself: why did this happen? Why all these languages? Some scholars have pointed out that actually it wasn't strictly necessary for the disciples to speak in all these different tongues and dialects, for the people described here were mostly religious Jews or proselytes who had come to Jerusalem to celebrate Pentecost, and they all spoke either Greek or Aramaic. Greek was the official language used by most people in the Roman empire, and Aramaic was spoken in the Middle East. One of those two languages was all one needed to know really, and if you threw in a little Latin, you were all set. Indeed, why all these different languages?

It cannot be otherwise than that this speaking in many other tongues holds a promise. The Gospel will be proclaimed to the ends of the earth. The church, which is called to this great mandate, will be enabled to speak to people everywhere in their own language. For it is in their own languages that people need to be approached with the one Word of God. Pentecost is thus placed in the context of a world-wide mission! The outpouring of the Holy Spirit in Jerusalem is not a happening of local, restricted significance, but an event of universal, cosmic magnitude.

THE PROMISE OF PENTECOST

This is the promise of Pentecost, made clear in that speaking in tongues: people everywhere will hear the Gospel proclaimed in their native tongue. There will not be any "special Gospel language" – some holy language which all have to learn first – but people will be approached in their own language with their own historical background and in their own cultural context. It is through this direct preaching in the local languages that people everywhere will come to faith. The preaching will not "transcend" languages and culture, but will use languages and cultural settings to bring people to faith.

Now, of course, this was in Jerusalem a miracle. The disciples were identified as Galileans (verse 7). They were by and large uneducated people, who spoke Aramaic or Greek with a Galilean accent. They had no degrees or university training. It was the Spirit who caused them to speak in these languages to demonstrate the power of Christ.

The text does not suggest that it will always go this way. Today our missionaries must undergo extensive language training. They must also learn to understand the culture in which they will work. This takes time and effort. But the fact remains: the Gospel *will* be made accessible to all nations through the work of dedicated men and women who come to speak to people in their own tongues.

This happened also in our lives. The Word of God has been proclaimed to us in our language, which is English. It was made clear to us in concepts and examples which relate to today, to our cultural and social setting. I do not say that we did not have any problems here. Perhaps our teachers threw in the odd Dutch word, maybe even a Greek or Latin one. Some of us learned to speak the Queen's English in Australia, and sometimes we noticed a bit of a cultural gap. There are those whose background is different from that of the majority; some even have a non-church background. But did all this not fall away when we could speak with each other from the Word of God about the mighty work of God in Christ?

The Gospel must be made accessible to us in our language, so that we can hear it, understand it, and receive it. So the Holy Spirit works personally and intimately in our hearts with words that we can follow. In our own language we learn to receive the Gospel and cherish it. Pentecost holds this promise which is fulfilled time and again.

MIGHTY WORKS

We want to take a look yet at the rich contents of this profession of the church at Pentecost. These people, who hear the disciples speaking, say, "We hear them telling in our own tongues the mighty works of God."

The mighty works of God, that is what the disciples were talking about on Pentecost. The original has here only one word, *magnalia,* a word so rich in meaning that we need two words to translate it. The question is: what is meant here by "the mighty works of God"?

Notice that it says *works,* in the plural. The disciples are speaking on Pentecost not just about one work of God, but of all His works. For God has been working ever since the creation of this world to bring people to the knowledge of salvation. Notice how these works are qualified as being mighty. The works of God are great and splendid, actually beyond adequate description and understanding. In these works God reveals Himself as unique, the only living God of heaven and earth who alone is to be praised for ever and ever. The Holy Spirit was poured out on Pentecost so that people everywhere, through the ministry of the church, would come to know how God worked salvation in this world in Jesus Christ.

MANIFEST IN CHRIST

For is it not in Him that God's mighty works are manifest? Does not the invisible God become visible to us in Jesus Christ? Is He not the One who has wrought for us so great a redemption? When you hear the expression "the mighty works of God," you may think of many wonderful things, but all these works find their core and focus in Jesus Christ! All God's efforts from the beginning of time, the Bible tells us, have their climax and completion in Jesus Christ, in His death, resurrection, ascension and the outpouring of His Holy Spirit.

The public profession of the Church is an *all-embracing* profession. It is about all God's mighty works, as demonstrated in history, as revealed in the Scriptures. But it is also a concentrated profession: it is about God's work *in Christ.* You can see this clearly in the sermon which the apostle Peter delivers on the day of Pentecost. See verse 32 and following: ". . .this Jesus God raised up, and of that we all are witnesses. Being therefore exalted at the right hand of God. . .He has poured out this which you see and hear." Jesus had been promised; He was born; He died and was raised; He ascended and was glorified; He sent His Spirit; and He is now preparing to come again to judge the living and the dead. These are the mighty works of God by which He glorifies Himself and redeems His people. This is the rich content of our profession.

This was the profession and proclamation of the disciples on Pentecost. And this very same profession is still made today. We believe all the mighty works of God, from creation to re-creation. It is still asked today, as it was then: do you believe that you receive the remission of sins in His blood and that by the power of the Holy Spirit you have become a member of Jesus Christ and His Church? Do you seek your life outside of yourself in Jesus Christ? And we say "yes"!

THE SPIRIT STILL WORKS

Is this not proof that the Spirit of God, who was poured out in Jerusalem, still works today? How do you think we would ever have come to this confession? On our own? Never! Through our own insight? Not a chance! It happened only because it has been Pentecost, and the Holy Spirit worked faith in us by the teaching of the Gospel in our own language.

We see here that the church – and all its members – have a great calling: they must speak of "the mighty works of God." The apostle Peter later wrote in his first letter (2:9), "You are . . .a royal priesthood. . .God's own people, that you may declare the wonderful deeds of Him Who called you out of darkness unto His marvellous light." The mighty works. The wonderful deeds. You have to speak of this, declare it to others by word and deed, show it in your life!

For this calling was not just given to the disciples in Jerusalem, but was placed on the entire church and on every member. In our profession of faith we committed ourselves to this before God and His church. We did so, believing that He who brought us this far in His immeasurable grace will also bring us further.

Do you know what the purpose is of our life? To rejoice in the mighty works of God, to praise Him, to let Him work in us more and more the life of holiness, which is a pleasure to Him and a blessing for our neighbour. The mighty works of God must become evident in our life. The church does not just *confess* a doctrine, but *lives* it! It is a doctrine which includes all time, past, present, and future, and a lifestyle which is directed by the Spirit of Christ.

You know, the people of old already sang of the mighty works of God, the one covenantal work in Christ. You see that in Psalm 111:

> Praised be the LORD! I shall impart
> My thanks to Him with all my heart
> Among the righteous congregation
> Great are the doings of the LORD,
> And all to whom they joy afford
> Will study them with dedication.

We today, after Pentecost, have even more reason than the Old Testament Church to praise God for His mighty works of redemption. For we know Him who is our eternal Saviour and who has anointed us with His Holy Spirit.

Let's go back for a moment to our professor. If Pentecost can be termed the "birthday of the congregation," we may congratulate each other. We may congratulate all Christians who professed their rebirth through the Holy Spirit and who, in response to God's promise, committed themselves to the Lord. It all started at Pentecost. We still see the reality of it today. It will be seen until the church is gathered out of all nations. The blessings come to us. The glory goes to God, the Father, the Son, and the Holy Spirit.

Pentecost: The Command and The Promise

"And Peter said to them: repent, and be baptized every one of you in the name of Jesus Christ for the forgiveness of your sins; and you shall receive the gift of the Holy Spirit".

(Acts 2: 38)

When the people in Jerusalem hear the sermon of the apostle Peter on the day of Pentecost, they are moved and disturbed, and they ask, "What shall we do?" (verse 37). It says that they were "cut to the heart." The sermon makes a strong impact on them so that they begin to ask about the way of salvation.

Now it has been suggested that this is the model for all preaching. Every sermon must lead the hearers to this question. Preaching has to make people concerned and restless, so that they begin to examine themselves and their lives and ask what they should do to be saved. And then, of course, the answer is always the same: repent and be baptized and receive the gift of the Holy Spirit.

"What must I do?" We can, in fact, come up with seven or more steps which must be followed – the seven steps of the evangelical Methodists – but they all come down to this: repentance, baptism, receiving of the Holy Spirit.

However, you will understand that preaching is more than leading people (time and again) to the initial question: what shall we do? We may not overlook the context in which these words were first spoken. We must be led by the Word beyond this question to a deeper understanding of the wondrous way of salvation in Christ.

We see something of this in the apostolic response to the question what people must do upon hearing the Gospel of the risen Lord Jesus Christ. This response includes a great command and a great promise.

REPEATING OR UNDERSTANDING?

Pentecost has been seen as the most mysterious happening in the Christian church, for who can fathom the work of the Holy Spirit? As we have noted before, many people have misunderstood it and sensationalized it. Just as Rome constantly repeats Golgotha – Christ's death – in the mass, so Pentecostals constantly attempt to repeat Pentecost, the outpouring of the Holy Spirit. But merely repeating something does not mean understanding it. Exactly what happened on that day of Pentecost in Jerusalem?

Well, the Spirit of God was poured out – once for all – over the church of Christ. That is the basic fact. The next question is then: what is the result of this outpouring? I mean, after all the signs have been taken away, what is the net result?

The result is that the apostle Peter preached a sermon. Yes, Pentecost ultimately leads to preaching. And a sermon has to have a text. Peter took as text for the sermon a word from the prophet Joel, from the well-known second chapter which speaks of the time when God would pour out His Spirit over all flesh, and when all Israel would be renewed. It was, according to Joel, the time that preceded the great judgment, the time of the "latter days."

A CHRISTOLOGICAL SERMON

The apostle Peter explained that text in a *Christological* manner. He said: this text of Joel is fulfilled today, because Christ has risen from the dead, and He "has poured out this which you see and hear" (verse 34). The outpouring of the Spirit, then, leads to a sermon about the resurrection and ascension, the glory of Christ Jesus. That is the heart of the preaching of the church, both in the Old and the New Testament: the mighty works of God in Jesus Christ.

Of course, you understand that for the hearers in Jerusalem this was a very disturbing message. For Peter ends this part of his sermon with a no-nonsense accusation: this Jesus whom you crucified! Most if not all of the hearers of that sermon remembered quite well what had happened during the previous Passover when Jesus of Nazareth was crucified. And now to hear that this Jesus had risen from the dead and had ascended into heaven? Now to see these miraculous signs of Pentecost and to hear these signs connected to the Man who had before already worked so many miracles? Indeed, it was a very disturbing message. And we can well understand that they were cut to the heart. For they shared a corporate responsibility for what had happened. It was the Jews who had said: His blood come over us and our children.

DIFFERING RESPONSES

What shall we do? It was the same question which the people asked when they heard the preaching of John the Baptist at the Jordan, some years before. Severe preaching it was, which led to a convicting of the consciences and to the question: how can we escape the pending wrath of God?

Now this was the *general* mood of the hearers. Do not think that everyone thought this way. We read in verse 41, "So those who received his word were baptized, about three thousand souls." Yes, a lot of people responded positively, but not all. The general mood, however, was indeed one of being touched, frightened, and disturbed, "Brothers, what shall we do?"

And it is in this situation that the apostle Peter responds with the words of our text: "Repent, and be baptized every one of you in the Name of Jesus for the forgiveness of your sins." This is the great command which always accompanies the preaching of the Gospel, first to Jews, and also to Greeks: repent and be baptized.

NO FREE CHOICE

We learn here that the Gospel does not leave us a free choice. It always comes with a serious command. We are called to choose for Christ. This must be a conscious act of ours which is made with our mind and our heart. Everyone who hears the Gospel has a tremendous responsibility. Everyone is called to make a positive response.

The apostle Peter does not say, when confronted with the question: well, don't worry, go home, think about it, and see what you come up with. But he says: repent, and the implication is: do it now, while you hear the Word. Repentance is not something to be postponed until tomorrow, it must take place today.

The word that the apostle uses here for "repent" means in the first place a change of thinking. There is also another word for repentance in the Greek which means a complete turning around, but here it is: a new way of thinking. Repentance is not merely an emotional reaction to a stirring sermon; it is also a new way of looking at things, which implies a change in attitude. The Jews must re-interpret the events surrounding Jesus in the light of the Scriptures and the subsequent facts. Those who hear the Word must, in the light of that Word, change their minds.

A CHANGE OF MIND

This is a hard thing to do. Usually when we have made up our mind, that's it. We will not change it. Some people are even proud of the fact that they never change their mind! They always think the same, so they say. They are stable and firm, or better: stubborn and hard. No change of mind, not ever! Is it wrong, is it weakness to change our mind about something, especially when the Scriptures cast a different light on it?

Of course not. The Gospel comes with the command: Get a different look on things. Start to see with the eyes of the Holy Spirit, in the light of the Scriptures. Re-evaluate God's work of redemption in Jesus Christ. Look again at His mighty deeds of salvation. And in that light, turn away from your sins.

For repentance always has to do with sin. It is always a turning away from sin to God. We know of the expression in Lord's Day 33 of the Heidelberg Catechism that we must have "godly grief" – that is, a grief worked by God – over our sin. And so we turn to Christ, our only Mediator, to be cleansed from all sin by His redeeming and atoning blood.

BE BAPTIZED

That is the significance of the next words: "be baptized every one of you in the Name of Jesus Christ for the forgiveness of your sins." The Jews of Jerusalem were not unfamiliar with the meaning of baptism. It meant a total cleansing. It meant a new start in life. It signified a transition from a former way of life to a new style of life. Only, they had never heard of the baptism in the Name of Jesus for the forgiveness of sins. This was the new element. If they were baptized in this Name, it meant that they acknowledged Him as their only Saviour and placed their lives under His dominion. It meant that they broke with the sins of their people – which were their own sins as well – and were gathered into the church of Christ. It meant a breaking with the old ways and a transition to the new covenant.

In that light we can understand the words of verse 40: save yourselves from this crooked generation. Save yourselves from the generation that has rejected the Christ and which is destined for judgment. Step out before it is too late. Make the transition now. Pentecost marks the ultimate separation between believers and unbelievers. I think here of what we find in Psalm 12, "O LORD, protect us from this generation, Forever save us from their ways of sin."

A PERSONALIZED COMMAND

This is the preaching of the New Testament Church: do not go under with this ungodly world, this crooked generation, but step over from the realm of darkness to the Kingdom of light. And baptism is a visible sign and seal of that transition. By that sign we are distinguished from unbelievers and incorporated visibly into the church of Christ.

It is hard to persuade grown men and women to make this choice. It is not something that you can give your children, not even through much instruction. Do not think that the people in Jerusalem gave themselves without any resistance to the apostolic preaching. Look at verse 40: he testified with many other words and exhorted them. . . . Office bearers need patience and perseverance in testifying from the Scriptures, in persuading and exhorting, and even then they must leave the fruit to the Spirit of God.

Notice also how the apostle makes this command a very personal one: be baptized every one of you in the Name of Jesus. Everyone has to make his/her own decision. It is a deeply personal commitment. We have a corporate responsibility as members of the human race, yes, but also an individual responsibility when the Word of God comes to us. Whoever hears the Gospel cannot hide away in the crowd, for the Lord comes with His Word to each one personally and says: what about you? And you? And you? And one day we shall all stand individually before the judgment seat of God and be judged personally.

INFANT BAPTISM HERE?

Do not conclude here now that this text is proof against infant baptism, since children cannot yet face up to this personal responsibility. Peter speaks here in the first place to adults, to mature Jews who knew the Scriptures and had seen many signs. All non-baptized adults who come to faith in Christ must be baptized as sign of their separation from the world and their incorporation into the body of Christ. But Peter also says that this extends to believers *and their children* (verse 39). The line of the covenant stands firm also in the New Testament: when adults come to faith and are baptized, their children share in the same promise and so receive the same sign. And as the children grow up, they themselves are faced with the command of the Gospel to be born again, to repent and believe, and so to respond to their baptism, to accept it joyously that God set them aside already in their youth and made them His children.

Repent and be baptized. Do you see how the Gospel demands of us a totally new life? Completely dedicated to God, fully separated from this world? This command comes to us with even more clarity and depth today that it did on that day in Jerusalem. We are not strangers to the Gospel. We have for the most part been taught it from our youth. To be baptized means for us: to be a living member of the Church of Christ. This is the calling that comes to us every Sunday again: look alive out there, be living members of Christ and of His church. But the command also has a rich promise. If we obey, we will more and more receive the gift of the Holy Spirit.

THE SURE PROMISE

For Peter adds, ". . .and you shall receive the gift of the Holy Spirit." Those who repent and are baptized will receive the Spirit. This is the promise of the Gospel. And the Gospel must always be preached with this specific and sure promise, as once on Pentecost.

"You shall receive the gift of the Holy Spirit." It is quite clear what the apostle Peter means. The disciples have manifested in their actions that they have received something special, but that gift is not for them only; it is for all believers. Pentecost is for all God's children. Those who repent and are baptized will receive the *same* gift as the apostles and the disciples.

We must read here carefully. It does not say: you shall all receive in the same measure the gifts (plural) of the Holy Spirit, but the gift (singular). This means: the gift which consists in the Holy Spirit Himself. Repent and be baptized, and you will receive the Holy Spirit. He will come to dwell in your hearts and in your lives.

Now someone may say: is this not turning the order around? Do we not teach in the Reformed Churches that we can only repent through the Spirit? Is it not first the Holy Spirit and then repentance? Or must we say – as do Arminians – first we must make our own free-will choice to repent and then the Holy Spirit will come to live with us? Is that what the apostle says? You do your bit first, and then God will do the rest?

A SPECIFIC ORDER?

Let us not make any problems here. The apostle does not prescribe a specific order. No one can repent except by the power of the Holy Spirit. No one can profess Jesus Christ except by the Spirit. In Acts 10, for example, it is the other way around: first they receive the Holy Spirit and then they are baptized. No order is established here. The point is that the initial work of the Holy Spirit in working repentance and faith is continued mightily when one places himself/herself in the communion of the church.

The Holy Spirit has been poured out over the church of Christ, which manifests itself according to His norms in its worship, office bearers, and members. By baptism, through profession of faith, we are placed in that church, we share in that communion and so we also receive the gift of the Holy Spirit. The Holy Spirit is given to us there where He is poured out, namely in the Church which Christ has purchased with His precious blood. It is in the church-gathering work of Jesus Christ that we receive and experience the gift of the Holy Spirit and nowhere else.

When we place ourselves faithfully under the preaching of the Word and give ourselves diligently to the service of the Lord, when we say, "I love thy saints, with them I am united" (Psalm 16), we will experience the renewing power and guiding strength of the Holy Spirit.

Pentecost means: the Spirit of God has been poured out over the Church of Christ. Therefore, when I in obedience to the Word of God maintain the unity of that church, I share in the gift of the Holy Spirit. He will then also live and work in my heart, in my life.

DO NOT SEPARATE WHAT GOD HAS JOINED TOGETHER

People often separate what God has joined together. Also Spirit and Church. Or Spirit and Word. Or Spirit and faithful office bearers. And they suggest that the Spirit works everywhere. But the promise of Pentecost is this: where the apostolic church is, there is the Spirit of God. Where the fountain is, there is the water of life.

No, we do not bind the Spirit in any way. The wind blows where it wills, and so it is with the Holy Spirit, and by His power fountains can appear suddenly in the driest deserts. But the Spirit of God binds and calls us to the place where He will fill our lives with the Word and the mercies of Christ, to the church which by God's grace is faithful to His Word.

"You shall receive the gift of the Holy Spirit." This means that whoever comes to Christ and publicly professes Him before many witnesses in the midst of the saints will be confirmed in the faith, confirmed and strengthened every week, every day again. For that is what this gift of the Spirit means: God Himself will dwell in us, God Himself will lead us and perfect us, keep us and preserve us, so that we may cross the finish line in His strength.

THE GREAT PROMISE OF THE GOSPEL

This is the great promise of the Gospel. The Holy Spirit will apply to us all the riches of Christ and cause us to persevere in the faith, the faith that all things come to us out of God's sovereign grace in Christ Jesus, by His perfect work alone.

This does not mean that there will not be trials and temptations. There may be times even of great doubt. We may still fall deeply into sin. We confess in the Canons of Dort, "Scripture testifies that believers in this life have to struggle with various doubts of the flesh and placed under severe temptation do not always feel the full assurance of faith and certainty of persevering." Life remains a discipline in living in God's grace (also after we have professed our faith). But the gift of the Spirit remains, for we also confess, in the same Canons, that God will "by the Holy Spirit again revive in [the believers] the certainty of persevering." So that in their deepest need believers may know: all my trials, Lord, will soon be over.

THE ONLY WAY OF SALVATION

The people asked Peter: what shall we do? And the answer was: repent and separate yourselves from this crooked generation. Be joined to the true Israel, the spiritual Israel, and the Spirit of God will abide with you forever. "The Spirit and the gifts are ours," said Martin Luther. This is still the command and the promise with which the Gospel is preached to everyone, indiscriminately, no matter what his place or standing. It is the only way of salvation, for the Jew and also for the Gentile, for us and for our children today.

When Peter preached his sermon on Joel 2, the church was not as far yet as it is today, when we may preach on Acts 2. Pentecost is not to be repeated; the new era is here, the last days have arrived. The reality of Pentecost is to be experienced, every day. Now we look forward to the day when Christ in glory will shine on the clouds of heaven, in the faith that "From heaven He sent His Spirit down, Christ keeps us by His power secure. We'll never be forsaken" (Hymn 31: 5, *Book of Praise*).

We will never be forsaken, for we have received the gift of the Holy Spirit.

Pentecost Confirmed

"And when they had prayed, the place in which they were gathered together was shaken; and they were all filled with the Holy Spirit and spoke the word of God with boldness".

(Acts 4: 31)

I have been explaining to you from Scripture how the outpouring of the Holy Spirit is a one-time event, which cannot be repeated and is not repeated. When the Spirit was poured out, He came to stay, permanently. You might say that this is the classic, Reformed position.

But there are various passages, also in the Book of Acts, which clearly state that the apostles and others were filled with the Holy Spirit after Pentecost. I think of what we read in our text, "and they were all filled with the Holy Spirit." Just compare that with Acts 2: 4 (the Pentecost story) and you find the same words. Does this not indicate that the "Pentecost experience" has been and can be repeated?

Now we will not deny that in various places after Pentecost we can read about people being filled with the Spirit. In Ephesians 5: 18, we even read the command, "And do not get drunk with wine, for that is debauchery, but be filled with the Holy Spirit." You should note, however, that in Ephesians 5 the apostle does not say: be filled with the Holy Spirit for the first time, for he uses the present imperative tense: be constantly filled with the Holy Spirit. Instead of constantly getting drunk, he writes, be constantly filled with the Spirit. Paul there does not say that we have to repeat Pentecost, but that must always live through the Holy Spirit who was once poured out and now dwells in the church.

REMARKABLE DIFFERENCES

Back to Acts 4. When you compare what happens in that chapter with what is reported in Acts 2, you notice some remarkable differences. First of all, the signs of Pentecost (tongues of fire, the sound of a mighty wind, speaking in other tongues) are not repeated. There is no massive gathering of people from everywhere who come to see and hear what is going on. There *is* a sign, the place where the disciples are gathered is shaken, but that is restricted to this one place. No one else notices it. Pentecost showed us mighty signs for the whole city, but Acts 4 gives us one sign for the small church. As much as Pentecost was a public affair meant for all, so Acts 4 is a private affair, restricted to the congregation.

And when it says in Acts 4 that they were all filled with the Holy Spirit, it means that the Spirit again powerfully came over them, but for a specific purpose, as we will see. That happened more often, earlier with Peter, later with Stephen, always in a special situation. May we rightly call these events a repetition of Pentecost?

We really see something different. Throughout the Book of Acts, on particular occasions, we see how the Lord Jesus *confirms* that it has been Pentecost, and that the Spirit will never leave the church by blood once bought. But confirmation is not the same as repetition. The situations, the signs, and the events described are all different from what happened at Pentecost. They are related, but not the same.

A CRITICAL SITUATION

Here in Acts 4 there is good reason for the Lord Jesus to reassure His church. For the situation is serious. The Jewish Sanhedrin has for the first time officially forbidden the apostles to speak in the Name of Jesus. It has underlined this with threats. The counter-attack is now beginning. And the question is: will that small church be able to withstand the pressure of a growing intimidation, yes, even the prospect of persecution?

What do we read in this text? Christ reassures His church that the Holy Spirit will not leave the church. He will enable His church, through the indwelling of the His Spirit, to withstand the opposition from the world, so that the progress of the Gospel is not impeded. So it will go, despite the cost and suffering, from this time forth, until the last one has been gathered in. That is the message of this text, which we will explore in a little more detail. We will see how this confirmation of Pentecost is a response to prayer, is revealed in power, and results in progress.

A TURN OF EVENTS

On Pentecost, we can say, the Lord Jesus Christ opened up a mighty evangelical campaign: the Gospel was preached everywhere in Jerusalem, many signs and wonders were done by the apostles, and on the first day there were tallied about three thousand souls. And so it continued, day after day. The new congregation showed that it was motivated and guided by Christian love, people kept coming to the church, and we read in 2: 47 that they experienced "favour with all the people."

A young, enthusiastic, growing church, and a very popular movement had sprung up. The apostles, we'd say, are really on a roll here. And we can be sure that they were excited about what was happening. It was a time of optimism and unexpected opportunities. No one offered any opposition to the church and its ministry.

Then comes the turn of events. After the healing of the lame man at the gate of the temple, Peter and John address a jubilant crowd. But suddenly the temple police, under the leadership of the priests and the Sadducees, come and arrest the two apostles. Since it is already evening, they are put in prison until the next day. And we read in chapter 4 how the Sanhedrin, the Jewish council, meets to deal with them. It becomes clear to everyone present that the Name of Jesus is the focal point, Jesus, whom they had crucified.

The Jewish council is rather stuck with the whole matter. They could not deny that a miracle had taken place. They did not dare at this time (yet) to take drastic measures, because the Christians were too popular with the general populace. What did they do? They came up with their first counter-measure: a prohibition to speak again in the Name of Jesus: "speak no more to anyone in this Name." And they threaten that further measures will be taken if the apostles continue with this preaching. Then they let the two men go.

CONCERN FOR THE FUTURE

This is a serious matter. The apostles could have expected that the repressive regime of the Sanhedrin would act sooner or later. They also know that the threats are not idle boasts, for the Sanhedrin has earlier demonstrated their determination and cunning. They turned the people against Jesus, and can also turn the people against the apostles. For the first time since Pentecost a major crisis has risen which will affect the ministry and life of the church.

We read in verse 23 that the two apostles went "to their friends" to report what the chief priests and elders had said to them. These friends, fellow-apostles and others, will have been gathered together, awaiting the outcome of the trial. They were under much stress, of course, as they waited to hear what had happened. And when Peter and John tell them about the prohibition to speak in Jesus' Name, everyone realizes how serious this is. There is gladness that Peter and John are released, and they praise God for this. But at the same time, there is great concern about the future. They know: if we continue to preach the Name of Jesus, and we must, then we will come to clash with the Sanhedrin. There's a storm brewing on the horizon. It may take some time yet to arrive, but it is coming.

A CONGREGATIONAL MEETING

We get the impression from verse 24 that some kind of a "congregational meeting" was held. The congregation did not shrug off the threats of the Sanhedrin and take a light-hearted approach. They did not build on their current popularity and momentum. They built only on the promises given in God's Word.

They all gathered for a special prayer meeting. It says in verse 24: they lifted their voices together in prayer to God. They felt the crisis. They sensed their need and peril. There was no triumphalism here, as if they would easily overcome all adversity. They humbled themselves before God.

There is a strong connection between this prayer and their "being filled with the Holy Spirit." Our text says: and when they had prayed, they were all filled with the Holy Spirit." The Holy Spirit, as we confess also in Lord's Day 45 of the Heidelberg Catechism, is given only to those who with hearty sighing unceasingly beg for Him. We can only receive the ongoing strength of the Spirit upon sincere and heartfelt prayer. But if we pray in that manner, we will be answered. We might even translate, "While they were yet praying, they were all filled with the Holy Spirit." The prayer is immediately answered, according to need.

PENTECOST LEADS TO CRISIS

We should therefore take a brief look at this prayer, and note its main features. First, they call upon the Lord as Sovereign. His power and Word surpasses all power and edicts of men. Second, they base their prayer on the Scriptures, by quoting from Psalm 2. Why Psalm 2? Because this Psalm speaks about the great conspiracy against God and His anointed, His Messiah.

And while the Psalm itself speaks of a battle between the LORD and the nations, the disciples see the Jewish leaders as siding with these ungodly nations against the Lord Jesus. They mention specifically Herod and Pontius Pilate with the Gentiles and the people of Israel. The apostles see things in a broad perspective. The fallen world and the false church rise up together against God and His Christ.

Now that's all they quote: the rebellion against the Christ of God. They indicate: the battle which has been going on for ages has now reached its final stage. Now the last persecutions will begin. Now the great tribulation will commence. Psalm 2 will find its ultimate fulfillment in the last showdown between Satan and the seed of the woman. And they all realize that this matter is too much for them.

You see, Pentecost brought about a great crisis in this world. Get away from the idyllic scenes of the first Christian church, whose members had everything in common and lived in the favour of all. The first shots have already been fired. Soon there will be the first casualties, Stephen and James, followed by many others. The church can not cease preaching and the world will not cease its destruction. This is the first confrontation which will lead to many, even more violent and widespread confrontations. The earth will turn red with the blood of the martyrs.

THE ULTIMATE COMMITMENT

There is a strong temptation here for the church. The apostles can still back off. The Sanhedrin has made it clear that they will not cease and desist. Now the disciples must make the ultimate commitment. This is the point of no return! Do you see what is taking place here in our text? No repetition of Pentecost, but the church facing the consequences of Pentecost.

It is not easy to remain a Christian when the tide is turning against you and when the ultimatum has been issued. This little congregation does not make light of the matter or exude any self-confidence. As they turn to Psalm 2, they also plead with the Lord to fulfill that Psalm in their lives and to grant them victory in the evil hour. Is it not the Lord God who precisely for this situation gave the promise and comfort of Psalm 2:

> Lo with a rod of iron Thou shalt break them
> Dash them in pieces like as potter's jar?

Turning to the Scriptures, they realize that it is not their fight, but the Lord's . Not their honour is at stake, but His glory. And they can stand in that battle only in the Lord's strength. Now that the final hostilities break loose, they ask, "Lord, look upon their threats, and grant to thy servants to speak with all boldness. . . ."

A POWERFUL CONFIRMATION

What the church will need in the last days is assurance, certainty, that the Lord Jesus, Who has all power in heaven and on earth, will thwart the evil designs of the ungodly and enable His people by the power of the Holy Spirit to persevere and remain faithful. If we ever need the comforting presence and the motivating power of the Holy Spirit, it is now.

The disciples are disturbed, but they are not dismayed. They open the Scriptures, and plead on God's own promises. And while they are still praying, "the place in which they were gathered together was shaken." When Pentecost is confirmed, it is confirmed in a very powerful and unmistakable manner! What is more powerful, humanly speaking, than an "earthquake," when the very building you are in is shaken?

Now the Greek text does not use here the normal word for earthquake. The word denotes more a strongly noticeable shaking and rattling. The ground did not really shake but the "place where they were gathered" (that is: the building) shook! This underscores that the sign was limited. Whoever was not in the building did not notice it. It is not a sign for all of Jerusalem, but only for the congregation. God does not want to shake up the city, He wants to strengthen His little church.

For that is the meaning of the shaking: God confirms His presence and power. The disciples knew that God's presence was often demonstrated in earthquakes, in the shaking of the environment. It is therefore a direct sign to them that the Lord has heard their prayer and responds to their needs. The shaking demonstrates, as it were, that God has come into motion from the throne in heaven.

> He Who sits in the heavens laughs,
> The LORD has them in derision (Psalm 2).

They pray: look upon their threats! The enemy is trying to close us down and shut us up. But God says: they can never turn back the clock. It has been Pentecost. The Holy Spirit has been poured out. I will not be stopped by them. And the whole house begins to move and shake.

EQUIPPED FOR THE CHALLENGE

And we read, "and they were all filled with the Holy Spirit." What? Had they not been filled with the Holy Spirit before? Yes, they had. Was that, then, not sufficient? Yes, it was. Did that filling with the Spirit "peter out"? No it didn't.

Why then this "filling with the Holy Spirit" now? Well, the Lord Jesus simply equips them to meet the challenge of the day, in the crisis of the times. Pentecost is confirmed. The disciples are enabled to face this new challenge in the assurance of the power of the Holy Spirit.

That is what they had asked for on the basis of God's Word, is it not? They had prayed, "grant to thy servants to speak thy word with all boldness." They had spoken with boldness before, even to the Sanhedrin (see how it says in verse 8, that Peter, *filled with the Holy Spirit,* addressed them). They asked: grant us in this new situation, now that we are under an express prohibition to speak, that we continue speaking with the same boldness, yes, even with more boldness than before.

It is the Lord Jesus who in this way at this precise moment makes clear to His church how true Psalm 2 really is. The Lord will not back down, but neither will His church. He will grant strength according to need, and so He will always confirm to His people the reality of Pentecost. When we need it, we will be filled with the Holy Spirit who dwells in the midst of His people and in our hearts.

What we need, also today, is not Pentecost redone, but Pentecost confirmed. We need to believe and experience the help and power of the Spirit of God in all the challenges of the last days. We need strength in trials. The trials differ from age to age and from time to time. The temptations and persecutions are not always of the same nature and intensity. But we need to be filled with the Spirit *always* to speak with boldness; to be confessing Christians in word and deed, regardless of opposition or consequence.

We have to pray for this, of course. There is a strong connection between prayer and being filled with the Spirit. We must bring our *specific* needs before God's throne and ask for ongoing spiritual strength to meet the challenges of the times, the trials of our life. When this is our constant prayer, we will be able to continue in our time, as the disciples in their time.

THE NEW ELEMENT

For notice the last words of our text: and they spoke the word of God with boldness. Here we see that it is not a repetition of Pentecost, for this is really nothing new. It was "new" on the day of Pentecost, but it is the order of the day since Pentecost. The new element is that they did not cease speaking. What was not forbidden on Pentecost is forbidden now, but they continue speaking with boldness.

That is the progress about which this text speaks. The church will not be muzzled. God's work must continue. Even if Jews and Gentiles band together against the LORD and His Anointed, the church will not be silenced.

They spoke the word with boldness not just in that house, but in the temple and in the streets, see verse 33. The disciples continue to preach that Jesus is truly risen from the dead. The order "do not speak anymore in the Name of Jesus" leads to the exact opposite: even more speaking in the Name of Jesus.

The word "boldness" literally means: speaking everywhere with courage. For courage is what the church needs in the latter days, in critical situations. It must be strong in Christ, firm in conviction, unceasing in testimony and preaching.

COURAGE TO CONTINUE

You see how in Acts 4 we are one step further than in Acts 2? In Acts 2, on Pentecost, the church moved from behind closed doors into the streets to speak of the risen Lord and Saviour. And in Acts 4 we read that this church will not be pushed back behind closed doors, but receives the courage and conviction to continue even in the face of prohibition and persecution.

The church prayed: Lord, let the initiative of Pentecost not be snuffed out. And Christ assured His church on the spot: do not worry, they can never turn back the clock, the Spirit is here to stay. As the ages unfolded, even until today, that courage is still Christ's gift to His church. It has been all progress since then.

Do not ask the Lord Jesus to repeat Pentecost. Ask Him to confirm His promises to you, to confirm in your life that it has been Pentecost and that the Spirit is also with you in your circumstances, to give you courage to face the challenges of life in a fallen and apostate world. And believe, also because of this text, that Christ will never desert you in the battle of faith.

And you will discover, as the church did in Jerusalem, that Christ will complete also in you what He has begun. He brings His people through the crises, by the power of the Holy Spirit. So that we do experience it: the Spirit is greater than any crisis which we face in life.

God is our refuge, He will shield us
And to our foes He will not yield us
He is our strength in troubles nigh
Our Help is He, the LORD most high (Psalm 46: 1, *Book of Praise*).

The Fruit of the Spirit Manifest in Our Lives

"But the fruit of the Spirit is love, joy, peace, patience, kindness, goodness, faithfulness, gentleness, self-control; against such there is no law".

(Galatians 5: 22, 23)

What effect does the outpouring of the Holy Spirit have in our lives? I mean, what practical effect? How does it change our lives, our thinking and our behaviour? We must deal with this question, otherwise the remembrance of Pentecost can become theoretical and formal.

Some may say: I don't really detect much difference in my life as a result of Pentecost. And this is where despair may set in: if the Holy Spirit is poured out, why do I see in my life so much of the works of the flesh and so little of the fruit of the Spirit? The works of the flesh can dominate us so strongly. And then it can become a matter of deep concern, for Paul writes, "I warn you as I warned you before that those who do such things shall not inherit the kingdom of God" (Galatians 5:21). We can feel so unclean and useless, so afraid and ashamed before God, because of the works of the flesh.

Paul makes it sound so easy, "Those who belong to Christ Jesus", he writes, "have crucified the flesh with its passions and desires" (Galatians 5: 24), but we realize in our lives that something which is being crucified is not necessarily dead. The "flesh with its passions and desires" may be nailed to the cross, but it is putting up a tremendous fight to stay alive. This causes difficulties for us all.

Pentecost reminds us of our great riches. The fullness of the Holy Spirit poured out over us means that we are partakers of the anointing of Christ. We have received much. But now we must also render much! God wants to receive out of the fullness which He Himself has given.

The comfort of Pentecost is that He *will* receive, because the Holy Spirit exercises this decisive power in our lives that they bring forth fruit. In this chapter we will take a closer look at the fruit of the Holy Spirit as it is manifested in the life of the believer. We take note of the purpose and the great variety of this fruit.

FAITH ALWAYS EVIDENT IN WORKS

The churches of Galatia who were the recipients of this letter had been brought to confusion by a false teaching. They were told that one is not saved by faith only, but also by the works of the law, specifically the ceremonial laws, such as circumcision. This is the Judaist heresy which in so many forms can plague the church of Christ.

But whenever we are warned against this heresy, and told that we are saved only by faith, through grace, we are reminded that faith becomes evident in good works. There is no such thing as faith without works.

This is what Paul wants to drive home in chapter 5 of his letter. The liberty which we have in Christ may not be turned into a licence to do all kinds of evil. We read in verse 13, "Do not use your freedom as an opportunity for the flesh."

MARKED CONTRAST

The "fruit of the Spirit" stands in contrast to the works of the flesh (see verse 19). That is why the text begins with the word but: "But the fruit of the Spirit. . . ."

I am convinced that the apostle, guided by the Holy Spirit, has chosen his words with great care and discernment. Works (plural) of the flesh over against fruit (singular) of the Spirit.

The works of the flesh. Plural, because there are so many of them. "Our countless misdeeds and transgressions prevail from day to day" (Psalm 65: 2, *Book of Praise*). Evil is abundant and pluriform; there is no end to sinful ingenuity. But *fruit* of the Spirit. Fruit, singular, because in all its variety it is one and the same thing, coming from one Source and having one purpose, namely the renewal and transformation of our life.

The word *works* (of the flesh) stresses our own evil *will.* These works are the things we do according to our natural inclination. The term indicates the preoccupation of the sinful flesh, the searching after evil. We are always, so to speak, working at the pursuit of evil.

The word fruit, however, stresses God's grace. Fruit is the product of growth, and growth is possible only through care and love. You cannot really grow something unless you nurture it with care and have patience with it as it grows.

GROWTH AND MATURITY

So we understand some of the beauty of this expression, "the fruit of the Spirit." The Holy Spirit has been poured out over the church, and He has only one purpose: our growth and development as children of God. He patiently seeks fruit in our lives. The Holy Spirit does this in the love of Christ. Never think small of the love of Christ with which the Holy Spirit nurtures us so that we may grow and bring forth fruit.

When you read the word "fruit," you must also think of maturity. We must produce ripe fruit, ready to be harvested. Now you know that all growth and development takes time. Ripe, fresh fruit does not appear overnight. It must have a starting-point, yes, but it must also go through a distinct process. Well, so it is with a Christian. We need time to mature, basking in the warmth of God's love, nurtured by the nourishment of God's Word. Then the Holy Spirit brings forth fruit in our lives. That means that then He develops in us a new nature, a new person, a Christian character, the mind of Christ. This is the purpose of the fruit of the Spirit: to show forth in us the mind of Christ.

HOW DOES FRUIT GROW?

Growth and maturity. This leads us to the question how things grow. The Bible has some beautiful passages on growth, especially spiritual growth.

I think of Psalm 1, the introduction to the whole Book of Psalms. It says there: the believer is like a tree "planted by streams of water that yields its fruit in its season" (verse 3). Planted in good soil, so that the roots can go deep. That is the first requirement for growth. And this is what the Lord Jesus Christ spoke about in the parable of the vine and the branches (John 15). We are rooted, in Christ. We are connected to Him by faith. And now the Holy Spirit draws up from Christ the fruit, an abundant fruit wherein the husbandman, the Father, is glorified.

The fruit of the Holy Spirit in us is the same as the fruit of Christ in us. He is the vine, and we are the branches, and the fruit is the result of His live-giving and life-sustaining power. We do not bring forth fruit on our own. We cannot do so. We must be connected to Christ by faith. See how all is related here: there is no separation between Father, Son and Spirit. They all work together in one purpose: the growth and perfection of the Church.

ADVERSE CONDITIONS

The first thing that the Spirit always does, therefore, is lead us to Christ, through the Word. He says: here is your Source, here is the only connection. Believe in Christ that all your sins are forgiven, and then start to grow in faith.

Can we understand this growth? I know that I do not see it enough in my life. Sometimes I think that there is no growth at all and that I am actually withering. Remember also that everything that grows takes a beating. Think of all the contrary conditions to growth for a little plant. There is the wind, the drought, the trampling underfoot. It is often amazing that the plant even survives. Psalm 80 speaks about the need for divine protection, when it says: "O God of hosts grant preservation, protect Thy vine from devastation. Help Thou the son of man to stand." The vine has no strength of its own. So it is with us. There is the leaven of sin, the weakness of the flesh, the temptations of the world, the power of the devil.

THE NEED FOR PRUNING

And when we do bring forth fruit, we get pruned. Christ said that "Every branch that does bear fruit, He prunes, so that it may bear more fruit" (John 15: 2). A pruned tree looks pitiful, stripped down, cut back, naked. Pruning hurts. But if you don't prune the vine, it becomes unfruitful. There will be nothing but leaves.

The fruit of the Spirit, then, is manifest despite many contrary conditions and through much pruning. The book of growth, the Book of Psalms, speaks of those conditions. But it also rejoices in the abundance of fruit which in the end does appear by God's grace.The same book which confesses that "our countless misdeeds and transgressions prevail from day to day" also says "the righteous man is like a tree which by the streams yields fruit abundantly."

The command to bring forth fruit is seriously meant. There must be fruit. Christ said: every branch that does not bear fruit is taken away and burned. At the same time it contains much comfort, for it is the Spirit who will bring forth this fruit. We should not think lightly of the effective power of the Holy Spirit, of the love of Christ, and of the boundless mercy of God, who does not quench the flickering flame or break the bruised reed. Don't give up, no matter how hard you fall, but flee to Christ, seek the Word, and pray for the fruit of the Spirit in your life.

ENDLESS VARIETY

The text continues by *describing* the fruit of the Spirit, and this description shows the variety of this fruit.

We should, incidentally, not confuse the expression "the fruit of the Spirit" with another Biblical expression, "the gifts of the Spirit," as we meet it, for example, in I Corinthians 12. When we read about the gifts of the Holy Spirit, we discover that the apostle means specific gifts which one believer may have in contrast to another. The gifts of the Holy Spirit are mentioned specifically as: wisdom, knowledge, faith, healing, miracles, prophecy, speaking in tongues, interpreting of tongues. Not every believer has these gifts, Paul writes. They are distributed among the members. That is why the word is in the plural. There are many different gifts – literally "charismata" – in the church, and not every one has the same.

It is different with the expression "the fruit of the Spirit." For this is given equally to and required equally of all believers. We do not all have the same spiritual gifts – and some of these, like speaking in tongues, have disappeared in the church – but the Lord requires of His church always, in Paul's days and today, the same fruit. So keep them distinct, "fruit" of the Spirit as constant and common, in contrast to "gifts" of the Spirit as changing and specific.

And when you look at the description of the fruit of the Spirit you notice indeed how varied it is. Just as varied as life itself. And yet it all belongs together. It is like the colours of the rainbow: many different colours, yet one rainbow, and the colours together make the whole effect. Variety in unity, in conformity to the one Law of God.

I should point out that this listing is not exhaustive. There are known manuscripts, other than the ones used for the text of the Revised Standard Version, which contain even more Christian virtues. And there are examples of other listings (Ephesians 5, Colossians 4) which bring forward different aspects. The point is that the Bible speaks about every area of our life, and therefore such a listing of virtues, of spiritual fruit, cannot be formal or fixed.

FRUIT IN CLUSTERS

Fruit tends to come in clusters. Variety of fruit means an abundance of fruit. Christ said, "By this my Father is glorified that you bring forth much fruit" (John 15: 8). We may think that we have produced enough, but the Lord always seeks more fruit in us. He looks for constant growth and development so that there is an ever greater yield.

Speaking of clusters: our text mentions nine virtues which some explainers have divided by three, so that there are three clusters of three virtues each. Such a grouping is indeed relevant for a better understanding of the text.

The first three words (love, joy, and peace) speak about an upward line, to God. They are especially the fruit of a living relationship with God. The second cluster (patience, kindness, and goodness) suggest an outward line; they are the fruit of a Christian fellowship with our neighbors. And the third cluster (faithfulness, gentleness, and self-control) give us more an inward line: they refer to the fruit of the Spirit in our personal life, the deep transformation of our character. The fruit of the Spirit is evident in all our relationships: with God, with our neighbor, and with ourselves.

NO CONDEMNATION

Our text also tells us that where this fruit appears there is true freedom and happiness. "Against such there is no law," writes Paul. That means: the law does not condemn such people. It can also mean: more than this, God does not ask. The Judaizers said: God wants to you keep the whole law of Moses, with all the ceremonies, or else you are condemned. But Paul says: no, where the varied fruit of the Spirit is evident over the entire spectrum of our life, where much fruit appears, there is no condemnation and there are no further demands. God asks only that we bring forth much fruit of gratitude; He does not ask that we save ourselves.

It is Christ Jesus who "full atonement made and brought to us salvation" (Hymn 24: 5). What we are doing, or better yet, what the Spirit of God is doing, is building on the foundation of salvation laid by Christ.

Do you see the practical daily effect of Pentecost? And do you realize that now the fruit of the Spirit must and will become evident? From my side, never enough is done. I always come up short. My countless misdeeds and transgressions prevail from day to day. Yes, the vine is devastated and the branches flounder. And yet the fruit appears, the varied fruit, the undeserved bounty. The Spirit works, and we grow in Christ. And we have this hope that one day the fruit will be mature and the harvest abundant.

The Return of Jesus Christ

Epilogue

THE BINDING OF SATAN

"Then I saw an angel descend down from heaven, holding in his hand the key of the bottomless pit and a great chain. And he seized the dragon, that ancient serpent, who is the Devil and Satan, and bound him for a thousand years, and threw him into the pit, and shut and sealed it over him, that he should deceive the nations no more, till the thousand years were ended. After that he must be loosed for a little while".

(Revelation 20: 1-3)

Every Easter we remember the fact that Christ's tomb, which had been closed and sealed, was powerfully opened by an angel from heaven whose face was like lightning and whose garments were of a dazzling whiteness. The appearing of this angel reminds us of another angel who came from heaven, this time not to open what was sealed, but to bind Satan, and to close and to seal the "bottomless pit" into which he was thrown.

You see the contrast. A sepulchre opened and the seals broken, but also a pit closed and sealed. Christ emerging in victory, but Satan going down to defeat. You will realize that these two events are closely related. And so, from the opening of the tomb we go to the sealing of the pit.

The binding of Satan is a popular topic. We live in an age and culture which thrives on speculation. One of the widespread speculations is that of the great millennium which – according to many – is to come at the end of time, and which will constitute a literal thousand years' reign of Christ in which the present state of Israel is to play a major role.

You can understand that during and after the Gulf War in the Middle East speculations about this so-called millennium were again rampant. There are, moreover, some similarities with the "new age" philosophy, which has also gained many adherents. According to that theory a "golden age" is coming soon, a time in which a "grand millennium" (in whatever form) will be realized. This causes optimism about the immediate future among many. They think that we stand on the brink of a golden era of peace and prosperity.

A MILLENNIUM?

Against this background, it is important for us to take a closer look at what the Bible reveals about this "millennium" and its significance for the church of Christ.

Let it be clear that we, too, believe in the existence of a "millennium," a time before judgment day, when Christ rules supreme over all the earth. In that sense, I am not ashamed to say: I am a millennialist. The main issue is, however, when this millennium begins and how it takes place.

For a proper understanding of the book of Revelation it is important not to see the events described in the various chapters as taking place in a chronological order, but rather to realize that the *same* events are being described from various aspects, from different angles. The book of Revelation has one very clear theme: the risen Saviour, Jesus Christ, is Lord over all, and He directs history to its end, the perfection of the kingdom of heaven.

ONE THEME; TWO ASPECTS

This theme, which is given in visionary form and symbolic language, has two aspects. We see the world being prepared for judgment and the coming to the ultimate manifestation of evil. We also see the church being gathered and preserved for its eternal glorification. So Revelation is a book which is truly meant for the comfort of the church of Christ in the last ages.

The binding and loosing of Satan must be understood within this framework. Amidst all the turmoil and the carnage of the latter days in which the church finds itself, we are fully assured: Satan is bound, and he cannot prevent the realization of the final outcome, which is Christ's glory in the gathering of His church. We see in this passage, then, how the risen Lord Jesus Christ comforts His church of the last ages by the vision of the binding of Satan. We will pay attention to the moment and the power of this binding.

TOWARDS THE GREAT DAY

Throughout the book of Revelation you can read of the great day of judgment. I think of Revelation 11: 18, ". . .the nations raged, but thy wrath came, and the time for the dead to be judged. . ." (echoes of Psalm 2?), and of 14: 20, about the treading of the wine press, and also of chapter 19, about the fall of Babylon and the lake of fire.

Everything is moving toward that great day. Time and again the theme is picked up and not merely repeated but deepened. Every time we receive further information about the flow of the last period of history and the forces which exert their influence.

Now a key line in the book of Revelation is that two beasts, that is two powers, are emerging on earth (Revelation 13). We cannot go into detail about that issue now, but let us get a brief picture, for it has everything to do with a proper understanding of this passage.

TWO BEASTS

One of the beasts is emerging out of the sea (the nations) and represents political (and military) power. This beast uses all its power against the saints to the advantage of the Serpent, Satan. Call this the power of the fallen, secular world.

The other beast, emerging out of the earth, represents the cultural and apostate religious institutions of this world, or as some would say, the apostate church, which causes everyone to worship the first beast. Now these two beasts – secular world and apostate church – form a mighty coalition which seems invincible. John will have shuddered when he saw it. How can the faithful church of Christ survive the brutal power and refined deceit of these two beasts who pool their resources?

Well, the downfall of this coalition is described in the chapters 18 and 19, which speak of the fall of Babylon the great, the harlot who committed fornication with the kings of the earth. This leads to the announcement of the marriage feast of the Lamb and the supper of the last judgment. We read in chapter 19: 20, ". . . and the beast was captured and with it the false prophet. . . ." Apostate world and false church are defeated, judged, and cast into the lake of fire.

Then follows chapter 20, the first verses of which form our text. Chapter 20 describes how the dragon, the ancient serpent, Satan, is bound. Now this is not meant as a new development which takes place after the defeat of the two beasts. We are simply given another aspect of the same process. In the destruction of those two beasts is included the binding and judgment of their master and leader, the devil. In all that is described in the book of Revelation we see not just the undoing of those two beasts, but also the binding of Satan and ultimately his total, final defeat.

THE UNDERLYING STRUGGLE

This new vision gives us further background information, deepening our knowledge of what we already know. For behind that corrupt world and that apostate church is the devil. History simply cannot unfold without his being bound, nor can it be completed without his downfall. And as John has described various events, all leading to the same final judgment, so he now describes the development from its ultimate vantage point, namely that of the struggle between Christ and Satan.

John writes, "Then I saw an angel coming. . . ." It says literally, "After this, I saw. . . ." Which means: John now sees a new sequence of events, which further explain the preceding. There is a strong connection with the preceding, but also a progression of thought.

We read about an angel coming from heaven, "holding in his hand the key of the bottomless pit and a great chain. And he seized the dragon. . .and bound him for a thousand years." Our question is: when did or does this binding take place? Of what moment in time does our text speak?

The vision itself, as it stands, does not give a clear answer. But within the context of the book of Revelation it is evident that the two beasts mentioned earlier could not have been destroyed without the binding and downfall of Satan. He is the unseen power behind the powers. He is called the "prince of this world", the ruler of darkness. He is the principal character with whom the church and its Head, Jesus Christ, must contend, not only in the last ages but throughout the history of the world. Paul wrote to the Ephesians that we do not have to contend with flesh and blood but with the spiritual hosts of wickedness! That evil spiritual host is led and dominated by the devil.

So, when was Satan bound? Or must this binding still take place, and will it be followed literally by a period of a thousand years, as millennialists say? You can only find the proper answer to this question when you compare Scripture with Scripture. And I want to mention a few important texts which underscore that we are not faced here in Revelation 20 with a chronological sequence of events but with a further explanation of the underlying struggle.

WHEN WAS SATAN BOUND?

This binding of Satan has everything to do with the earthly ministry of Christ. When He came into the flesh, He manifested Himself as the Son of God.

In Him the Kingdom of Heaven decisively broke through, and this is the time when Satan was bound.

We read of this in Matthew 12, where it is described how Christ cast out a demon. The Pharisees claimed that Christ casts out demons by the power of Beelzebub, the prince of demons. But Christ shows how ludicrous this suggestion is. How can someone cast out a demon if he has not first overpowered the lord of the demons? Christ says, "How can one enter a strong man's house and plunder his goods unless he first binds the strong man"? The word binding is used there, the same as in our text. That strong man who is being bound by Christ is Satan. Indeed, how could Christ cast out demons, if He had not first overpowered and bound the prince of the demons?

In Luke 10 it is described how the seventy disciples, who were sent out to preach, come back to Christ jubilantly, saying, "Even the demons are subject to us in your Name." And Christ answers, "I saw Satan fall like lightning from heaven!" The demons are subjected because their master, Satan, has fallen.

In John 12, when a voice is heard from heaven, Christ says, "Now is the judgment of this world, now shall the ruler of this world be cast out, and I when I am lifted up from the earth, will draw all men to myself." And finally, in Revelation 12, we read that Satan is cast out of heaven, when the child (Christ) is caught up to God and His throne.

So the binding of Satan, the fall of Satan and his being cast out of heaven is connected to the earthly ministry of Christ. Then it started. And it is an accomplished fact when Christ rises from the grave and ascends into heaven. In the completion of Christ's earthly ministry, His victory over sin and death, lies the essence of the binding of Satan.

When the apostle John in chapter 20 receives background information concerning the break-up of the coalition of the beasts, he sees how an angel comes from heaven and binds Satan. This binding takes place at the time of the resurrection and ascension of Christ and it sets the tone for the entire latter days. Throughout the latter days, from Christ's ascension to His glorious return, Satan is bound.

IN THE MILLENNIUM

The so-called "millennium," therefore, is not a time that is yet to come, but a time in which we at present find ourselves. The great millennium is now.

The comfort of the church is not that there will come a time when Satan will be bound, but precisely that He is already bound! That is why the diabolic coalition of the fallen world and the apostate church cannot succeed against those who are faithful to Christ. They are unsuccessful because the devil is restricted. The church of the latter days, in John's time as well as in our own, may know: Satan is bound, and he can really do nothing against Christ and His church.

Connected with this understanding is our interpretation of the number 1000. We read in our text that the dragon is bound for a thousand years.You know that in the book of Revelation numbers often have a symbolic meaning. The root of 1000 is ten, the number denoting fullness and completion. When multiplied by 10 times 10 it denotes entirety. So the number 1000 simply means the whole period of the time, the full span of time, that God has allowed for the last ages. It means the time from the resurrection/ascension – with which the book of Revelation begins – to the period just before the return of Christ, when the final act of history will unfold. Throughout this time, Christ rules supreme and Satan is bound.

So we may know, whatever happens throughout all the terrors of the latter days, Satan does not exercise power and authority. Did not Christ say when He ascended: to Me is given all power in heaven and on earth? This is evident in the binding of Satan, as described in Revelation 20.

CHRIST'S GREAT POWER

In order to be comforted by this all the more, John may see the great power with which Satan is bound. For you must be impressed by this vivid description. The angel, it says, seized the dragon. This word indicates power. He grabs him, as it were, by the throat and instantly immobilizes him. Some explainers see in this "angel" the Lord Jesus, but I think that when the Lord Himself appears (also in Revelation) He is usually depicted in a different manner. This angel is obviously endowed with the strength and the power of the Lord and so manages to subdue the devil.

Notice how we are told that the angel has in his hand the key of the bottomless pit and a great chain. Of course, it is Christ who holds all the keys, to the Kingdom of heaven and to the bottomless pit. The key is a symbol of authority. The great chain is symbolic of the power which comes with the authority. With that chain, I presume, the angel binds the dragon. It is not just a rope which may be broken, but a chain so strong that its shackles can never be undone.

Satan is subsequently cast into what is called "the bottomless pit." Literally it says: the abyss. An abyss is an endlessly deep hole, an old form of prison, from which it is impossible to escape. It seems to be the place where God keeps the fallen angels which have become demons or evil spirits, to restrict their movement.

Let me give you another reference to this "abyss." In Luke 9 we read that Jesus casts out demons from a possessed man in the region of the Garasenes. When Jesus asks the demon what his name is, he says "Legion," for many devils had entered the man. We also read, "And they [the demons] begged Him not to command them to depart into the abyss." They beg not to be locked up. This request is granted, and the demons enter, as you know, into a herd of swine. So the abyss is the place where demons were kept and restrained so that they cannot do on earth as they please.

Some explainers see in this abyss the same place as Sheol, where the unbelieving dead are kept until the day of judgment. But that is not clear from Scripture. It is also not the place called "hell," for that is described later as "the lake of fire." You may see this abyss as being a specific place where evil spirits are curtailed. It is also the place where the prince of demons, Satan, is cast, thrown down with great power.

Notice how John lists all the names by which the devil has become known through the ages: the devouring dragon, the ancient serpent who misled mankind from the beginning. In case it is still not clear, the names "devil" and "Satan" are also included. "Devil" means the one who continually causes havoc and deception, a name which shows the evil methods of the evil one. "Satan" means opponent or antagonist, and it shows the evil character and purpose of the devil: to oppose Christ and His church to the bitter end. Well, no matter what he is called and what power he may have manifested in the past, now he is bound and cast into the bottomless pit.

SHUT AND SEALED

And this pit, as we read, is shut and sealed. The devil will not get out of this prison until he is let loose. He is chained in a pit with a sealed entrance. He is gone, powerless, and cannot exercise his demonic power until someone lets him out. This shows you again one of the themes of the book of Revelation: also the devil, as a fallen creature, is at all times subject to the power of Jesus Christ, the risen Lord. The power of this binding is definite and effective.

Now the objection to this interpretation is always the same. People say: if the millennium has already started and the devil is presently chained and bound, how is it that he still exerts so much influence? What do we really see of this binding of Satan? It looks much more like a future event than a present reality. Why is the devil still going about, as Peter writes, like a roaring lion, seeking whom he can devour? In Revelation 12 we read that the devil goes to the earth to make war on the woman and her children, the church.

Therefore, does our understanding of this vision accord with reality? For a chained and imprisoned dragon, he still exerts a lot of power. If this binding has already taken place, how powerful, how effective is it really?

THE BINDING QUALIFIED

We should note that this binding of Satan is qualified in our text. It says that he was thrown into the pit which was sealed over him, in order that "he should deceive the nations no more" until the thousand years are ended. After that he must be loosed for a little while. The main thrust is here that "he should deceive the nations no more." The binding of Satan does apparently not imply that he exerts no power whatsoever, but specifically that he can not anymore deceive the nations!

We must ask a few questions here. Who are meant by the nations? It is clear from Scripture that the text refers to the heathen nations, who did not (yet) know the Gospel. During the past centuries of world history, these nations by and large were in total darkness, in the grip of Satan. Only in Israel was the light of God's grace. But that world-wide dominion of Satan has come to an end with the resurrection and ascension of Christ. In his missionary sermons the apostle Paul spoke about former "times of ignorance" among the heathens, which have come to an end through the resurrection of Christ (Acts 17: 30). If God previously let the nations go their way, *now* they will be confronted with the claims of the risen Lord. He says the same in Acts 14, "In past generations he let all the nations walk in their own ways. . .," but that is now no longer the case. Now is the time for the world-wide proclamation of the Gospel of the Lord Jesus Christ.

WORLD-WIDE MISSION

The point is, then, that Satan cannot in any way prevent this world-wide mission. He will deceive the nations no more. The Gospel will be preached everywhere, and all over the world people will turn to Christ. Satan cannot keep the nations under in his deceptive lies, but must watch and see how the Gospel is preached throughout the world.

We find the same thought expressed by the apostle Paul in II Thessalonians 2, where we read about the man of lawlessness being restrained so that the Gospel may advance freely, all over the world. And when this has been accomplished, the son of lawlessness will reveal himself in all his ugliness and evil by the power of Satan, to be destroyed by Jesus Christ.

Here, in Revelation 20, we read also about the end of the thousand years – that is after the Gospel has been preached throughout the world and the church has been gathered. Then Satan will be let loose for a little while. He will not break loose, but be let loose, and only for a while. Then he will try once more, in a last-ditch effort, to destroy Christ and His church. He may even succeed in uniting all the world in this final campaign. But he will not be successful. When he is finally let loose, it is too late for him. He will go to meet his final destruction.

A COMFORTING VISION

You must remember that when all this was revealed to John on Patmos, there was much persecution and oppression of the church. The Christians could be tempted to doubt the power of Christ. What did they see of it? But John may comfort them with this vision: the Gospel *will* find its way victoriously throughout the world. Satan cannot prevent it. And we today know how true this vision has proven to be. The Gospel went, against all odds, from Jerusalem, to Rome, throughout the world, and it is still being preached everywhere. The amazing success of the mission work by which millions have been saved since this vision underscores the truth of the vision.

The church of John's days was immensely comforted by the vision. It is still today our comfort and motivation. Christ rules, not Satan. And when Satan is loosed toward the end of the ages and unleashes his final terrible furore against the church of God, God Himself, said Jesus, will shorten the days, so that the elect may stand firm.

We do not know how far we have progressed in the millennium. But it is clear that the Gospel has been preached almost everywhere. Many have been called. Millions have heard the Gospel. Satan could not prevent the progress of the preaching. And every day we come nearer to the time when Satan will be loosed, when the world will be steeped in global apostasy and lawlessness. In that sense we have no reason for false optimism and must be on our guard. We have no future here, but we look for the kingdom of heaven.

But the bottom line is: the risen Lord rules supreme throughout the latter days, and when Satan is loosed, Christ will crush him definitely. That is the reality of Easter and Ascension in which we live and work. Therefore we are never without hope, even when we see how much resistance demonic forces still exert in this world, in our own lives. Christ will fulfill His purpose in us, for us, and also through us. Therefore we can sing, looking to Christ,

> The prince of darkness grim,
> We tremble not for him.
> His rage we can endure,
> For lo! his doom is sure;
> One little word shall fell him (Hymn 41: 3, *Book of Praise*)

I do not underestimate the devil. He scares me, rattling his chain from the bottomless pit. But I'm glad that he is chained and bound. We live under God's dominion. And under God's dominion have saints their triumphs won.

THE HEAVENLY GLORY OF THE SAINTS

"Then I saw thrones and seated on them were those to whom judgment was committed. Also I saw the souls of those who had been beheaded for their testimony to Jesus and for the word of God, and who had not worshipped the beast or its image and had not received its marks on their forehead or their hands. They came to life, and reigned with Christ a thousand years. The rest of the dead did not come to life until the thousand years were ended. This is the first resurrection. Blessed and holy is he who shares in the first resurrection! Over such the second death has no power, but they shall be priests of God and of Christ, and they shall reign with Him a thousand years".

(Revelation 20: 4-6)

In the previous section I wrote about the binding of Satan as it was revealed to the apostle John in visionary form and recorded in the first three verses of Revelation 20. I concluded that this binding of Satan, lasting a thousand years (which denotes a full and complete period of time) takes place with the completion of Christ's earthly ministry and His ascension to heaven.

We also saw how this "millennium" is characterized as a time in which the progress of the Gospel will continue unto the ends of the earth. Satan loses his control of the world, so that he cannot deceive the nations any more. The mandate which Christ gave to His apostles, "To Me is given all authority in heaven and on earth. . .go therefore and make disciples of all nations. . ." (Matthew 28: 18, 19) is a difficult task but not an impossible mandate.

MANY MARTYRS

I suggested that this vision will have been of immense comfort for the believers in John's time who were being persecuted and killed for their faith in Jesus. John himself was exiled, and many others were put to death for refusing to offer incense to the Roman emperor.

It is evident from the entire book of Revelation that the "binding of Satan" does not mean that there will not be any casualties on the earth. A fierce battle is going on, and while Satan is bound and cannot stop the progress of the Gospel and prevent the gathering of the holy catholic church, he still persecutes the believers. In the latter days they have entered "the great tribulation" (Revelation 7: 14).

It is clear, then, that the millennium is not an age of undisturbed peace. Many will have to give their lives for the faith. Others will be sorely pressed not to succumb to the cult of the beast. The question arises, "What will happen to those who die in that period of time? Will they, in fact, not go under in Satan's campaign, despite the glorious rule of Christ?"

THE SCENE SHIFTS

The vision continues in this passage. But now the scene shifts from earth to heaven. John may see and proclaim what happens to those who during this time die in the Lord Jesus Christ. We are told that they reign with Christ in heaven and so consciously await the great day of the coming of the Lord.

It is not the first time in the book of Revelation that John has seen and recorded such visions of the heavenly glory of the saints. In chapter 6 he gives us the vision of the souls under the altar. Chapter 7 provides us with the vision of the great multitude before the throne of God. This is repeated in chapter 14, where the 144,000 are mentioned. From various angles the same comfort has been made known. And now, in chapter 20, it is made known again, and in even greater depth and riches, so that we will never doubt that Christ is risen and has ascended and that we may sit with Him in the heavenly places (Ephesians 2: 6)

We now examine the vision concerning the heavenly glory of the saints during the time when Satan is bound. We will see how their earthly faithfulness is vindicated and their heavenly bliss ensured.

THRONES AND SOULS

After the binding of Satan, we read in verse 4, "Then I saw thrones, and seated on them were those to whom judgment was committed. . . ." It does not say here exactly where these thrones are located. Many scholars who believe in a literal millennium – Christ returning to earth to rule for exactly 1000 years – assume that these thrones are located on the earth, most likely in the city of Jerusalem from where, according to them, Christ will reign during that time. But it should be noted that whenever thrones are mentioned in the book of Revelation, these are always presented as being in heaven. Consistent exegesis, therefore, will take these thrones also as located in heaven.

The number of the thrones is not specified either. It remains indefinite. That is in keeping with the dynamic character of the last ages. What is made clear is the position of those who sit on the thrones. A "throne" symbolically indicates a place of honour, of rulership and judgment. So it says that those seated on the thrones are "those to whom to judgment was committed."

Note well, it does not say *the* judgment, as if the final judgement is given to those on the thrones, for it is reserved for Christ, who will come to judge the living and the dead. It says only "judgment." This means that those on the thrones have the right and authority to make certain judgments in keeping with God's will, and so to partake in Christ's heavenly rule and authority.

Those who sit on the thrones do not have this right of themselves, for it is committed to them, literally: *given* to them. Also in heaven, rule by God's children is not a matter of merit but of grace. God's sovereign grace extends from earth to heaven.

So far we still have not clearly identified who are seated on these thrones. But John continues the description. We read, "Also I saw the souls of those who had been beheaded for their testimony to Jesus and for the Word of God, and who had not worshipped the beast or its image and had not received its mark on their foreheads or their hands." It is clear that those seated on the thrones are the same as "the souls" which John sees. For of these "souls" we read that they "came to life and reigned with Christ a thousand years." This reigning with Christ is evident in their being seated on the thrones.

So it is clear who are seated on the thrones. They are the saints who have died. Their "souls" are taken up to Christ in heaven where they may rule with Him. It says in verse 4 that "they came to life, and reigned with Christ a thousand years," but we can best translate "and they *lived* and reigned with Christ a thousand years." They did not, as it were, die for a while and then come to life again, but they lived with Christ from the moment they left this life on earth. I'll come back to that later.

TWO GROUPS OF SAINTS?

In the description of the saints in heaven, John makes a distinction which has led to some discussion. It appears that there are two "groups" – if I may use that word – of saints in heaven: those who have been beheaded for their testimony to Jesus and the Word of God – the martyrs – and those who had not worshipped the beast and its image and had not received its mark on their foreheads or their hands – the other faithful. Some explainers take these words to denote one and the same group: only the martyrs. Others admit that two groups are mentioned here, but conclude that only the martyred saints (those beheaded) come to sit on thrones in heaven while the others do not receive this special honour.

What to think of this? In the book of Revelation special mention is indeed made of those who gave their lives in the service of the Lord. But not everyone is called to make that sacrifice. Everyone is called to be faithful to the Lord Jesus and to serve Him alone. Here in our text both groups – the martyrs and the other faithful who were perhaps not martyred – are mentioned in one breath. I therefore understand it in this way: they all live and they may all reign with Christ throughout the time of the millennium.

Rather than noticing any distinction, I see here the *unity* of the heavenly church. All those who have remained faithful, even unto death when required, may go to Christ and rule with Him in heaven. That is the simple and yet awesome significance of what John sees.

VINDICATION IN HEAVEN

So the souls of faithful believers are taken up to heaven and there they may share already in the glory and victory of Christ, reigning with Him for the duration of the thousand years, that is, until Christ returns in glory on the clouds of heaven. They take an active part in the millennium, praising God before His throne, calling upon Him, making righteous judgments, reflecting His glory.

All who die in the Lord are glorified and beatified. We may even use the word vindicated. For that is what is described here in this text. Just think of it, on earth these people were vilified and persecuted. They were stripped of their rights and lost their possessions. They were constantly being forced to the fringe of society, set under a massive boycott. They did not receive any consideration or compassion but were treated brutally and cruelly as the worst elements of human society.

But in heaven they are immediately vindicated for their faithfulness on earth, even unto death. Their earthly work and suffering were not in vain, but reap a great reward of grace.

FAITHFULNESS ON EARTH

Notice how this earthly faithfulness is described. They have, first, remained faithful to "the testimony of Jesus and the Word of God." They did not deny Christ before men, but lived and spoke as Christians. They stood for the truth of the Word of God. They were at all times confessing Christians who in word and deed showed their faith.

It also says: they had not worshipped the beast or its image. They did not partake in the idolatry of the last ages. They kept the antithesis between church and world. Therefore they "did not receive the mark of the beast on their foreheads or on their hands." They were not a part of the grey mass of sinners and idolaters, but were known by another mark, Holy Baptism, which is the ensign of Christ and the sign of their being set aside from this world in fellowship with Him and His saints.

Because of their faithfulness while on earth, they are granted heavenly glory. You realize that this portrait of earthly faithfulness is given also for our instruction. Here on earth is where the decision falls. Here it is where we must show forth our Christian character and example, where we must be professing Christians who are not ashamed of Christ and His Word, and do not partake in the sinful culture and cultus (false worship) of this world. This is difficult in itself, and will become even more difficult as time progresses and the delusion of mankind increases.

Here lies the great test and task for every generation, for us as well. Will we keep the testimony of Jesus and the Word of God? Will we not go under in the delusion and deception which is growing steadily? This text is an appeal from God that we today discern the real issues, fight the good fight of faith, run the race to the end. We must endure! I think of what we find in Hymn 39, "If we endure – so Christ has said – we'll also reign with Him our Head."

When our earthly faithfulness has thus been shown, our heavenly bliss is ensured.

THE REST OF THE DEAD

It says in verse 5, "The rest of the dead did not come to life until the thousand years were ended. This is the first resurrection." These are difficult and much disputed words, but we'll try to understand them in the light of the context.

It is clear that faithful believers will *live* with Christ in heaven throughout the millennium (verse 4). If we accept that as the proper understanding of verse 4, then the "rest of the dead" must mean those who have died in unbelief. The "souls" in heaven are indeed the souls of people who have also died. When they die, their bodies go into the grave, and their souls to Christ.

But it is not so with "the rest of the dead". It says of them that "they did not come to life" until the thousand years were ended. It is again better to translate: they did not *live* until the thousand years were ended. That means: they died and were in the state of death until the return of Christ when the great resurrection of all people takes place. Until that time, they are kept in the realm of the dead, in Sheol. I think here of Psalm 49: 4:

> Into Sheol like sheep they headlong run
> Their shepherd, Death, stands by to urge them on

They all go down directly to the grave. . .
But God will pay my ransom and not leave me,
For He into His glory will receive me.

THE FIRST RESURRECTION

The words, "this is the first resurrection," have given rise to various interpretations. Literal millennialists take them to mean: when the thousand year reign comes, only the believers will rise; the unbelievers will follow after the "millennium." So the first resurrection would be that of the believers, and the second that of the unbelievers. But that is not consistent with biblical teaching, which makes clear that there is essentially only one resurrection, either to eternal glory or eternal agony.

Therefore the words "the first resurrection" must refer to the saints who go to heaven at their death. It is used, then, in a figurative sense. Some who follow this line of thinking disagree on the detail whether all the saints go to heaven or just the martyred ones. As indicated, I see here the same reality for all who die in the Lord. They all participate in the glory of heaven according to the measure of God's grace.This is called "the first resurrection." It is not the final resurrection, when their souls are united with their bodies, but the first one.

Is this not in keeping with Christ's teaching, for example in John 11, in the history of Lazarus? When Jesus said to Martha, "Your brother shall rise again," Martha took it to refer to the great resurrection. Christ did not deny that, but said something much more profound, "I am the resurrection and the life; he who believes in Me, though he die, yet shall he live, and whoever lives and believes in Me shall never die" (11: 25, 26). Is this not an awesome reality of which Israel already sang in Psalm 17,

But I, when I awake, shall see
Thy face in righteousness and glory
O with Thy likeness then before me
How rich and full my joy shall be!

Dead, yet alive. Dead for the world; alive before Christ. Who lives and believes, shall never die. When we die, we indeed leave behind our earthly bodies, but it is a dying unto sin and an entrance into eternal life (Lord's Day 16). It is not a dying in the final and devastating sense of the word, for we experience at our death "the first resurrection"! In that sense it can be said of the believers that they shall never die.

THE SECOND DEATH

Notice how we then read in our text a beatitude: "Blessed is he who shares in the first resurrection. Over such the second death has no power." If there is a *first* resurrection, there is apparently also a *second* death. With this "second death" is meant "the lake of fire" (see verse 14); it is a being consigned to hell as righteous punishment for sin.

What John writes is consistent. Those who partake in the first resurrection, who go to Christ when they die, shall not go under in the second death, that is, be cast into hell on the day of judgement, but they shall enter into everlasting blessedness. Of this eternal bliss John may assure the church.

If there is a *second* death, there is also a *first* death. The first is when we leave this earth. We have seen that for believers this is already called "the first resurrection." Death for a child of God is not a sinking into darkness but an entrance into eternal life. The unbelievers are also resurrected, but only to be cast into the lake of fire. They go from death to death, from being dead temporarily to eternal death, an everlasting experiencing of God's wrath.

But those who share in the first resurrection have nothing to fear from the second death. Instead they are called "blessed." We read that "they shall be priests of God and of Christ," already during the thousand years. Priests and kings. Is that not the designation of God's people in the Scriptures? Think of what Peter wrote in his first letter, "You are a chosen race, a royal priesthood, a holy nation, God's own people, that you may declare the wonderful deeds of Him who called you out of the darkness to His marvellous light. . ." (I Peter 2: 9).

A royal priesthood. You do not always see that here on earth. But it is surely evident in heaven, throughout the latter ages. And on Christ's great day it will become evident in all its final glory, for then comes for the believers (to continue the phraseology of the text) the second resurrection, the great resurrection, when their souls are reunited with their bodies and they may live on the new earth together with God in perfect harmony! Only then is God's work of restoration complete and is the restoration of life perfect.

HOW LONG, O LORD?

Until that day of Christ's coming, the saints – in heaven and on earth – do not cease to call out: how long, O Lord? For the vision of the glory of the saints during the binding of Satan gives us a picture of an interim period, not of the final situation. As much as we appreciate the interim situation, we still long for the finale and the finish: the day of the great resurrection and the restoration of body and soul on the new earth.

This vision concerning the glory of the saints in heaven is given to the church so that we would be comforted in all trials and motivated to steadfastness in service. And as we progress in time, and Satan is loosed for a little while, we will have to fall back more and more on the truth of this vision. When everything in this world is taken away from us, this will be our surety and hope.

The Lord knows how difficult it is for us to persevere. It takes much struggle and prayer. In Revelation 2 the church at Smyrna is specifically warned about coming tribulation. The Lord knows what His children must suffer for His sake. But He says there, "Be faithful unto death, and I will give you the crown of life. . . . He who conquers shall not be hurt by the second death" (2: 11).

Christ said it already when He was still on earth with His disciples: "Do not fear those who kill the body but cannot kill the soul; rather fear Him who can destroy both body and soul in hell" (Matthew 10:28). Do not fear the world. Do not fear the first death. Fear only God, for He alone can save us from eternal damnation.

Let this be our surety and hope, also in times when we are faced not with persecution but certainly with much deception. Do not be fooled, the deception today is massive and widespread. Do not worship the beast or wear its mark. For then you face certain doom. But keep the testimony of Jesus and the Word of God. Fear Him who redeems you, body and soul, from everlasting damnation. And let it be here and now in this life your song:

> Surely the righteous will adore Thee
> And give their thanks to Thy great Name
> The upright all will stand before Thee
> And there Thy faithfulness proclaim" (Psalm 140: 10).

THE DEFINITE DESTRUCTION OF THE DEVIL

"And when the thousand years are ended, Satan will be loosed from his prison and will come out to deceive the nations which are at the four corners of the earth, that is, Gog and Magog, to gather them for battle; their number is like the sand of the sea. And they marched up over the broad earth and surrounded the camp of the saints and the beloved city; but fire came down from heaven and consumed them, and the devil who had deceived them was thrown into the lake of fire and sulphur where the beast and the false prophet were, and they will be tormented day and night for ever and ever."

(Revelation 20: 7-10)

We have now for a while followed the Word of God as expressed in the vision concerning the binding of Satan during the great "millennium," which I have characterized as the time from Christ's ascension to His return on the clouds of heaven.

We have drawn two major conclusions. First, during this time Satan cannot deceive the nations, that is, he cannot hinder the progress of the Gospel and prevent the gathering of the church out of all nations (20:1-3). Second, Christians who during this time die in persevering faith may rule with Christ in heaven, there already enjoying a foretaste of the glory which will be received in full on the new earth (20: 4-6).

THE COMFORT CONTINUED

This vision has been and still is of immense comfort to the church of the Lord Jesus Christ. But we know from verse 3 that this binding of Satan will come to an end. It says there: after the thousand years are ended, Satan must be loosed for a little while. And the vision now takes up that element: how in the last phase of world history, Satan will be loosed to deceive the nations.

It is obvious from this passage and from other parts of Scripture that this will be a difficult, almost devastating time for the church of Christ. At the same time, the outcome of this phase of history is never in doubt. The struggle will be severe, but the triumph is certain. Therefore we know that this section of the vision is not meant to frighten us, but to encourage us all the more. Even Satan's last concerted campaign will not be enough to overcome the power of Jesus Christ and to devour the church. In keeping with the entire line of this vision, we see how the church of Christ is comforted by the sure knowledge of the definite destruction of the devil. Even though Satan gathers all the nations for battle and goes so far as to surround the camp of the saints, he meets the fire of God's final judgment.

TWO DESCENTS?

Let us at this point refresh our memory with respect to the so-called "millennialist" view of this chapter and passage. Millennialists believe that Christ will come down to earth to rule for a thousand years in the city of Jerusalem, that all Jews (all Israel) will then accept Christ as Messiah, and that at the end of this period Christ will ascend again to heaven so that Satan will gain world control.

In fact, then, according to millennialists, Christ will retreat to heaven after the thousand-year period and give this world over to Satan. This also implies a second descent in glory for the great final battle, often referred to as the battle of Armageddon (see Revelation 16: 16).

But let me ask: where do we read that Christ will return to heaven after the "millennium"? Where do we read in this whole chapter of two descents? Only one return of Christ is mentioned in Scripture. And, we may add, even in this phase when the thousand years come to an end and Satan is loosed, Christ certainly does not give him free reign on earth by retreating to heaven.That would indeed take the comfort out of this vision. Imagine the devil having a free hand on earth.

CHRIST IN CONTROL ALWAYS

We read something quite different. From the beginning to the end of this vision there is a clear affirmation that Christ is also fully in control when Satan is loosed. He exercises this government *from heaven* where He is seated at God's right hand. Throughout the millennium and at its conclusion Christ rules sovereign and supreme, and when He lets Satan loose, this has a specific purpose.

We read in verse 3: Satan must be loosed. This is a divine necessity, a decision from above. It is not Satan who decides that he will have freedom to act. It is not Satan who after much struggle manages to break out of his prison. Throughout this vision, it is evident that Satan never takes the initiative, is never in control, and never has the ability to win. It is Christ who fulfills the counsel of God and completes the divine work of salvation from beginning to end.

UNCHAINED YET UNCHANGED

Satan is *let* loose. It says, "When the thousand years are ended, Satan will be loosed from his prison. . . ." Just as it is upon God's command that Satan is bound, so it is also upon God's permission that he is loosed. Now, when Satan is loosed, it appears that he has not changed at all during his imprisonment. It says that he will come out "to deceive the nations that are at the four corners of the earth. . . ."

There is a sense of urgency and purpose here. The devil has not changed at all. Note that point. You'd think that after a "thousand years" in jail, even the devil might have "reformed" or mellowed a little. Satan, however, would have *us* mellow and relax in the course of our life, but he does not change in his hatred of Christ. The choice of Satan and his fallen angels is irreversible. Satan's frustrated anger has increased throughout the time that he was restricted. And so, upon being loosed, he wastes no time but proceeds immediately to recruit and muster his forces for a final battle.

Now when Satan was bound, the emphasis lay on the fact that he could no longer deceive the nations. When he is loosed the opposite is true: Satan is enabled to deceive the nations. He now gets the opportunity to realize a global campaign of deception to unify the world against Christ and His Church. In passing, I want to point out how the apostle Paul in his second letter to the Thessalonians charts the extent of this deception. Satan will be successful in achieving a world-wide delusion, leading all nations astray for his cause. A global wave of fanatic intolerance will wash against what is left of the Christian Church.

DECEIVING THE NATIONS

We read here particularly that Satan will succeed in deceiving the "nations which are at the four corners of the earth, that is, Gog and Magog, to gather them for battle. . . ." We should inquire as to what is meant by these nations, especially by Gog and Magog. And this leads us to the prophecy of Ezechiel 38 and 39, where Gog and Magog are mentioned in a similar role against Israel, the people of God.

Actually the name "Magog" is mentioned for the first time in the genealogy of Japheth in Genesis 10. It is widely accepted that Gog and Magog should be taken as the names of the nations that were the farthest removed geographically from Israel. Therefore also in our text we find the expression "the nations which are at the four corners of the earth," that is, the most removed to the north, west, east, and south.

These far-away nations – descendants of Japheth – were not traditionally enemies of Israel. Israel usually had to battle with the descendants of Ham (Canaan). The immediate and constant enemies of God's people were such nations as Moab and Edom, brother-nations, or regional super-powers like Egypt, Syria, Babylonia, and Persia. At no time was Israel threatened by such far-away peoples as Gog and Magog. These nations were in the background, at the periphery of the circle of nations surrounding Israel.

GOD'S DESIGN

But already Ezechiel prophesied that one day these remote nations would unite with Israel's traditional enemies and form a coalition against God's people. This would happen *after* the great restoration and unification of Israel described in Ezechiel 37. Now, this concerted attack was not by accident or human design. From Ezechiel 38 and 39 it is clear that God calls up these nations, that is – in terms of the text in Revelation 20 – that He lets Satan gather these nations. Ezechiel 38 says, "Thus says the LORD. . .I will bring you forth and all your army. . .a great company. . .Persia, Put and Cush are with them. . .many peoples are with you. . .you will bestir yourself. . .a great host, a mighty army. . .you will come up against my people Israel, like a cloud covering the land. In the latter days I will bring you against my land. . . ."

What has not happened before, says Ezechiel, will happen. Far-away peoples will come to attack the city of God in great number and force. Now it is not easy to identify exactly which nations are meant in Ezechiel 38 and 39. The main attack seems to come from the north-east (the north being the great "unknown," uncharted area of that time): Persia, Iran, India, Mongolia. But it will also come from the south, the black nations from Ethiopia and farther down will be involved. And it is clear that this attack is to be expected in the "latter days" when Israel has been restored, that is, in the time when the great Messiah rules. The battle against Gog and Magog was therefore seen by Israel as the last and definitive battle, when all the world would be massed against them. So we come again to Revelation 20 where this prophecy of Ezechiel obviously finds fulfillment.

WHICH NATIONS?

Millennialists have gone to great lengths to identify exactly which nations are meant. At one time it was fashionable to think of the Russians and the (communist) Chinese. Recently the attention shifted to Iran and Iraq. It was Saddam Hussein who got things going by styling himself a new Nebuchadnezzar and referring to "the mother of all battles," but, as we now know, it turned out to be "the mother of all retreats." It is usually the perceived enemy of the day that is identified as Gog and Magog.

It is better not to make such hasty connections. We need not think only of military power, for the power of spiritual deception and delusion will also be used. Let it suffice to say that all the world will be involved. Satan will mobilize even the nations which have perhaps not yet played a major role in world history. From far and wide they will come to attack the people of God. To know this is enough; we need not speculate, but should believe that also this massive attack will be unsuccessful.

AN OVERWHELMING NUMBER

Satan succeeds in gathering the nations for battle. And, as we also saw in the prophecy of Ezechiel, the number of the enemy is simply overwhelming. Ezechiel spoke of a great company, a mighty host, armed to the teeth. Our text says that "their number is like the sand of the sea." In other words, an innumerable horde, a sea of men and armour.

As massive military campaigns go, this one is initially very successful. We read in the text that "they marched up over the broad earth. . . ." Over the broad earth means that they could move forward from all sides without any resistance. The earth was for this mighty host like a flat terrain over which they could advance unopposed and at great speed. We get the picture of a real "blitzkrieg," column after column of armored divisions rolling forward to one focal point.

For the record, we read about this same battle in Revelation 16, where the place of battle is called Armageddon, and it says there that "the great river Euphrates was dried up to prepare the way for the kings from the east." This means that nothing could stop this army, not even mighty rivers or high mountain ranges. We can put it this way: God just lets them move on and on to that one destination, taking away even natural barriers so that they may progress freely.

Obviously it has to come to a point of battle. We read that "they surrounded the camp of the saints and the beloved city." This mighty army encircles the city of God and everything is moved into position for the ultimate slaughter. Surrounded, the saints are. Cut off from all sides, with no way out.

THE BELOVED CITY

Of course, the question is: what is meant by "the camp of the saints" and "the beloved city"? To begin with the "city," this obviously refers to Jerusalem. You get the impression that the "saints" have previously gathered in Jerusalem or retreated in the face of this massive onslaught and have camped in and around the city of Jerusalem. So "city" and "camp" are really congruous. Imagine the retreat to the city in and around which the saints will make their "last stand." And it *will* be a last stand, for there is no way out, no way to win. It looks like a real massacre in the making.

Now some millennialists think of the literal Jerusalem in Palestine. All remaining Christians will come from everywhere during the "millennium" to gather in Israel and seek refuge in and around Jerusalem, where the final battle is to take place. What to think of this "literal" interpretation?

It is important for us to note that in the New Testament "the beloved city," Jerusalem, no longer means the earthly Jerusalem. Did not Christ Himself say to the Samaritan woman, ". . .believe Me, the hour is coming when neither on this mountain (Samaria) nor in Jerusalem will you worship the Father" (John 6: 21)? Christ specifically prophesied to His disciples the destruction of Jerusalem and its temple as places of worship, when He said, pointing to the temple, ". . .there will not be one stone left upon another."

The New Testament tells us that "Jerusalem" as the place of the great King, to which we direct ourselves in worship, is the Jerusalem above (Galatians 4: 26). From Revelation 21 we know that the holy city Jerusalem comes down from heaven. So we should not think here in this text literally of Jerusalem in Palestine, for that is incompatible with New Testament teaching.

FINAL ATTACK ON THE CHURCH

It can then only mean that Christians everywhere will be under attack, wherever they are. For Jerusalem is manifest here on earth in the believers, the saints. Jerusalem, the heart of the kingdom of heaven, is apparent in the gathering and assembly of the church on earth.This text simply tells us that the persecution of the church of Christ will be extreme and worldwide. Christians everywhere will be outnumbered and surrounded, relentlessly hounded, boycotted, and persecuted. Christians will be on the defensive, accused, and robbed of rights. The great discrimination and tribulation will break loose as never before.

Our Lord Jesus Christ spoke of that time in these terms, "then there will be great tribulation, such as has not been from the beginning of the world until now, no, and never will be. And if those days had not been shortened, no human being would be saved, but for the sake of the elect those days will be shortened" (Matthew 24: 21,22). United and directed by Satan, the world will seek to destroy the church in a last concerted effort. And the enemy will come very close to succeeding.

VISIONS OF GRANDEUR?

Millennialists sometimes have visions of grandeur: they see the millennium as a golden era for the church with world-wide acceptance of Christianity and millions of converts flocking to Christ. Evangelism Explosion. Church Growth Movement. I am not at all against organized evangelical activity and outreach, but we should realize that much modern evangelism is rooted in this false millennialist idealism.

"All the world for Christ by the year 2000" is a typical slogan in this connection. I hear this theme repeated constantly on television. Evangelism 2000. Some television preachers are convinced that we stand on the brink of the great millennium with church expansion world-wide.

But the Bible really shows us something different. The church will be fully gathered, but the opposition will steadily grow and the numbers of believers dwindle, so that Christ can ask, "When the Son of man returns, will He still find the faith on earth?" The message, method, and expectation of evangelism must be guided by Scriptural reality and not by false optimism, which is more idealistic than biblical.

The nations will gather all right, but not for baptism but for battle. Our comfort remains that in the end Satan, who has been loosed for a little while, will be cast into the lake of fire.

UNDOUBTED OUTCOME

I wrote earlier that the outcome is never in doubt. We are being prepared for the struggle but also assured of the triumph. That is God's way. Actually, there is in this text almost a sort of an anti-climax. It does not really come to an outright battle. Just when the stage is set, by way of speaking, the curtain falls. The enemies surround the beloved city, poised for the final attack, but, we read, "fire came down from heaven and consumed them." Not only the nations are destroyed, but we read that the devil himself is thrown into the lake of fire and sulphur, where his cronies, the beast and the false prophet, are.

Notice that this fire comes from heaven. The "saints" do not break out in a courageous attack to surprise the enemy and gain an unexpected victory. For at the end of history it is the same as at the beginning: the victory is the Lord's. Soli Deo Gloria! Numbers are not important. The saints may be outnumbered, just as the prophet Elijah once was when they came to arrest him, but fire comes down from heaven and consumes the enemy. We see here at the close of history what has really preserved the church throughout history: the sovereign grace of the Almighty God who reveals His glory in Jesus Christ.

Notice also the suddenness of the ending. All things seem to be going the way of Satan and his army. He is ready for a great victory. His golden era is about to begin. He's ready for a millennium of his own. But the end is sudden and swift, unmistakable and decisive. Last opportunity. Time is up. The day of the judgment of God has come. He is treading out the vintage where the grapes of wrath are stored.

FINAL CONCLUSION

Now we do not necessarily have to think of one single event. There have been numbers of times when the church was in great peril. But it will go to one final conclusion.

The church is greatly comforted here. For being cast into the lake of fire is more than being chained in the bottomless pit. The bottomless pit was a temporary prison. The lake of fire is an eternal hell. It does not say without reason: "and they will be tormented day and night for ever and ever." Strictly speaking, there is no "day and night" in hell. It simply means: constantly, without any interruption, and so, eternally.

A last question. Why does God give the devil this final opportunity? Why this great tribulation and trial for the church and this vain attempt of Satan and the nations? Why let Satan loose for a short time?

Why? There are two reasons. First, the power of lawlessness must come to its zenith. Sin must become manifest in all its maturity and ugliness. What is inside the devil and the nations must come out. So that the righteousness of God may be fully apparent.

Secondly, the victory of Christ must be demonstrated as complete and final. Satan was not defeated at his weakest moment. Satan was destroyed when he was at the peak of his power. He received all opportunity and was given access to all the power of this world. But it was not enough. For the Kingdom, and the Power, and the Glory belong to God and to His Christ, forever and ever. This is what must be conclusively demonstrated at the close of history.

We see it in faith, do we not?

> ". . . the depths of hell before Thee
> trembling and defeated bow"

And we? We shall seek the things that are above! Await the city of God, the new Jerusalem from heaven. Do that, while knowing that we shall be tried like ore in the furnace, that we will be surrounded and outnumbered, but also that we will be brought into a spacious place (Psalm 66). We shall sing of the miraculous escape, the song of sudden and total deliverance. Psalm 124: if the LORD had not our right maintained, we'd surely have been swallowed up alive. But blest be the LORD who made us not their prey. He gave us escape and freedom. Forever.

The Day of Judgement

"Then I saw a great white throne and him who sat upon it; from his presence earth and sky fled away, and no place was found for them. And I saw the dead, great and small, standing before the throne, and the books were opened. Also another book was opened, which is the book of life. And the dead were judged by what was written in the books, by what they had done. And the sea gave up the dead in it, Death and Hades gave up the dead in them, and all were judged by what they had done. Then Death and Hades were thrown into the lake of fire. This is the second death, the lake of fire; and if any one's name was not found written in the book of life, he was thrown into the lake of fire."

(Revelation 20: 11-15)

We come to the last of the events described in the vision of the binding of Satan. We know that Satan has been cast into the lake of fire, into hell, with the two beasts who served his cause on earth, and in that sense the vision has come full circle. Satan is bound, eternally, not just in the bottomless pit, but in the fire of hell.

That is undoubtedly an awful fate. Still, the vision has not ended. Now follows, after the judgment of Satan, a very vivid description of the judgment of *all people.*

ONE RETURN; ONE RESURRECTION

It is clear from this passage and from the context in which it is placed that as there is one return of Christ, so there is only one physical resurrection, and subsequently one full and final judgment. No one who ever lived on this earth will be able to escape that judgment. There are no absentees, there is no exemption; everyone will be individually judged by Christ according to what he has done in the body on earth, as Paul writes in his second letter to the Corinthians (5: 10).

I mentioned earlier that the vision of the binding of Satan is given to the church for our comfort. We must keep this in mind also when we look at these last verses of the vision. The Lord Jesus does not want to frighten us so that we will expect this day with fear and trembling. He wishes to comfort us here so that we may – as the Belgic Confession puts it so beautifully in Article 37 – anticipate it with great joy. For it is not a day of the church's annihilation, but one of vindication, one for which the saints by God's grace have longed throughout the centuries.

OPENING OF BOOKS

A key element in this last part of the vision is the opening of books. "Judgment" means that books are opened and that by them the evidence is presented to determine the outcome of the verdict. And it is on these books and their opening that I want to focus in particular.

We see, then, how after the casting of Satan into hell, the Lord opens the books on the day of judgment. Reference is made to *all* the books of our lives, as well as to the opening of the *one book of life.*

The history of this world does not end with the casting of Satan into the lake of fire. We read in the text, "Then I saw a great white throne and Him Who sat on it." The stage is being set, as it were, for an official event, namely the final judgment. This "throne," reminiscent of what Daniel wrote of many centuries before, was introduced earlier in Revelation 4, but is now more fully described. First we note that it is a great throne, denoting the greatness and glory of God to whom the throne belongs. It is also called a white throne, and, as you know, the colour "white" in the book Revelation denotes holiness and righteousness. He who is seated on the throne will judge according to His absolute holiness and in complete righteousness.

NO ESCAPE FROM JUDGMENT

Notice that John does not give a description of the One sitting on the throne. We may think of God, the Father, of whom we know that He inhabits this throne. We may also think here of the Son of God, our Lord Jesus Christ, who has been designated as the One who will judge the living and the dead.

It is remarkable that the very appearance of God on His throne is so awesome that it causes all creation to flee. We read, " . . . from His presence earth and sky fled away, and no place was found for them." What do these words mean? I think that we must understand, first of all, that there is no escape from the last judgment. Everything, all creation will be affected. Not one person will be able to find a place to hide. But secondly, these words indicate that "earth and sky" (denoting our world as we know it) will disappear. The present world will cease to exist. The judgment of God marks the end of this world, this earth, as we know it.

John does not describe in detail how this will take place. But elsewhere, in II Peter 3: 10-13, we do read what will happen. As the dead rise to face the throne of judgment, this present world will be burnt down. Peter writes: the elements will be dissolved with fire, and the earth and the works that are upon it will be burnt up. This world with all its great monuments of human achievement, the proud architecture of fallen man, will simply be melted down by the fire of God's judgment, and out of those elements God will fashion a new earth for His children.

ALL MANKIND JUDGED

John does not describe that aspect. He is more concerned with the judgment of mankind. We read in verse 12, "And I saw the dead, great and small, standing before the throne . . . ." Notice also in this connection what we read in verse 13, "And the sea gave up the dead in it, Death and Hades gave up the dead in them. . . ."

It is clear that this judgment will include all who ever lived. The earthly distinctions of position and rank have no more bearing. The dead include great and small, and by this John means those who were powerful and mighty (the great) and those who had no position (the small). Whether you were a king or a subject, a prince or a pauper, an aristocrat or a commoner on this earth has no bearing on your entering into judgment, nor does it affect the outcome of the judgment.

It also does not matter any more how you died. Notice how the dead are brought back from the realms of Death and Hades. There was perhaps no trace left of any human remains. Think of those whose bodies were burned to ashes, and whose ashes were spread out over the waves. Who could ever imagine that such bodies would ever rise, fully intact, completely restored?

There are those who insist that their bodies be cremated, the bones pulverized, and the ashes cast out into the wind. Some may think that by doing so they can prevent any possible resurrection. How could God ever raise such disintegrated flesh and bone? Dead is dead, gone is gone, never to rise again. But, in the light of God's Word and power, how foolish are such notions.

God knows exactly each one of the dead, and He raises them all, believers and unbelievers alike, so that each person will stand individually before His throne of judgement. There is no one who lived who can escape.

Even the "sea," that mass-burial place with no markers or tombstones, that place from which no human returns, gives up the dead. God doesn't need a tombstone or marker to locate anyone, for by His simple command they all rise to stand before Him.

STANDING BEFORE THE JUDGE

Now it is not easy for us to picture what John saw and describes. We read of the dead standing before the throne, and it conjures up an image of a multitude of people (billions upon billions) standing before a single throne, something very hard for us to understand from our perspective of space. But the word "standing" here denotes a certain posture. Just as a defendant must rise in the courtroom to face the judge, so all people must stand before God, in great awe, with total reverence, in full recognition of the solemnity of the moment, to hear the verdict that will be pronounced.

This is how we must interpret the word "standing." No contempt of court is allowed here, for the Judge of heaven and earth is about to speak His verdict. It is as if the bailiff says, "All rise." And all stand as the judge ascends the bench, in this case, the throne. The moment of absolute truth has arrived. That is the impact of these words.

BOOKS OPENED

Then we read, "books were opened." It is an unqualified word, books (plural) denoting many . A little further we read that these books are actually record books in which our deeds have been written.

This text reminds us of what we find in Daniel 10: 9-11, where the judgment of God is also described: ". . .ten thousand times ten thousand stood before Him; the court sat in judgment and books were opened."

This notion of books being opened may seem frightening, at first reading, but it is done because of God's righteousness. When justice is to be done, nothing may be charged wrongly. At the same time, all the evil which we have done must be brought forward as proper evidence. For God judges not on the basis of rumour or hear-say, but on the basis of the facts. You may be assured of this, that God will not charge anyone with something he didn't do, nor will He overlook the evil that someone did do.

BOOKS AND CONSCIENCES?

Books were opened. For many years the Reformed churches understood this expression to mean that the consciences were opened. That is how we had it in the Belgic Confession, Article 37, "the books that is, the consciences of men were opened." The word "consciences" was dropped in 1983, although the notion itself has not completely disappeared from the article.

The idea was that when we are confronted with all our sins we will also admit to them. Our lives will pass before our very eyes. God will present us with such clear evidence and proof that we will not deny it but admit that what has been written is fully correct.

The same is said regarding the ungodly and the wicked. We read in Article 37, "the wicked shall be convicted by the testimony of their own consciences. . . ." As much as ungodly people denied sin and wrongdoing during their life, even until the day they died, so they will have to admit fully before God and will know in their own hearts: yes, we have sinned, wilfully, knowingly, and with dedication. There will be no one who comes up with any lawful excuse. No one will blame another, for everyone will see the true facts, as recorded by God in His infallible righteousness: yes, this is indeed what I said and did.

Books are opened. God will open to us all the books of our lives. And we will have to admit that we have sinned and are worthy of death. On that day, it will be clear to us as never before how depraved we were by nature and how often and how deeply this showed throughout our lives.

RENDERING ACCOUNT

The Belgic Confession puts it this way: ". . .all people will render account for every careless word they utter, which the world regards as mere jest and amusement. The secrets and hypocrisies of men will then be publicly uncovered in the sight of all."

Every evil word you said, even in jest. Every dirty joke, every foul word, all misuse of God's Name, it's in the book. Every secret sin, which no one saw except God, it's in the book. Every hypocritical act, insincerity and untruthfulness of which people did not know and which they could never even surmise, it's in the book.

And did you notice that the confession says: this will be publicly uncovered in the sight of all? Is that not frightening? There goes my carefully built and protected reputation, my almost impeccable name for which I worked so hard.

Do you know on what Bible passages these words of our confession are based? On such texts as Matthew 12: 36,37: "I tell you, on the day of judgment men will render account for every careless word they utter; for by your words you will be justified and by your words you will be condemned." Woe to those who have publicly condemned others for certain sins, but secretly done the same or worse themselves. It will come out publicly on that day.

Remember what Jesus said to His disciples when He warned them for the leaven – the hypocrisy – of the Pharisees, "Nothing is covered up that will not be revealed, or hidden that will not be known. Therefore, whatever you have said in the dark will be heard in the light, and what you have whispered in private rooms shall be proclaimed from the rooftops" (Luke 12: 2, 3). We will not get away with anything on that day, no matter what we got away with in this life.

It's in the books, and when the books are opened, it will come out, and all will see and we will know that it is true. There will be no excuses, no cover-up, no pointing to others. I, wretched sinner, I am guilty of all these things written in the books, I am deserving of eternal death.

It reminds us of a *public* trial, where the facts are presented, verified, and published, so that everyone may know for sure, without a doubt: this person here is guilty as charged. There is no room for error, no margin for mistakes, for the books are one hundred per cent accurate.

A FRIGHTENING PROSPECT?

Again, this is not meant to frighten us. For if we have honestly and humbly in this life confessed our sins, and if we have walked sincerely with our God, without hypocrisy, will be we afraid of the truth? Ashamed? Yes! But afraid? No! We need only be frightened if we nurture our sins, harbour them in secret pleasure, and refuse to confess them and repent of them.

It is not meant to frighten us, but it is meant to make us very serious in our Christian life and very honest before God and our fellow men. Why should we pile up shame upon shame for that day? We should never think, "Oh, well, I'm saved anyway, so I can go ahead and do this or that evil." On the contrary, knowing the seriousness of the day of judgment, when the books of our lives are opened, we will battle our sinful nature unceasingly. Therefore, daily conversion is so important, especially with a view to that day, so that we need not shrink back at Christ's coming, but may have full confidence to face Him in the sure knowledge that our names are also written in that other book, the book of Life!

THE BOOK OF LIFE

For if the books of our deeds were the only ones to be opened on that day, we'd all be in deep trouble and face a hopeless reality of eternal despair. But John writes, "Also another book was opened, which is the book of life." The same term returns at the end of this text: if anyone's name was not found written in the book of life, he was thrown into the lake of fire."

There is a book of life. Notice here "book" in the singular. One book, expressing the unity of God's eternal decree, which contains the names of all God's children. And, of course, we understand that this book contains the names of those whom God has chosen in Christ before the foundation of the world. He knows them by name, and has written these names in that one book of life, the book which symbolizes eternal and blessed life.

This "book of life" is in many ways a marvellous book. It contains not only the names of the saints, but also their trials and sufferings for Christ's sake. It is not the first time that we read of a "book of life," an exact record of those who are saved.The prophet Daniel already was able to speak of this book, chapter 12: 1: "at that time [the time of the end, that is, the resurrection] your people shall be delivered, every one whose name shall be found written in the book." God remembers His own in their trials to deliver them and to raise them to glory on the great day. I think of Psalm 56: 8, "Thou has kept count of my tossing; put Thou my tears in Thy bottle! Are they not in Thy book?"

Who can count the number of times we toss and turn in turmoil during sleepless nights? But God knows! He keeps track of our anguish and pain. He records not just our sins, but also our trials. He knows of our silent prayers and quiet pleas. He counts each and every tear that we cry in and for His service. Would anyone really think that all God does is keep a record of our sins and not of our trials and our battles?

THE WONDER OF THE BOOK OF LIFE

There are some beautiful texts about the book of life in the Bible. In Matthew 10, when the seventy who were sent out returned jubilantly because even the demons had to obey them, Christ said, ". . .do not rejoice at this that the spirits are subject to you, but that your names are written in heaven." Of what advantage are earthly conquests if our heavenly safety is not guaranteed? What is more important, experiencing a victory here on earth or being assured of victory on the new earth: our names written in heaven?

In his letter to the Philippians, Paul writes of various people, Euodia and Syntyche (two women in the congregation) and Clement and the rest of his fellow workers, that their "names are written in the book of life." They were not perfect people, for just a little earlier he was admonishing them to stop quarrelling and to be one in the Lord! You see, you do not have to be perfect to be in that book, but you must love the Lord and serve Him.

HOW DO I KNOW?

Now the question may be asked: how do I know if *my name* is in that book of life? We can sometimes struggle with this question. Let me ask another question first. How do you know that you are in those other books? I know that I am in those other books, because I believe and confess that I am a sinner. This I know, because the Bible tells me so! Precisely. And so I know that I am in the book of life because I believe that Christ has paid for my sins. This too I know, because the Bible tells me so!

It is by faith alone in Christ that we can sing, "For in the book of life Thou didst engrave me, Thou hast upheld me, foes could not enslave me" (Psalm 56). I know by faith alone that I am in that book.

This is what the Holy Spirit confirms in our hearts by the preaching of the Gospel. Of this we see the fruits in our life. Of this we receive the necessary assurance. There are never enough fruits. Sometimes the assurance is not felt. We ride all the crests of the waves of human emotions. But by faith we do know: my name is in that book of life!

Not that we deserve it. The books of our life convict us. Our own conscience accuses us. The facts cannot be denied or hidden. It is by grace alone in Christ through faith. On that day, God will open the book of life, and He will say: you who have believed in the Son of God, enter into the glory of your Lord! It is Christ who gives us a place in the book of life.

GREATER THAN MOSES

Let me illustrate this clearly. When the LORD God was going to destroy Israel for making a golden calf and worshipping it, Moses once made this rather bold statement to the LORD. He said, "Alas, this people have sinned a great sin; they have made for themselves gods of gold. But now, if Thou wilt forgive their sin – but if not, I pray Thee, blot me out of Thy book which Thou hast written" (Exodus 32: 31, 32).

Moses volunteers to stand in Israel's place and be blotted out of God's book for their sake! Is this a bold word? Well, Moses was the "mediator of the old covenant." But God would not accept Moses' offer. He said, "Whoever has sinned against Me, him will I blot out of My book."

Do you see the implication? Only Jesus Christ, the true and eternal Mediator, greater than Moses, could atone in our place, so that our names could be maintained in the book of life. Not Moses, but Christ was "blotted out," underwent the agony of hell and eternal death, so that our names might be inscribed forever in God's book of life.

We read in Hebrews 9: 15, "Therefore [Christ] is the Mediator of a new covenant, so that those who are called may receive the promised inheritance. . . ." Moses could not atone for God's people; Christ could and did.

THE FINAL QUESTION

No one or nothing can erase our name from the book of life, except God. Therefore God's service does remain a serious matter. Is it not amazing that David in Psalm 69 dares to ask of God about his foes, "Blot Thou their names out of the book of life, let them not be enroled among the righteous"? Did you ever take careful notice of those words? Blot thou their names out of the book of life! Is that possible?

If you're written in, can you be written out? Was David being vindictive here? No, David is appealing to the justice of the LORD over those who bear the sign of God's covenant but who oppose God's Word and reject His anointed. David uses here a terminology that is similar to our speaking of "excommunication." David is making the connection: the gift of life is extended only to God's children who serve Him with joy and zeal. If they do not, they should be removed from Israel.

But only God, not man, determines who is in that book. He alone bestows eternal life or eternal death. And He has written into the book of life the names of those whom in His sovereign grace He saved in Christ.

Saved in Christ. The question is not: am I written in the book of life? The question is: do I believe in the Lord Jesus Christ, the anointed of God, the only Messiah? Do I serve Him with all my heart? I am God's covenant child, do I also live like one? If you answer "yes" to these questions, you should have and will have no problem with that other one, "Am I written in the book of life?" It will not be a question, but a joyous confession:

> We, too, shall stand before the throne,
> Then shall our names be found
> Recorded in the book of life.
> How shall our joy abound. (Hymn 55).

Joy after much struggle. Struggle against sin and Satan. Struggle with much weakness. But always with the certainty of triumph in Christ. Now the vision of the binding of Satan has really ended, the eternal binding of Satan and all ungodly people; and the eternal liberation and glorification of all who have hoped in Christ Jesus and longed for His Day have really begun.

Don't be afraid of that day. The Belgic Confession concludes as follows: "Therefore we look forward to that great day with a great longing to enjoy to the full the promises of God in Jesus Christ, our Lord."

Come, Lord Jesus.